Praise for
Lonely Girl, Gracious God

God's grace often touches us in the most unexpected ways and it is those gracious blessings that powerfully impact our lives. So it was for me as God graced me through my association with Farema. From the time I began working with Farema on the ice I was encouraged by her passion for skating. Every challenge for her became a lesson for me; every triumph for Farema became mine, as well. I received far more from Farema in those instructional sessions than she ever could have learned from me. I was witnessing the grace of God in the brightness of Farema's eyes when she focused on my instruction; the confidence in her movements as she glided across the ice; the resilience in her recovery when she fell on the ice; the joy on her face when she completed a skating program; and the sense of ease in her belonging when she skated and socialized with her fellow skaters. Every moment with Farema was a privilege and the memory of that time will forever remain among my most treasured life experiences. In *Lonely Girl, Gracious God*, Lauri Khodabandehloo shares the story a special young woman, her determined and devoted mother and the power of God's grace.

LUCINDA "CINDY" JENSEN, PSA MASTER RATED COACH, RETIRED MANAGER
AND SKATING DIRECTOR OF THE LANE COUNTY ICE CENTER

I was first introduced to Lauri and Farema when I had the pleasure of reading Lauri's submission to *Chicken Soup for the Soul: Children with Special Needs*. It was an honor to read their entire story *Lonely Girl, Gracious God* and what happens when a parent stands against the odds, armed with love, perseverance, and faith. Lauri's first novel is heart breaking, heart wrenching and achingly honest and most importantly, triumphant.

HEATHER MCNAMARA ,CO-AUTHOR, *CHICKEN SOUP FOR THE SOUL:
CHILDREN WITH SPECIAL NEEDS* & *CHICKEN SOUP FOR THE UNSINKABLE SOUL*

Lonely Girl, Gracious God is a pow͏ ͏ Lauri Khodabandehloo's object is not sc ͏ ld with autism creates sometimes unbeara ͏ ͏es. *Lonely Girl, Gracious God* is, abov͏͏ ͏r of a family's faith, the need to balance ͏ ͏ with those of

her siblings and parents, and the struggles of a husband and wife, and their resilience, in facing each difficult transition in their daughter's journey to adulthood. It is a gift to all of us.

KAREN SIMMONS, CO-AUTHOR, *CHICKEN SOUP FOR THE SOUL: CHILDREN WITH SPECIAL NEEDS, THE OFFICIAL AUTISM 101 MANUAL & AUTISM TOMORROW,* FOUNDER & CEO AUTISM TODAY

Lonely Girl, Gracious God really touched me. (Lauri is) a fabulous writer; (she has) created images in my mind and I'm sure, also in any other readers' minds, that seem real and at the same time unreal, beyond reality....

HAROLD (HAL) SPENCER, PRESIDENT OF MANNA MUSIC, INC., SONG WRITER/COMPOSER, AND AUTHOR

Lonely Girl, GRACIOUS GOD

Lonely Girl, GRACIOUS GOD

A Mother's Story of Autism's Devastation
and God's Promise of Enduring Love

LAURI KHODABANDEHLOO

Deep River
B O O K S

LONELY GIRL, GRACIOUS GOD
PUBLISHED BY DEEP RIVER BOOKS
Sisters, Oregon
http://www.deepriverbooks.com

Visit www.lonelygirlgraciousgod.com for autism resources and more.

[Information and resources on autism spectrum disorder that are presented in this book are not intended to replace or supplement the advice of qualified medical professionals regarding the diagnosis and treatment of this disorder. The author and publisher specifically disclaim liability, loss, or risk, personal or otherwise, which is incurred as a consequence, directly or indirectly, of the use or application of any of the contents of this book.]

All Scripture quotations, unless otherwise indicated, are taken from the Holy Bible, New Living Translation, copyright © 1996. Used by permission of Tyndale House Publishers Inc., Wheaton, Illinois 60189. All rights reserved.

[Some names and identifying details have been changed to protect the persons involved.]

ISBN-10 1-935265-46-6
ISBN-13 9781935265467

Library of Congress Cataloging-in-Publication Data Control: 2011922002

Printed in the United States of America
2001—First Edition

10 9 8 7 6 5 4 3 2 1

Cover and interior design by Robin Black, www.blackbirdcreative.biz

Dedication

TO ALL THE ANGELS

To Lisa, Lainee, and Farah for loving their little sister and sacrificing hours, days, and even years, to help her experience a fulfilling life, if only for a while—I thank you from the bottom of my heart. You are the loveliest of angels.

For the kindness and compassion of all the angels at the ice rink where Farema found a place to shine, especially to Lucinda Jenson, who saw potential in an autistic child, and to Scott Hamilton for his tireless and selfless devotion to children and adults with special needs: I cannot begin to thank you adequately. You have all blessed Farema and our family beyond what mere words can say.

Where would we be without all of you precious earthly angels?

A special thank-you to Jennifer Lonas of Refiner's Touch Editorial Services: your encouragement and prayers during the hard times of reliving the past were just the icing on the cake of your most excellent editing, helping me to lay the foundation for this book and shape the initial chapters! And to Rachel Starr Thomson, fellow author and editor with Deep River Books: for your gentle way of ushering me along the narrow and focused path of pulling this story together in a finished product, I offer my sincere gratitude.

To both of you—I am so very grateful.

What a wonderful God we have—he is the Father of our Lord Jesus Christ, the source of every mercy, and the one who so wonderfully comforts and strengthens us in our hardships and trials. And why does he do this? So that when others are troubled, needing our sympathy and encouragement, we can pass on to them this same help and comfort God has given us.

—2 Corinthians 1:3–4, Living Bible

CONTENTS

ALIEN BABY

W hat's that?" My teenage daughter's question was followed by a hearty laugh. I was standing at the kitchen sink, drying a glass I'd just washed. I set the glass on the counter and folded the towel before looking over my shoulder to see what Lisa found so amusing.

My three older daughters were giggling themselves silly over little Fee, a nickname her seven-year-old sister, Farah, had given her. Farema, my youngest, was around fourteen months old.

I walked into the dining area where the girls were seated around the kitchen table finishing their pancake breakfast, and I stared in disbelief at my baby daughter. She had smeared maple syrup into every strand of her long, curly hair, but that wasn't what the girls were giggling about.

Little Fee was sitting rigid in her high chair, her thin little arms stretched out in front of her, her tiny hands stiff, palms parallel. She was staring straight ahead, a fixed smile on her face, her index fingers pointing inward, almost touching, and vibrating as if an invisible current of electricity was passing between them. Her eyes sparkled more than usual as her tiny body quivered, and I wondered momentarily whether she was having some kind of seizure.

"Look at that!" Lisa squealed. "She looks like an alien! Mom, she's an alien baby!"

I pasted a smile on my face as I moved closer and acted as if Farema was just trying to amuse her sisters. But as I watched her bizarre movements, my heart sank in my chest.

The girls continued to laugh at their baby sister, and Lisa planted a cluster of kisses all over Farema's syrup-covered face.

Then, as quickly as the puzzling display had begun, it was over. It had lasted only a few seconds, but it left a deep sense of dread in my soul. I'd never seen anything like it. My three older girls had never behaved like that when they were babies, and I had spent enough time around other people's children to know that what I had just observed wasn't normal.

My fifteen-year-old daughter, Lainee, was my investigator, never letting anything get past her without careful consideration.

"That's kinda strange, isn't it, Mom?" she asked, her eyebrows knitted together in concern.

I didn't want to answer her, so I ignored the question and went back to my dishes.

"Mom," Lainee persisted, "isn't it?"

"Well, honey," I finally responded, "Farema's pretty smart, and I think she just wants to keep up with the rest of you and do something funny to make you laugh."

As I spoke the words, I hoped against hope that they were true. I watched from the kitchen sink as my contemplative, sometimes overly intuitive teenager sat quietly surveying her baby sister with a much-too-serious look on her face. I was afraid that downplaying the incident wasn't going to work, and it was just a matter of time before Lainee would start asking me about other strange behaviors she'd noticed. But my greatest fear was that she would tell her stepfather, Cody, drawing his attention to something I really didn't want him to know about. It would only confuse and upset him—and add to my stress.

Farema's alien-baby routine wasn't the first peculiar behavior I'd observed, nor would it be the last. From the moment she had craned her tiny newborn neck in the delivery room and stared with keen intent at the ceiling lights, I'd realized there was something very different about my little one. The nurse had held her up naked and wriggling so I could look at her face, but nothing could pull her eyes away from those lights.

Even the nurses had noticed.

"She's the most alert newborn we've ever had in here!" one of them remarked. "All of us are amazed at how observant she is!"

The nurse had smiled as she said it. I gazed with a mix of pride and awe at my newborn. She looked like a tiny fairy child, with golden-brown ringlets framing her delicate face. As she fussed in my arms, my thoughts drifted back to the long, hard road that had led up to this moment.

Chapter 1

A ROUGH START

W hen I found out I was pregnant in July of 1980, it took me completely by surprise. But instead of feeling overjoyed about the news, I dreaded telling my husband. For seven long years, Cody had been working hard to save up enough money to buy his own restaurant, and it looked as if his American dream was finally going to come true. A fourth child would put an additional strain on our finances and might even jeopardize Cody's plans, which was the last thing I wanted to see happen.

We had also agreed five years earlier, after our daughter Farah was born, that we wouldn't have any more children. Cody had desperately wanted a son, but he had come to terms with his disappointment and accepted that it wasn't meant to be. Since then, I had been on birth control and never dreamed I would end up pregnant again.

Now it looked as if Cody might get his boy-child after all, but I wasn't sure how he'd react, so I decided to put off telling him for a few months—at least until I began to show.

By September, I realized I couldn't conceal my secret any longer, so I thought up a roundabout way of breaking the news.

After dinner one evening, Cody retreated to the living room and settled into his usual spot on the couch for a little television. I had strategically placed a greeting card on a side table next to the couch so he would be sure to notice it. The card was black and had only one word in gold script across the front: *Congratulations!* Inside, I had simply written ". . . on number four."

I watched from the kitchen doorway as Cody checked to see what was on the news and then glanced at the card, just as I'd hoped he would. I held my breath as he reached over and picked it up, read the front, and then opened it to see what was inside.

He stared at the card for a moment and then turned to look at me. I could feel his eyes burning a hole in my head as he waited for me to respond, but I pretended not to notice, fixing my attention on the TV screen.

After a moment, he said in a quiet voice, "For real?"

I nodded silently without looking at him, then turned and retreated to the kitchen to busy myself with cleaning up. I couldn't bear to see his reaction as the news began to sink in.

Cody didn't say a word about the pregnancy for several weeks, and I wasn't about to bring up the subject for discussion. Doing so would only have ignited a conflict I didn't want to have. It seemed the better part of wisdom to give him plenty of time and space to process things. I knew he'd say something when he was ready.

When Cody finally broke his silence, he told me he wanted to schedule a vasectomy. He seemed just as shocked as I had been that I was pregnant. We couldn't understand how something like this could have happened when we'd been so careful.

Having another baby was the last thing either of us wanted at this point in our marriage. Cody didn't want, or need, another mouth to feed as he was preparing to buy his first restaurant, and I had grown weary of the responsibilities of being a mother.

For years I had been longing for a life of my own that would allow me the freedom to experience things I felt I'd missed out on because I had married so young. I had practically been a child when I married my high school sweetheart at eighteen, and by the time I was twenty, I had two baby girls to care for. I wasn't ready to take on such weighty responsibilities, but ready or not, I had to grow up fast and learn how to meet the needs of the little ones who were depending on me.

At twenty-five, I had gone through a painful divorce and struggled to cope with the demands of caring for two young daughters on my own. Then I met Cody. We both worked at a restaurant in San Jose, he as a busboy and I as a waitress. This handsome, dark-skinned man from Iran had the whitest teeth

I'd ever seen and a sparkling personality to match. He spoke very little English, and what he did say was always laced with a thick Middle Eastern accent. He charmed me with his dazzling white smile and wit, and he showered attention on me and my girls.

In just a matter of weeks, I found myself strangely attracted to this man who came from a part of the world I knew nothing about. Even though Cody and I barely knew each other and certainly didn't love each other, marriage held undeniable benefits for us both. A couple of turbulent years trying to survive as a single mother had taken their toll, and I couldn't handle the stress anymore. Marrying Cody seemed like the best solution, especially for my girls. Many years later I'd learn that Cody never believed in "falling in love." In his country, a couple are married first—love and respect come later.

After a whirlwind courtship, Cody and I took a weekend trip to Reno, Nevada, and got married at the county courthouse on June 12, 1972. Before the ceremony, my heart had screamed at me not to go through with it. I even prayed that God would intervene. But the terror of going on alone with two young daughters to care for overpowered common sense, and I ignored any reservations I had.

As Cody and I left the courthouse that day, I told myself that I had married for the sake of my children and would learn to love Cody in time.

Three years later, Farah made her grand entry into the world, and I resigned myself to another long wait before I could spread my wings and fly.

Now, at thirty-three, I was pregnant with my fourth child and knew that I would be stuck in my stay-at-home-mom role for another five or six years. Freedom had been so close, I could taste it. My teenage daughters, Lisa and Lainee, were involved with their own friends and activities, and my six-year-old, Farah, had just started kindergarten. With all of my girls in school, I had been looking forward to time to myself in the mornings to run errands or talk on the phone without interruption, plan a coffee klatch with my girlfriend Randee, or just sit and watch a TV program that didn't contain the loud and silly antics of colorful cartoon characters. But my wings had been clipped once again, and I was devastated.

Some women in my situation might have considered terminating the pregnancy, but that was never an option for me. I had no right to end a life that God had created. In my heart I knew he had a reason for letting me become pregnant, though I didn't have a clue what it was. I was also living with the painful memories of a D&C procedure I'd had after Cody and I married. I never knew whether I had actually been pregnant; the doctor said the test was inconclusive but that after seven weeks he'd be unable to proceed with any kind of "remedy." Though I'd consented to go ahead as planned, I couldn't bear the thought that I might have naively allowed the doctor to end a life that was a few weeks along. The experience left me devastated and overwhelmed with guilt, nearly plunging me into a breakdown. No, I would never allow that to happen again under any circumstance! Besides, no matter how I felt about having another child, I just couldn't deprive Cody of one last chance to have a son.

This fourth pregnancy turned out to be the most difficult one I'd ever experienced. Early on, I sensed that something wasn't right, but I couldn't put my finger on it. Then, at around five and a half months, the baby started kicking. I thought it would taper off in time, but instead, the jabbing became relentless, making my days miserable and robbing me of the few precious hours of sleep I so desperately needed.

As the weeks passed, the pain and lack of sleep became unbearable, reducing me to tears at all hours of the day and night. I finally pleaded with my obstetrician to take the baby by C-section, but he just shook his head and looked at me as if I had to be kidding.

I wasn't.

"It feels like I'm being beat up from the inside!" I pleaded with him, trying to describe the pain. "I can't take it anymore!"

The doctor responded sympathetically, but I suspected he thought I was overreacting. I also knew that as a devout Catholic, he would never perform a C-section at this stage of the pregnancy if there was even the slightest risk to the baby or me.

When I told him how difficult it was to get even an hour of sleep at night, he showed me how to lie on my side to ease the pain without causing the baby any discomfort. I had already tried that—I had tried everything I could think of to find relief—but I decided it would do no good to argue with him. I had great respect for this man who had taken care of me through all my pregnancies, and I knew he meant well even though he didn't understand what I was going through. I resigned myself to crying my nights away and coping as best I could until the baby arrived.

At seven months into the pregnancy, I began to feel an overwhelming sense of foreboding. It wasn't the normal apprehension and fears most women experience during pregnancy as their bodies change and hormone levels fluctuate. It was a deep knowing, an intuition that something was terribly wrong with my unborn child.

One evening at home, I cried out to God, "Please let this baby be okay." I felt desperately alone as I sobbed and rocked back and forth on the couch. Even though I hadn't wanted or planned to have another baby, I couldn't bear the thought that this child might not be normal and healthy.

These ominous feelings hung over me like a storm cloud throughout the rest of my pregnancy. I didn't understand why I felt this way, but it seemed as if something, or someone, was whispering in my ear, telling me that I needed to accept what was coming.

One afternoon as I was taking a nap, I dreamed that I heard a loud flapping outside the house. When I got up and opened the front door, I saw thousands of angels filling the sky, their white robes shimmering in the sun as they soared heavenward. I stepped out onto the porch, longing to go with them, but an angel with a white beard looked at me and shook his head. I knew immediately that he was telling me I needed to stay put; it wasn't my time to go.

When I awoke from my nap, the dream seemed so real that I got up and went outside to see if it had actually happened.

Strange dreams are common during pregnancy, but I felt certain that God was speaking to me, telling me that I needed to wait on him no matter how difficult the pregnancy was.

As my delivery date approached, I could hardly wait to be free of the burden I'd been carrying the past nine months. I imagined the relief I would feel when my agony finally came to an end. I mentally ticked off the days, until late in the evening on February 19, I felt my water break and told Cody that it was time to go to the hospital.

We promised our girls that we would call as soon as we had some news, and then we headed for Sacred Heart Hospital. All of my children had been born there, so I knew the baby and I would be in good hands. The familiar surroundings and the kind, upbeat nurses always put me at ease.

Cody and I were lost in our own thoughts on the drive to the hospital. All I could think about was that this war going on inside my belly would be over in a few short hours. I was certain this rambunctious child was a boy and that Cody would be elated. But those thoughts didn't soften the jarring reality that I would soon be the reluctant mother of four.

When we arrived at the hospital, I waddled into the ER with Cody by my side. The receptionist at the front desk welcomed me with a warm smile and summoned an attendant with a wheelchair. Since I'd already dispensed with the admissions paperwork a few days earlier, I was immediately taken to a large, open room on the maternity floor, where other expectant mothers in various stages of labor were waiting in smaller curtained areas for their turn in the delivery room. I could hear the low hum of private conversations throughout the room, punctuated by loud groans that issued from behind closed curtains.

The attendant wheeled me over to an empty exam area and helped me transfer my big belly onto a rolling gurney that would be whisked down the hall when my time came. As I shifted my weight around to get comfortable, a nurse arrived to examine me and announced that I'd be giving birth in the next few hours. I felt confident that this delivery would be quick and easy since my labors had become shorter with each of my previous deliveries.

After about an hour, I was moved out of the exam area into a private room to wait for my labor to begin. With my other children, labor had started immediately after my water broke, but this time, I felt nothing. Cody kept vigil with me but had trouble staying awake. The long hours he'd been putting in at El Kiosco, his restaurant, were taking their toll, so I convinced him to go home and get some sleep. I assured him I would call as soon as the contractions started.

After Cody left, I decided I might as well get a few precious moments of sleep before the agonies of childbirth began. I had started feeling some intermittent labor pains by this time, but they were so light I could easily ignore them.

I dozed off, grateful for the relative calm and hoping that the rest would give me extra stamina for the work ahead.

All of a sudden, searing jolts of pain in my lower back jarred me awake. I had no idea how long I'd been asleep, but as the pain increased and I struggled to focus on my breathing, I found myself thinking that I was way too old to be doing this again. Somehow I had a feeling that this delivery wasn't going to be as quick and easy as I'd assumed it would be.

Waves of pain came and went, and I waited for what seemed like hours before a nurse finally appeared and announced, "We'll take you to the delivery room when we have one available, but for now, we'll just put you down the hallway. It shouldn't be too long."

Before I could ask what she meant, she whisked me out of the room, parked my gurney along the wall, and scurried off to assist a woman who was screaming so loudly I was sure she could be heard for miles. When the nurse finally returned, she examined me right there in the hallway, with hospital personnel and patients passing at will, and wondered aloud whether I could "hold off" until the delivery room was available. By then, my labor pains were so intense, I couldn't have cared less about privacy. *Just get this baby out of me!* I silently screamed.

When I heard her say, "Okay, I think we can take you into delivery now!" I breathed a sigh of relief.

Someone grabbed the end of the gurney and sped me through an open door into the delivery room. The doctor immediately positioned himself at my feet, and I heard his familiar urgings, "Okay, now push!"

The nurse placed her hand between my shoulders and helped me raise up enough to give it my all. But nothing happened.

Again I heard the doctor say, "Now, Lauri, give me a good push!" And again my body failed me. I had no strength, no urge to push—nothing.

I could hear the urgency in the nurse's voice as she came around to the head of the gurney to make sure I understood that I had to help deliver this baby before complications arose. But no matter how hard I tried to force my belly to expel this lingering infant, I had nothing to offer.

Another nurse came over to help out, and as the doctor urged me to try harder, he and both nurses put their hands on my stomach and tried to push the baby out. I kept telling them I didn't know what was wrong. I couldn't push. I couldn't feel anything.

The doctor's voice betrayed his concern as he firmly instructed his assistants as to what they should do next. I was near panic. Everyone kept assuring me that the baby was coming, but I was alarmed that my body was refusing to respond as it should. This had never happened during my other three births.

Finally the doctor pulled the baby free and quickly placed the newborn in the waiting arms of one of the nurses. As she rushed out of the delivery room, I caught a glimpse of the pale blue form in her hands.

"Is my baby okay?" I called to anyone within earshot. "Do you know if my baby's okay?"

But no one seemed to hear me. All the attention was focused on the tiny infant, who had been taken to a small window-enclosed area adjoining the delivery room. I lifted my head to see the nurses bustling back and forth in the room and hovering over my newborn. Thankful for the care my little one was receiving, I rested quietly on the gurney, patiently waiting for someone to tell me what had happened. A faint cry reached my ears from the other room. Whatever was wrong, at least my baby was breathing.

Eventually, one of the white-gowned nurses came over and assured me that all was well. Rushing the baby out of the delivery room had been a "precautionary procedure," she told me. They had just wanted to make sure the baby's airway was clear so she could get plenty of oxygen.

She? The nurse smiled and announced that I had delivered a little girl—six pounds, five ounces. It really didn't matter to me whether it was a boy or girl; I was just relieved the baby was all right. Nine months of agony had finally come to a welcome end.

Minutes later, another nurse entered the room carrying my newborn. She lifted the baby into the air so I could get a good look at her and then plopped her down on my chest. While I waited for Cody to arrive, I caressed her feather-soft head and gazed at her tiny body. I was amazed that such a small thing had caused so much turmoil.

When Cody finally entered the room and came over to where I lay, I knew what he was expecting to hear. I had been assuring him for months that he would finally have his boy-child.

"No baby girl ever felt like this!" I had insisted. "I'm positive this one's a boy!"

I swallowed hard as I glanced at Cody and announced the news with as much enthusiasm as I could muster. I hoped he would give me a smile, a reassuring look, any sign that he was happy I had given him another little girl. But instead, a look of bitter disappointment washed over his face. His final hope of having a son had been crushed.

I knew that Cody would eventually get over his disappointment and embrace his youngest daughter with the same fatherly love he had always shown our other girls. But I was sad that I hadn't been able to give him the baby boy he had wanted so badly.

Later, when I was settled in my hospital room, the nurse brought my newborn to me so I could breastfeed her.

"So you named her Farina—like the cereal?" she asked as she placed the baby in my waiting arms.

"Actually, it's Fah-ree-*mah*," I corrected, emphasizing the *m* sound. "My husband is Persian, and this name is popular in his country."

As I held my little one, I noticed that she was having trouble sucking, but I didn't think there was any need for concern. She had just gone through a traumatic delivery, so I really wasn't surprised that she'd be too weak to suckle. With a little practice, she'd soon be nursing as well as any hungry newborn.

Farema looked so perfect as she lay fussing in my arms. All my worst fears of the past nine months melted away as I gazed at her angelic face. A baby this beautiful couldn't possibly have anything wrong with her.

This fourth and last child of mine was already curling her tiny baby fingers around my heart. There was something extraordinary about her, and I sensed that God had something very special planned for her life.

What I didn't know was that little Fee would turn my world upside down.

Chapter 2

INCONSOLABLE

From the moment we brought our tiny newborn home from the hospital, she whimpered softly like a wounded animal. In all my years of mothering, I had never heard anything quite like it, but I wasn't overly concerned. The delivery had been hard, so it made perfect sense that she might need a little time to recover.

I could tell she was still having problems nursing and wondered whether she was getting enough nourishment. Breastfeeding had come so naturally to my other girls, but this little one didn't seem to know how. Even so, I felt compelled to keep trying. I knew that mother's milk would give her the best start in life so she would grow up healthy and strong like her sisters.

That first night, I tried in vain to get Farema to nurse. In a daze, I gently laid her in her crib and shuffled back to bed, unhappy that I had failed. I dozed for what seemed like only a few minutes before hearing her faint cries and padding back down the hallway for another attempt at breastfeeding. I knew the drill—up and down several times a night to nurse and burp, pace and rock, and try to catch a few precious minutes of sleep. But this time "the drill" wasn't having the usual effects.

The next morning, Farema still didn't seem to be getting any milk, so I called the hospital, hoping the maternity nurses would be able to help. But their advice only fueled my anxieties.

In a warning tone, one of the nurses said, "Make sure she's getting milk. You don't want her to get dehydrated or too weak to nurse if nothing is coming out."

I hung up the phone feeling like a terrible mother. I tried to revive my flagging confidence by reminding myself that I had successfully nursed three other children. But the harder I tried to get Farema to breastfeed, the more distressed I became. She was only three days old, but I was sure she was starving to death. In a panic, I called my friend Randee, whose mother was a registered nurse.

After I explained the problem, Randee called her mom, and the two rushed over to help. Within minutes, Cathy confirmed what I feared: Farema wasn't getting enough milk. We immediately prepared a bottle of formula and nudged it between her waiting lips. We were relieved to seek how quickly she took the bottle, sucking with every ounce of energy in her little body. After she had downed some formula, I patiently encouraged her to breastfeed, hoping she would eventually catch on. Alternating from bottle to breast, we were finally able to get enough milk into Farema's little tummy, and she quieted down.

I couldn't have been more grateful for Cathy's help that afternoon. As I walked Randee and her mom to the door, I gave them each a big hug and expressed my heartfelt thanks. Cathy left me with some final instructions and a promise to check back to see how I was doing.

Breathing a sigh of relief, I carried my precious newborn back to her room and settled into the rocking chair for a peaceful moment with her in my arms. Moments later, the crying began again.

Exasperated, I rose wearily and began pacing the floor, rubbing Farema's tiny back in the hope that she just needed to let out a good burp. But that didn't stop her crying. Bewildered, I couldn't imagine what was causing so much angst. I mentally ticked off the list of possibilities. I'd just fed her, so I knew she couldn't be hungry. I'd burped her and changed her diaper. I'd rocked her, walked the floor with her, patted and rubbed her back. I'd done everything I could think of, but no amount of rocking, soothing, or nursing seemed to console her.

I decided it had to be colic.

The following evening around bedtime, I noticed a thin line of blood trickling down Farema's neck from her left ear. Alarmed, I didn't know whether to take her to the emergency room or wait until morning to call the pediatrician. Since her cries hadn't intensified, Cody and I concluded that it would probably be okay to wait, as long as I kept a watchful eye on her through the night.

In the morning, I called the doctor's office, and the receptionist told me to come right in. I quickly dressed and carried Farema out to the car for the short drive across town. As I looked at my little one sitting in her car seat, I prayed that the bleeding wouldn't be anything serious.

"She has a severe ear infection," the pediatrician told me after completing his exam. "It probably began while she was in the womb and blossomed into a full-blown infection over the past few days."

I'd never heard of such a thing. He smiled at me. "It's nothing to worry about. A course of antibiotics should do the trick. Bring her back in ten days or so and I'll check her again. I'm sure she'll be just fine."

Thanking the doctor, I slipped the prescription into my purse and gathered Farema in my arms, relieved that I finally knew why my little one was so miserable. On the drive home, I daydreamed about the prospect of a relatively peaceful night's sleep. Relief was just around the corner.

჻

The thick pink liquid the doctor prescribed cleared up Farema's ear infection, yet she continued to cry. I had been so sure the infection was the culprit and Farema would start behaving like a typical newborn as soon as it healed. I was wrong. If anything, she was crying harder and louder and longer now.

When I took Farema back to the doctor the following week, he agreed it could be colic and suggested I give her more water. I was willing to try anything just to get her to stop crying.

Stressful days and sleepless nights soon began to take their toll. I shuffled around the house like a zombie, my eyes burning and my mind in a fog. I tried every single colic remedy I'd ever heard of to quiet my bawling infant—even the age-old peppermint oil in water trick—but they all failed.

I checked and rechecked Farema's diaper, offered her milk when I knew she was full, rocked her gently in my arms, and paced the house while holding her over my shoulder. If by some miracle she happened to doze off, I ever so carefully laid her in her crib and prayed that she would give me a blessed hour or two of relief. But in a short time, the crying would start up again.

Cody couldn't take all the noise and insisted that I pick the baby up. I carried her around with me most of the time anyway and knew it would make no difference, but I complied to keep the peace. Even the girls helped out, but Farema was so small and frail, I was afraid to leave her in their arms for too long.

My mother felt that I held the baby too much, and she frequently scolded me about it.

"Do you ever put that baby down?" she asked, irritation tinging her voice. "I can't believe how much you carry her around, and she still isn't happy!"

I shrugged. "Cody wants me to hold her. You know how nervous he gets when she cries."

Mom grew up back in the days when children, especially small ones, were to be seen, not heard. She didn't believe in catering to their demands and made it abundantly clear that's exactly what she thought I was doing. She reminded me that I'd had colic as a baby, and she had just let me scream in my crib.

"You were such a bawler," she said, "but you turned out perfect without any coddling or spoiling!"

I bit my lip to avoid saying something I'd regret. I knew she thought she'd done the right thing as a mother, but I had always been jealous of kids whose parents had cuddled and kissed them and told them "I love you." I felt as if I'd missed out.

When I had kids of my own, I made sure to give them plenty of hugs and kisses and "I love you's" so they'd never feel deprived of affection.

In contrast to my mother, Cody didn't feel I was doing enough to pacify the baby. He was juggling a day job at a local restaurant and spending every spare minute on nights and weekends overseeing the interior remodeling of El Kiosco. With the grand opening scheduled for May, he had been working extremely long hours, and on the rare occasions when he was home, all he wanted to do was stretch out on the couch for a few hours of undisturbed sleep. Keeping a colicky baby quiet was next to impossible, but I tried my best.

From day one, I was pretty much on my own in caring for the baby and our three girls, not to mention keeping the house from falling apart around us. Cody had tried to help out with Farema at first, but it was too much with the demands of work.

As the crying persisted, he became increasingly irritated.

"What is the matter with that baby?" he asked one day, looking at me as if I should know the answer. I didn't.

I told him it was probably colic and silently prayed that it would pass before I lost my mind.

About a month into the crying marathon, Cody had finally had all he could take.

"I don't want to hear that baby crying anymore!" he screamed. "If she's crying, I want one of you to pick her up and hold her until she stops!"

I knew he was at his wit's end and didn't know what else to say. We were *all* at our wits' end. We just wanted the noise to cease.

Lisa, Lainee, and Farah did their best to entertain their little sister. They dangled rattles in front of her, made silly faces, squeezed squeaky rubber toys, and tried anything else they could think of to distract her, but nothing worked. Farema paid no attention to them or their antics. No one could make her stop crying.

After a few minutes, Lisa and Lainee would give up and escape the mayhem to hang out with their friends. I couldn't blame them, and I felt bad that I couldn't give them the attention they needed.

Five-year-old Farah treated her baby sister like a live doll, trying continuously to make her smile and laugh. But like Lisa and Lainee, she would eventually give up.

Farah often had to fend for herself while I was consumed with trying to figure out what was wrong with Farema. But she never complained and was always eager to help. She seemed to be handling everything so well that I rarely worried about her. It wasn't until years later that I began to realize what a toll my neglect had taken on all the girls.

The guilt I felt about neglecting my three older children was only the tip of a massive iceberg. Secretly I wondered whether my own ambivalence about having another child had anything to do with Farema's problems. Had she sensed that I didn't want her? Whether she had or not, I believed I was to blame for her misery. It was my fault that she had come so close to starving, and somehow, her ear infection was my fault too. Maybe I hadn't been attentive enough when I was bathing her. I was convinced that God was punishing me for not wanting this baby in the first place. I was getting exactly what I deserved. Perhaps I was even being punished for my past sins: divorcing my first husband, taking my two little girls away from their daddy, and then marrying Cody on the rebound, a man I didn't even know or love at the time. I kept the guilt hidden so deep inside that no one but God knew how I really felt.

As days melted into weeks, tensions in our house ran high. I was harried and exhausted trying to soothe a screeching, discontented infant, and the girls pretty much ran wild. When nerves were on edge, they would take off to play with their friends or withdraw to their rooms. Chaos and noise usually put Cody in a bad mood, so whenever he was home, we all tried to stay out of his way. As long as Cody didn't have to hear the baby, he was happy, so I took her out of earshot, wandering the backyard and pacing with her in remote areas of the house.

Mercifully, I found a few moments of relative calm here and there when she drifted off from sheer exhaustion. During those quiet times, I tried to catch up on household chores while fighting off the exhaustion that threatened to envelop me. Friends often stopped by, giving me a chance to blow off steam and complain about Farema's colic and my lack of sleep. Their visits were a saving grace in the midst of the chaos.

Somehow during those mind-numbing days, I managed to hold on to the tattered edges of my optimism, telling myself that things would begin to look up soon. The crying wouldn't last forever. Or so I thought.

Chapter 3

SEARCHING FOR ANSWERS

By the time Farema was a year old, I knew she was slow in reaching certain milestones essential for normal development. I didn't need my doctor to tell me that she was in the low percentile for weight, because she was very small. And when I took her to her well-baby appointment for a checkup, I found that she was well below the average age to roll over, sit up, or babble the way babies do when they're beginning to imitate words. She was more than a month behind the typical age to lift her head and look around when lying on her stomach or push with her arms to roll over onto her back. I blamed it on her small size and difficult birth. I told myself she hadn't been able to catch up yet because of all the attention from her sisters and me. We were the reason she was so immature.

My friend Peggy, whose daughter Brittany was only three months older, agreed. "If you and the girls let her cry a little longer without rushing to help, she might try harder to push herself up or learn to crawl to find you."

We had always been in tune with running to satisfy the baby in order to keep the peace. But now it seemed that wasn't the best thing for Farema. Peggy was confident that Farema would eventually catch up. She reassured me, saying that the reason for her slowness was that she had "four mommies" to attend her.

And yet for all the milestones Farema was slow to attain, she proved herself a contradiction when, at less than ten months old, she was able to pull herself up on the chair or the sofa. She took off walking unaided a month later.

Farema's learning to walk at about the same age as her sisters reinforced my assurance that she was going to be fine and that her development was on track; still, I paid close attention to what Peggy and her husband did for little Britt.

Peggy had begun reading to Brittany before she was a year old. In fact, she and her husband were reading to her while she was still in the womb. I'd thought they were overdoing it, but if it helped their child do well later on, I'd give them credit for trying. After Farema had her first birthday and still spoke no words, I wished I'd tried it myself. And later, when I did try to encourage Farema's vocabulary, my attempts were fruitless.

"Once upon a time," I began as I read a little storybook for toddlers while holding Farema close on my lap. Almost immediately my little girl would begin to wriggle and squirm, trying to release herself from my grasp. It happened many times. Almost as if my voice was irritating her, she would let her body go limp and slide down to the floor to sit quietly alone. As often as I tried to retrieve her, she'd determine to be free, whining incessantly as she dropped all her weight to hang there, arms straight up, making it impossible for me to hold her fast. Even as an infant, Farema would stiffen and throw herself backward as if to force me to let her go in midair. One day, after nearly dropping the arching toddler, I noted how both actions gave her the same result—Farema wanted to be anywhere but folded safely in her mother's arms.

While I tried to find peaceable ground with a one-year-old, I was busy trying to understand the complex world of teenagers. My two little girls, Lisa and Lainee, suddenly developed into young ladies who wanted to taste the delicacies of freedom out in the world. Just as quickly, my focus directed on how I'd prevent that from ever happening.

I'd been a late bloomer, and the girls were much the same. But when Lisa turned seventeen, it was as if the daughter I'd known all those years vanished. In her place was a foreign being—part child, part woman—with a mix of some unknown entity that clashed with every plan I'd held dear for her unfolding future. Lainee was right behind her.

At first, Lisa only wanted some minor freedoms that her stepfather, raised in a culture where daughters were never allowed to be alone with a boy, would never agree to. But I knew she had no intention of doing anything indecent; that, like mine at her age, her interest in the opposite sex was still at a very immature and infant stage.

Lisa was nearly six feet tall, with startling blue eyes and blonde Farrah Fawcett hair that flowed like a mane around her shoulders. She had an infectious, laid-back personality that attracted everyone to her. And although she had no lack of boys at school interested in being her boyfriend, I trusted her to keep all the boys she knew as "just friends." She'd shown no interest in any one young man, and for me that was enough. But Cody came from a culture that prohibited dating, and he would not allow it. And so the battle lines were drawn. Little did Cody know the wiles of a woman. Lisa found ways to be with her peers who went to movies and dances at the school, and eventually she found ways to date, but at great cost to peace and serenity under our roof. Soon after, when Lainee became interested in going out with boys, Cody was less oppositional, though never totally accepting of the American tradition.

As the months passed and the older girls tugged at the invisible ties that bound them to me and to our home, I felt pulled by another unseen force—Farema's odd behaviors, imperceptible to all but me. I felt a gnawing in my gut that something was just not completely right.

While struggling to keep track of my teen's comings and goings, I found myself caring for a baby who had developed a knack for disappearing as soon as she was able to walk. More than a couple times each day I shouted—and begged—for someone to "help me find the baby!"

Farema couldn't get far at first—her little legs didn't travel so fast at one year old—but as the months passed and she was able to go faster and farther, Farah was elected to help me look in closets, under beds, and out the back door on the deck. Farema never answered our calls for her, but she met us with a happy grin when we finally found her. Farah kept me semi-sane with all her help, but years later I would regret the burden I'd laid on her young shoulders.

As life became more unmanageable with my older girls wanting to live like their American friends, Cody escaped for long days and nights in the restaurant, and I was home alone with Farah and little Fee.

Farah played with her friends in the neighborhood, and I spent a lot of time watching over my toddler. While I watched, I wondered—why did she seem so different from my first three babies?

Chapter 4

FLASHBACK

Farema still didn't sleep at night. As I immersed myself in caring for her, my life before her quickly faded into a hazy memory. I did remember feeling during those years that life couldn't possibly get any harder. How wrong I'd been. I let my mind drift back to the year I first met Cody.

᠅

"How many teeth do you have?" I couldn't believe what I was saying.

The handsome, dark-skinned young man standing next to me had the biggest smile and the whitest teeth I'd ever seen. We'd just finished our shift at the Brave Bull Restaurant, where I'd been working for a couple weeks, and I was waiting to sign off on the sheet of paper kept at the podium near the front entrance where the employees recorded their hours each day.

As I stood there with a silly smile on my face, Cody turned and looked straight at me. He said nothing for a few seconds, then he flashed a huge white smile at me and answered with a strong Middle Eastern accent, "About one hundred and twenty."

I laughed, surprised at his wit, and found myself strangely attracted to this man who came from a part of the world I knew nothing about.

Cody had come to the United States from Iran on a student visa in the spring of 1970 and enrolled as a freshman at Gavilan College in Gilroy, California. He'd always wanted to come to America, and when an Iranian friend had immigrated, Cody decided to follow as soon as he had the chance.

Shortly after Cody arrived in the States, his friend helped him get a job as a busboy at the Brave Bull in San Jose, where the manager was also from Iran and spoke Farsi.

That same year, hundreds of miles away in Portland, Oregon, I was in the midst of a divorce.

Larry and I had met during our junior year of high school in Springfield, Oregon. We dated through our junior and senior years. Dad was a traveling salesman at the time, working for a Christian publishing company, while my mother traveled to California to record albums and perform across the country, singing in a childlike voice and speaking through her puppet, Little Marcy, to teach children the love of Jesus.

After graduation, Larry went to visit his father in Seattle and work for the summer, and I held down a job cooking and serving hamburgers at The King Cole, a popular fast-food restaurant. We wrote letters to each other, and when he returned to Springfield in the fall, we picked up where we'd left off.

We'd talked about getting married, but I told him that meant I'd have to marry a Christian. I had attended Sunday School and church since I could remember, and I knew the importance of putting God first in my life. At the age of ten, I'd gone forward at my home church in San Jose one Sunday and asked Jesus into my heart. I still remembered the immense freedom I felt after that. My sins were forgiven, and one day I knew I'd go to heaven. Though Larry had gone to church as a child, he hadn't gone forward and made a public confession of faith. One Sunday morning when we were in church together, he stood up and walked to the front to accept Christ as his personal Savior. My prayers were answered.

On a sunny day in June of 1965, Larry and I exchanged vows and were married in a beautiful church wedding. His best friend, Pete, and two younger brothers, Bruce and Mark, stood beside him, and my sister, Dianna, and best friend, Randee, supported me. Pink roses accented the pink satin bridesmaids' dresses, and my heart was filled with everlasting love. I believed on that day that we'd be together for the rest of our lives, just like we promised in the vows we made to each other. That day would be the most wonderful day of my life, as well as one that would change the landscape of my life forever.

Six months later, our first daughter, Lisa, was born on Christmas Day. I was only nineteen years old, just a child myself, but when I looked at Lisa, my heart swelled with the joy that only a mother can know. She looked just like her father, and she was the most beautiful baby we'd ever seen. We called her our Christmas Angel.

The timing of my pregnancy deeply disappointed and embarrassed my parents. Being raised in a Christian home and becoming a Christian at an early age hadn't safeguarded me from the unbridled passions and poor decisions of adolescence. And in spite of growing up during the sexual revolution of the sixties, I was very naive. All I knew was that I loved Larry and wanted to be with him for all of my life. I believed in happily ever after.

At first we were happy to be together, all grown up and on our own. But with the sudden responsibilities of a newborn, I began to feel overwhelmed and insecure. For my teenage husband, the pressure of having to support a family in less than six months took its toll. And though he worked hard in the mill in Springfield and consented to living with my parents until we could afford our own apartment, the marriage was fraught with problems from the start.

I'd been raised by a mother whose upbringing was strictly religious by anyone's standards. Dad had come from a large family that also followed the biblical laws of God, and until my junior year in high school, in response to my ceaseless pleadings to let me attend the school dances with my friends, I'd known little of the typical teenage lifestyle of the times. I was sheltered and unaware of the obstacles and temptations the world held that might chip away at a marriage that was already on shaky ground.

Larry's home life was more normal. Larry had a stepfather, a big man with a big voice and a gentle and kind heart. His mother was a beautiful, petite woman, with the same smile I'd first noticed on her son—a smile that had captured my heart at first sight. Larry's younger brothers, Bruce and Mark, were wonderful to me, thinking it very cool that they now had a sister. And I loved them all back.

Before Lisa was a year old, my father helped Larry land a job with Decca Records in Portland. The move took me away from family and friends, but I thought I'd do fine with Larry and our baby, and we would be the happy family I'd longed for. The job meant travel, and I was often home alone, wondering when my husband would come home to me. I found out quickly that "happily ever after" is not something that can be counted on. Life isn't a fairy tale, and people are vulnerable to stresses and shortcomings. Larry was too young and full of life to stay home like the dutiful husband, and I was too immature to know how to be the perfect wife.

Larry's having to be on the road for work, living a life of freedom while I was homebound with first Lisa and then Lainee, made it hard to bond as a family. Parenting when we were both so young and immature put stresses on our marriage right from the start. We scarcely knew how to care for each other, much less a family. And the world was becoming a different place as the sixties and the free-minded ways of America tempted my young husband to stray.

I had meant my marriage vows, but instead of turning to God to heal what was broken, I allowed selfish pride to flourish and grow in the garden of my heart. Without warning, my life suddenly stretched out in front of me like a forked road, and I was faced with the decision of which way to go. I could fall to my knees, hand over my pain and the shattered pieces of my heart, and patiently wait for God to lead according to his will, trusting him to heal and mend our marriage—or I could take the path of my own choosing. I recklessly set out to find my own happiness. Little did I know then that a lifetime of guilt and shame would sprout and thrive from my choices.

The day I presented Larry with the divorce papers, he looked at me with tears in his eyes and said that he didn't want a divorce. But he signed the papers anyway. I felt like a lost soul. The happily-ever-after dream of a perfect life with my one and only love had dissolved in an instant, and a piece of my heart was gone forever. I was terrified to raise my young girls alone. Immature and naive in the ways of the world, I believed nothing could ever hurt me more. Feeling abandoned and crushed, I covered my brokenness with a sunny smile, never knowing that my pain and disappointment had only begun.

In the summer of 1970, my divorce from Larry was finalized. I felt devastated and shattered, and the crack in my heart was almost too painful to bear. I made up my mind to find a way to leave my past behind.

I called a friend in San Jose who'd been close to our family in Los Gatos when my parents were young. She invited me to stay with her and her husband until I found a place for my girls and me. Within a month I had my own apartment, and she'd introduced me to a potential employer at a very exclusive restaurant.

The manager, Kavyan, interviewed me and hired me on the spot. Then he looked at me gravely as he explained the rules. "You may speak only when I tell you to speak, or when I ask you a question, or when you are taking dinner orders from a customer. When you aren't attending to the customers, you are to stand at your station, and you are not to say a word. Do you understand? Not one word. We don't talk to each other; we only attend to the diners."

Kayvan continued to instruct me on my new job duties, and with a wave of his arm, he pointed out three small bus stations along one wall. It was clear that he ran a tight ship. I was immediately intimidated by his strictness and his foreign accent. But he also had a certain charm about him. If he hadn't, I'd have looked elsewhere for work. I promised to abide by the rules and then went shopping for a long black skirt and white blouse. An elegant look for a waitress, I thought.

On my first day at the restaurant, I met Cody, who was assigned to bus my tables. He was a hard worker, and I could see how he tried to make my tip bigger by attending to my tables especially well, constantly pouring glasses full of water and bringing anything that might run low before the patrons had a chance to request anything. I realized right away that he was working much harder for me than for the other waitresses, and when a male customer acted too interested in talking to me, I thought I felt a wave of resentment from this young man with the huge smile. I was flattered by his attention, and whenever I turned around I could tell he'd been watching me. I tried to talk to him, but our conversations were almost nonexistent. He knew some broken English, but very little, and I spoke no Farsi. But since we weren't permitted to talk while we worked, it didn't really matter. I tried to express my gratitude with a smile every time our eyes met. Before long, I realized our eyes were meeting on a regular basis.

The restaurant was one of the finest dining locations in San Jose, and the strict rules we had to follow as employees were well worth the trouble. I was hopeful that I would be able to afford living on my own with the girls and no longer worry about where the money would come from.

Lisa had turned six on Christmas Day and would be starting first grade in September, and Lainee, at five years of age, would attend kindergarten. I hoped both of them would love California as much as I had growing up, and I was determined to meet and marry someone who would give them the love and stability they deserved. I prayed that my heart would one day mend and I'd be happy and complete.

My life was back on track for the most part. I was terribly lonely, but I kept it well hidden behind a bright smile and a positive, energetic attitude. I knew that I would eventually make some friends at work, and as I stood at my post by the bus station, waiting to deliver food or take dinner orders, the young, dark-skinned men I worked with flashed welcoming smiles at me. But Cody's big white smile outdid them all.

In only a matter of weeks, my relationship with Cody began to change. We spent a day with the girls at the beach in Santa Cruz, and he was the perfect gentleman. He treated the girls as if they were his own, taking them into the ocean and playing with them on the sandy beach. Soon he was stopping by after work to visit at our apartment. I helped him improve his English, and he showered my two little daughters and me with attention. He made sure the girls were the first he paid attention to, and within a few weeks he gently smiled his way into our hearts. But when kisses good night and a hug here and there led to his wanting more in our relationship, I told him I'd never again become seriously involved with someone unless we were married.

"Okay, let's get married," he replied.

Before I had time to consider what I was jumping into, I had consented, and we were planning a weekend trip to Reno. I wasn't at all sure what was going to happen once we got there. Before we left, I tried to call Larry once more, but I couldn't reach him, and a letter I'd sent him when I first moved to California had gone unanswered.

The night before we left for Reno, I took the time to sit alone at the kitchen table in our little apartment after the girls were tucked in bed and whisper a prayer.

"Dear Heavenly Father, I know this is way too fast. I know this man is someone I hardly know anything about. But I'm alone, and I'm afraid. I don't want to raise my girls all by myself, and I think if it's all right with you, we might have a happy family together. Please stop me if this isn't what you want me to do! In Jesus' name, amen."

When Cody and I walked up the steps of the Reno County Courthouse that weekend, on June 12, 1972, I felt desperate and numb. My heart was screaming at me to stop this madness, but I refused to listen. God hadn't stepped in and saved me from this moment, so it had to be the right thing to do. At least that's what I kept telling myself. An hour later, Cody and I stood before the justice of the peace and exchanged vows. I knew I was diving head-first into another possible mistake, but I prayed and told God how scared I was to be alone. I was terrified to raise my girls in a world so full of sadness and disappointment. My outlook on life was very different now.

Once we were back in San Jose, Cody moved into my apartment, and Kavyan promoted him from busboy to cook at the Brave Bull. I called my parents as soon as we returned and told them I was married.

"You what?" Mother's voice sounded small and quiet. I repeated the simple statement, "I got married this weekend." She simply answered, "Oh."

I was confident my parents would see the big friendly smile on my new husband and be grateful I hadn't picked someone they couldn't warm up to. Years later I reflected on how very dangerous my decision might have been. I could have been entrusting my life and the lives of my children to almost anything, considering how little I knew about Cody. Once more I'd trusted my own decisions rather than waiting patiently and prayerfully as I'd been taught to do as a child. I had leaned on my own understanding, completely in opposition to what I'd once read in my Bible. And yet, God was certainly protecting me even then, while I was still determined to stumble mindlessly into a life without his direction.

When I found out I could be pregnant just three months into our marriage, I knew I wasn't ready to have a child. I still wasn't sure what I had gotten myself into when I married this man from another culture and faith. Cody apparently wasn't ready for another child either. When I told him I was afraid I might be pregnant, he immediately encouraged me to have a D&C for the assurance that there was no baby. He didn't think we could make it financially if we had another mouth to feed. I had misgivings, but I decided to go through with it anyway.

I had already survived what felt like a near-fatal broken heart, and the last thing I was planning to do was be caught in another broken marriage that would be much more difficult with a third baby in the middle. My mind was unstable. All I could be sure of was that if this didn't work, the less baggage between us, the better. I could feel the hardening of my heart.

Around the end of the year, my father called and told us about a small tract house for sale in Eugene. He offered to put a down payment on the house if we were interested. I was ready to go home, wanting the security of being near my parents and the place where I felt I really belonged. My girls missed their grandparents, and I thought once we were home together I'd find the

perfect life I'd always dreamed of. Cody thought this would move us closer
to his dream of buying his own restaurant, and we both knew we could never
afford to buy a home without my dad's help. Life with Cody and my girls was
beginning to look like the perfect new beginning. A couple of weeks later we
packed up and headed north. This was a new world for Cody, but the girls and
I were on our way back home.

Within days of the move, Cody was hired at at a local restaurant as a cook.
When the owner saw how good he was in the kitchen, he offered Cody a pro-
motion to head chef. Cody was elated that he'd finally be able to start saving
up for his own restaurant. I was proud of him. He was an excellent chef and a
very hard worker, and I knew it was only a matter of time before he'd be able
to buy his own place.

I was able to work full-time as a hostess at a new restaurant in an upscale
hotel right next door to where Cody worked. Lisa and Lainee stayed with
neighbor girls or my teenage cousins while we worked, and we were never
home too late. I enjoyed getting out of the house and helping with the finances.

Life was going to be okay, I thought to myself. But it wasn't easy getting
used to a new world of customs and culture, and at night when we went to bed,
I would pray aloud for my Moslem husband, that one day he might love Jesus
and believe in him as the Son of God. As soon as he heard my "Amen," Cody
would pray to Allah in Farsi, and at the end would say in English, "And please
show my wife, Lauri, that Allah is the only one true God." I ignored him the
best I could, all the while assuring myself that one day he would change and
find the truth of God's Son, Jesus.

By the time Farah was born in August of 1975, I'd felt the guilt of expecting my husband to raise my own two girls and have none of his own. Farah's
birth was the result of an agreement: I had told Cody that if he wanted to, I
would agree to have one more baby, and it would most likely be a boy. But no
matter what the child's gender, there would be no more little ones. I was completely content with the two girls alone. Cody didn't insist, which made me
all the more willing to give birth to one more child. My husband had proven
his devotion to me and to the sanctity of our marriage, though our religious
views were as different as night and day. He honored me as his wife, never once
forgetting to call and tell me if he would be home late, often assuring me that
I was the only woman in his heart. It meant so much more than I could ever

express. And in the years after we'd married, the girls warmed up to him—though they never forgot their daddy, Larry, for a second.

When Farah was only a few months old, I hired my cousins to assist Lisa and Lainee as babysitters and returned to my waitress and hostess job. My daughters meant everything to me, but I also enjoyed the hours when the older girls were able to help care for their baby sister and give me some independence and freedom.

ॐ

Farema's screaming jarred me back to the present. I knew that God had a reason for all the things he'd allowed to occur in my life up to that point, and I knew he had promised to make everything work together for good. But I couldn't help but wonder how different my life might have been if I hadn't filed those divorce papers so many years ago. Somehow, it didn't matter much. Although the years had changed my youthful belief that dreams always do come true, I had learned to be content. All I needed now, I told myself, was to find a reason why this baby was so different from her sisters—and to learn to survive until she grew out of it.

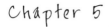

Chapter 5

STRANGER THAN FICTION

A
s many twists and turns as my life had taken before Farema came along, now that she was here it was stranger than fiction. I was certain that no one would believe me even if I dared to confide my day-to-day experiences of caring for little Fee—not even Cody. Unlike her sisters before her, baby Fee never turned her head to the sound of my voice. She stared at the wall, gazed at the ceiling, and seemed fixated on the light fixtures, but not once would she look at my face. As far as I knew, I was the only one who noticed. And while she seemed uninterested in the mommy who coddled and cuddled her, she flashed wide-eyed excitement and smiles at the sight of our big German Shepherd dog, Bear, the moment she caught sight of him through the glass sliding doors. I interpreted this to mean she was brilliant—a child with extraordinary ability, at only a few weeks old, to recognize a furry, lovable friend. But I constantly worked to get my baby to look up at me. She never did.

Other things were missing in my baby's development, but I had reasons to excuse them. When she never reached up to touch the musical mobile that hung temptingly over her crib, I told myself she was born small—her difficult birth would cause her to have delays. That was normal. Lisa and Lainee tried repeatedly to get their baby sister to grasp a rattle or small toy, to no avail. I was quick to make the same excuses.

Adding to the pressure, Cody's parents would call from Tehran and ask if she was saying any words yet. I sometimes became angry with their undue interest in her learning to talk, and I snapped back at Cody when he brought it up after a telephone conversation with his family.

"Who cares! Farah was two when she started to talk, so who would expect Farema would be any different?" Then I exited the room and wondered why I reacted so negatively to kind concern from my husband's family.

Although I'd only taken a few weeks off work when Farah was born, after Farema's birth I took my time returning to my job at the Rodeway Inn. Cody had been working at the motel restaurant next door to the Rodeway for more than nine years by the time he finally told his boss that he needed to quit and focus on El Kiosco. His dream was in full bloom, and I stayed at home with the girls, working a short shift here and there if someone was sick or on vacation. It was on one of those days, while I was home getting ready to work the lunch hour for someone who needed the day off, when I experienced the unexplainable.

Farema and I were home alone that morning, and I propped her up in front of some cartoons that were playing on the television in the family room. When I noticed she'd fallen asleep, I switched the television off and returned to where I'd been brushing my hair into a ponytail in front of the mirror in the small adjoining bathroom.

Then I heard the sound that at first made me wonder if Lisa and Lainee had come home and turned the TV back on. I hurried out to tell them to turn it off so as not to wake the baby. No one was there. I shrugged it off and went back to combing my hair. Again, I heard the singing:

"Snap makes the world go 'round! Snap! Crackle! Pop! Rice Krispies!"

I stopped and turned my head to better listen to the sound of the "Snap, Crackle, Pop" song that I recognized from a Rice Krispies commercial. For a moment, when I stepped back into the room again to be certain the television was indeed off, I wondered if I was imagining things. Was my mind playing a trick on me? I walked quietly across the carpet, and when I peeked over the baby-bumper seat to look at Farema, I found she was awake, smiling at the darkened screen in front of her. I was sure no one else was home.

But my fifteen-month-old couldn't possibly be the one singing.

The voice I'd heard sounded sweet and childlike, much like the cartoon voice in the commercial. Maybe one of the girls had come home early, I thought, as I walked through the house looking into the hall bathroom and each bedroom. Farah might have unexpectedly returned from an overnight with her cousin Jennifer at her grandmother's house—but no, there was no sign of her. The front door was locked, and no one was in the living room or kitchen. "Hello? Girls? Lisa? Farah?" I called out. No one answered.

I returned to the little bathroom and sat on the toilet seat lid to listen intently and contemplate what was happening. Either I was imagining this, or Farema, who'd only ever chattered in her babbling baby talk, had learned to sing the "Snap, Crackle, Pop" song. I knew that wasn't possible. How could it be? I waited for what seemed like a long time to hear more, but the singing had stopped.

I didn't say a word to the girls about it when they came home an hour later, just in time for me to go to work.

Lisa and Lainee headed straight for the kitchen to look for something to eat. I stopped at the breakfast counter and told them what was in the fridge for lunch if they wanted it, and then I asked them one question.

"Were either of you here a little while ago? Or did you just come in for the first time when I opened the door?"

They both responded with blank looks. Before they had a chance to ask why I thought they'd been there, I knew something very strange had happened that morning. I entertained the thought that this baby of mine, the one who used no real words but "talked" constantly in her own baby babble, might be keeping a huge secret from us.

"No way," I mumbled aloud. "That is just too weird."

Later that afternoon, on my way home from work, I mulled the morning's event over and over in my mind. The sounds I'd heard earlier that day had seemed so real. One thing I knew for sure: if it had been Farema singing, my worries about her learning to talk were over. I felt a sense of relief at the prospect that maybe we would soon see for ourselves what secrets this smarter-than-we-knew child held in store for us!

I never mentioned the singing to anyone, not even Randee. I knew it sounded unbelievable, and I wasn't sure anyone would believe me if I told them. I would keep it a secret, and if Farema did it again, if she had done it at all, someone else would be witness to it. And I didn't ignore the fact that since Farema's birth I'd been deprived of sleep. Wasn't it true that after three days' loss of sleep one becomes delusional and can even have hallucinations? I'd read that somewhere.

Farema would not sing again or utter one recognizable word, and the questions about my little girl's peculiarities continued to haunt me like a chilling draft. She was different in ways that I couldn't put my finger on, yet at other times she was just a normal, busy, constantly moving toddler.

Farema had been walking all over the house since she was less than a year old. Her ability to get around on her own came with new worries for me.

Our home was in a suburban neighborhood, but our house backed up to a long strip of land that spread out to about five acres owned by the city. The land went up for sale, and I begged Cody to see if we could offer a couple thousand dollars on a whim in case they'd take so little an offer. To my amazement, they did, and my dream of putting a horse on the property behind our house was a dream come true. Misty was a small pinto mare. With my knowledge of horses from my own childhood, I knew she would be safe even if Farema somehow ended up in her corral. In the years we lived there, we eventually added a pair of ducks, chickens, a couple of dogs and cats, and a family of rabbits to our backyard menagerie. Although Misty posed no danger, Farema had a lot of room to get lost, on our land and all through the neighborhood.

While Farema ignored things that might attract other children, like objects under the sink or in open kitchen drawers, she was attracted to things that made a fast whirling motion. She was fascinated by spinning toy tops. She liked to watch the overhead ceiling fan in the family room when it was on, and she would stare at the whirring blades until her little neck wore out.

When the hot sunny afternoons prompted me to set up a big square fan in the doorway, it soon became a center of attention for her and a dangerous dilemma for me.

As soon as I'd switch it on, Farema would waddle over, sit as close as she could to the whirring fan, and put her face close to the grate, letting the air blow onto her skin. All my pulling her away and trying to deter her from sitting up against the fan didn't work, and one day, fearing she might stick a tiny finger inside to the dangerous sharp blades, I switched the fan off and put it away.

Then Farema found a spin without blades.

One warm Sunday afternoon while Farah was playing with her friends in the yard, I asked her to let Farema join them for a short time. Farema had been watching the children while they took turns to see who could spin fast on bare feet in the grass the longest before falling down. Right away, Farema joined in. I heard the kids laughing and clapping for her and came out to the porch to see her stamping her tiny baby feet to turn as fast as she could, round and round, till she fell down. Then she got up and did it again. I was laughing too; it was cute and very funny to see her spindly legs moving so fast; but Cody didn't like it. When he came outside he told me to make her stop. He said that in Iran, spinning in circles was a sign of madness. If he really believed that, I knew it had to be something he'd heard as a boy in a country where superstitions and stories told from generation to generation are seldom based on scientific evidence.

"Cody, how can you believe that old wives' tale?" I said. "When I was a little girl I loved to spin around in the backyard, out on the lawn, until I'd get so dizzy I'd fall down, and it was fun! We kids all did it!" Cody only shook his head and went in the house, Farema in hand.

Disagreements about beliefs such as these were only one of many ways our cultures clashed, resulting in years of disagreements and angry tears between two people joined together with little common ground. Our religious faiths, cultures, and upbringings were as far apart as the east is from the west. But though we so often found little to agree on, we both believed our baby girl had a problem. As I wondered what it could be, I secretly trekked to the Springfield Library in search of answers whenever I had a chance to go alone.

I'd been visiting the library for short periods of time as often as possible since Farema was only weeks old. In the beginning I'd wanted to be sure there was nothing seriously wrong with her. By the time she began to exhibit some unusual behaviors, I went to read childhood development books just so I could discount the possibility that something *could* be wrong. Though I expected to find relief, each reading adventure brought more unanswered questions.

One possibility haunted me. I read books about children whose odd indifference to other people, including children their own age, corresponding with deficits in communication and responses, had once been diagnosed as *Childhood Schizophrenia*. In the 1940s, a doctor recognized differences in some children within that group and put a new name to their diagnosis—*Autism*.

In 1949, German-born psychiatrist Dr. Leo Kanner attributed autism to a "genuine lack of maternal warmth" in the parents of autistic children, and the "Refrigerator Mother" theory of autism was born. Bruno Bettleheim, another psychologist, wrote articles in the 1950s and '60s that caused Kanner's idea to spread: it was the cold, refrigerator-like mother who created a child with autism. I'd heard the phrase "Refrigerator Mother" before, but I couldn't remember when or where, and although the history was interesting to read, it prompted memories of how reluctant I'd been to have this last child. A slight shudder passed over me as I forced the thought from my mind.

Autistic behaviors themselves were strange and frightening. The more I read about this peculiar group of children and the bizarre behaviors they exhibited, the more I knew I could never be one of those people who cares for a child with a disability—and certainly not one with something so frightening as autism.

Chapter 6

THE CHURCH LADY

One summer afternoon, my neighbor Lois came to my front door with an older woman I'd never seen before.

"This is my friend Emily Watson," Lois said brightly. "She wanted to tell you about the new class she's teaching at Vacation Bible School this August."

Lois had one of those faces that always seemed to smile, even when she wasn't particularly happy. She and her husband, Steve, lived in the house next to ours with their three children, Shandy, Stephanie, and Stephen. A visit from Lois and her family was always a welcome event at our house.

I invited Lois and Emily into my living room and gestured for them to sit on the couch. I settled onto the piano bench across from them and pulled a sleepy Farema onto my lap.

Emily smiled and said, "Lois mentioned that you have a toddler who is too young to attend VBS with your other daughter, so I thought you might be interested in the new class we're offering this year. We want to minister to mothers in the community by giving them a little time to themselves during VBS. Would you like to sign Farema up for the class?"

"I'd love to have her attend if you think it's okay," I answered. I was thrilled to have a couple of hours to myself, if only for a week. I didn't think Farema would cause the teachers any trouble. She would probably just sit quietly on the floor the entire time. It amazed me that a toddler could sit for hours so contentedly without seeming to need any interaction with others.

Of course, at times she could be incredibly active and almost hyper—but I hoped for the best.

Emily sat on the edge of the couch holding a small Polaroid camera and fixing her gaze on Farema as we spoke. Farema was hanging over my arm like a rag doll, a vacant expression on her face. She always looked this way when she was in need of a nap.

I normally wouldn't have let anyone see my baby until she was more rested and animated, but I had let down my guard when I saw Lois at the door. Now I felt my defenses scrambling back to high alert under Emily's scrutiny. I was becoming increasingly sensitive about the way my toddler looked and acted, especially when she seemed so disconnected from the world around her, and I felt a fierce need to shield her from stares and unwelcome comments.

"Farema's about to pop off," I quickly explained. "I was just on my way to lay her down when I saw you coming to the door."

In the past seventeen months, I'd become adept at offering explanations and excuses for Farema's odd behaviors. I could pull any number of responses out of my hat at a moment's notice if someone looked askance at my little girl.

On more than one occasion at the grocery store or mall, Farema had thrown herself on the floor without warning and begun to shriek in terror. Every eye would turn in our direction, and I feared that someone would suspect me of child abuse. I never knew when an explosion was coming, and when it did, no amount of consoling would appease my distraught child.

"Oh, you poor thing," I'd coo in my most soothing voice. "You shouldn't have missed that nap!"

Making sure my comment was loud enough to reach nearby gawkers, I'd bend over, scoop my screeching child off the filthy floor, and quickly carry her out the nearest exit.

I'd left countless baskets of groceries abandoned in aisles and collections of toiletries and clothing heaped in the strangest places. My apologies were often only silent thoughts directed toward the confused and irritated shoppers transfixed before me. I knew that taking away the noise was the kindest thing I could do for them. I'd long given up trying to make Farema stop her tantrums: even smacking her on the diapered bottom when she'd throw herself on the floor at home didn't do anything except make her screech louder and look up at me as if I were an unknown attacker trying to hurt her for no reason.

But on this particular occasion, it was Farema's rag-doll listlessness, not a temper tantrum, that was drawing unwelcome attention from the stranger across from me.

Emily smiled and nodded sympathetically, but instead of taking my excuse as a cue to leave, she kept on talking. "Do you mind if I take a picture of you and your little one for the class? We need to have one for safety reasons."

Her request made sense to me, but I didn't want anyone taking a picture of my daughter when she looked so worn out. That afternoon, Farema seemed especially detached for some reason. I tried to get her to sit up in my lap and smile, but she just slumped limply and stared off into space, a glazed look in her eyes. I knew that the moment I put her down she would fall asleep, but I wanted my company to leave first so I could sit in her room and watch her sleep for a while.

I'd been watching Farema a lot more recently, trying to understand what was so different about her. But I couldn't put my finger on it. I had been concerned for some time about the way she seemed to separate herself from the rest of us. She didn't care to cuddle much, which was so unlike my other girls, who had thrived on my hugs and kisses as toddlers. The only time Farema would allow me to hold her was when she was just about to nod off. I'd rock her to sleep in my arms, then put her in her crib for her nap.

Emily and Lois continued talking about VBS, and weariness filled my body as I listened halfheartedly. When they finally got up to leave, I mustered a smile and walked them to the door. I sighed with relief as soon as the door closed behind them, then I carried Farema into her room and laid her in her crib. Instantly she was asleep. I sat on the twin bed next to her crib and gazed at her, my mind spinning as I thought about how different she was from her sisters.

The fact that she didn't interact or communicate with other children her age bothered me the most. It wasn't just the absence of verbal communication that concerned me: she completely ignored the children playing around her. My older girls had always loved playing with their little friends and had been willing participants in nearly every activity. One moment they would chase one another around the house, giggling wildly; the next, they would get into a fight over the same toy when there were dozens of others to enjoy. But Farema would do neither. No matter how much her playmates tried to coax her into joining the communal fun, she just sat slumped over in the middle of the action, seemingly oblivious to what was happening around her. Nothing seemed to move her, upset her, or elicit any sort of reaction at all. It didn't matter whether another child tried to get her attention in a nice way or self-ishly grabbed a toy from her, she had no interest in interacting with anyone. She had no real playmates to speak of, and I had come to think of Farema as a loner.

Even noises, loud or soft, couldn't seem to distract her or get her atten-tion—except when certain noises, at odd times, would scare her to death or throw her into a tantrum. Still, she didn't seem to be hearing normally. As I sat by Farema's crib and watched the rise and fall of her chest, I wondered whether she might have a hearing problem. That could explain why she didn't mind being alone, I mused. Maybe, just maybe, this poor little child had given up on trying to interact normally because she couldn't understand what was actually going on around her!

⁂

The summer of 1982 came to an end, and fall settled over Eugene. Chilly late-September breezes were blowing, and warm winter coats would soon be taken out of mothballs. Memories of summer were fading, though at times I wist-fully recalled that blissful VBS week in August when I'd had several precious hours to myself, enjoying a luxurious bubble bath and going shopping without any interruptions. I hadn't been able to do that since Farema was born.

One afternoon, I donned my waitress uniform and primped in front of the bathroom mirror before heading to work. It was Cody's day off, and I had agreed to work the evening shift at a nearby restaurant for a good friend who was having emergency surgery.

"Okay, I'm leaving!" I called out.

I walked into the bedroom, picked up my purse, and rooted around for my car keys. No luck.

"Cody, have you seen my keys? I lost 'em again."

I hurried into the living room and ran my hands along the sides of the couch, wondering if my keys, like so many other items, had disappeared into the bottomless pit that existed beneath the cushions.

Still no keys.

After looking in the bathroom and kitchen, I finally spotted them on the bedroom floor, where they'd apparently fallen out of my purse. I made my way back down the hall and stuck my head into the family room to say good-bye to Cody, but he was fast asleep on the couch. Farema was in her crib sleeping as well, so I tiptoed to the front door. I didn't want to disturb such a rare, peaceful scene, especially since Farema was still up crying several times a night with gas pains or earaches or something. None of us had been getting much sleep, and more than a year of nightly vigils was taking a toll.

Earlier that afternoon, Lisa and Lainee had gone off with friends who lived down the street, and they had taken little Farah with them. I knew they'd be gone for a while and that my twenty-month-old probably wouldn't wake up until after Cody had finished his nap. Even if she did, Cody would hear her on the baby monitor.

As I retraced my steps to the door, I happened to glance outside and notice a woman coming up the walk.

"Good grief," I muttered under my breath. "Who could that be?"

I didn't want to wake poor Cody, so I opened the door, slipped outside, and quickly pulled it shut before turning to face the stranger on my porch.

"Oh!" the woman gasped, stepping back awkwardly and looking as startled as she sounded.

"Can I help you?" I said, forcing a slight smile as I waited to hear what she was selling.

"Do you remember me, Lauri?" she asked, looking flustered. She stepped back again and teetered precariously on the edge of the porch.

"Uh . . . well . . . not really," I answered, surprised that she knew my name. The gray-haired woman looked somewhat familiar, but I couldn't seem to place her.

"I'm Emily Watson—from the church where your two little daughters attended VBS this summer."

Then it came to me. This was the woman who had come by with Lois in July to talk about VBS and take a picture of Farema for the Birth-to-Two class.

"Oh, yes, I remember," I said. "I'd love to chat with you, Emily, but I really need to go. I'm on my way to work, and I'm almost running late."

Somehow I felt uneasy about Emily's spontaneous visit, but I wasn't sure why.

"I really do need to speak with you for a few minutes. I was hoping we could go inside and talk. . ."

I tensed even more. The urgency in Emily's voice bothered me. No, it frightened me.

"You see," she continued, "ever since Farema attended my class, I've been feeling that I need to tell you something, but I didn't want to be the one. I've been praying about this for weeks, trying to convince myself it isn't necessary. Every time I thought about coming over or calling, I talked myself out of it. But now, I honestly feel that God sent me here today."

I was dumbfounded. For a fleeting moment, I wanted someone else with me on the porch to hold me steady. Something about this woman's body language, the tone of her voice, and the words she spoke sent a cold shiver through my bones. I tried to force a smile, but it was useless. I could hear my heart pounding as I stared at her in stunned silence. My mind was churning with incomplete retorts, but I couldn't think clearly enough to ask why she felt that God had sent her to talk to me.

Where are my girls? I need them! The thought screamed inside my head. I wanted my children near to shield me from whatever this woman was about to say. I felt a sudden impulse to run to my car and leave her standing on my porch. I didn't want to hear another word.

As I gazed at Emily, I realized that she looked older than I remembered her. Her face was lined and careworn, and her gray hair was pulled back in a small bun, which made her look even older. With thin, frail-looking fingers, she captured a few strands of hair that were blowing free in the breeze and absentmindedly rolled them back into place.

I'd never been able to be purposely rude to anyone, so I knew I wouldn't get away until I'd heard her out. I started toward the car in an attempt to lead her closer to hers, but after a few steps, I realized she hadn't moved. I stopped and turned to face her, bracing myself for what she would say next.

"When I saw your little girl the first time I visited with Lois," she began, "I felt there was something familiar about her. She reminded me of my oldest son, Robert. Robert was born with severe mental retardation, and by the time I had our second child, he was so big that we had to put him in an institution to keep him from possibly harming the baby."

As I listened to this insanity, I wondered if the woman standing before me was crazy. I stood frozen in place as my brain tried to process what I was hearing.

"Of course, I'm not suggesting you should do what we did," she continued. "Times are different now . . ."

"What exactly are you trying to say?" I finally managed. "Do you think there's something wrong with Farema?" My voice came out too shrill, too blunt. I knew I sounded like the crazy one now.

"Well . . . yes," she answered slowly, her eyes fixed on mine. "I do believe that she may be retarded—and possibly autistic."

She'd done it now. I couldn't listen another minute. I'd too spent many afternoons in the library, secretly flipping through childhood development books, and whenever the *A* word came up, I'd turn the page as fast as I could. I wouldn't, I couldn't go there.

"I have to go to work," I said woodenly; then I turned and walked around my car to the driver's side door.

I was glad that Cody had slept through this unwelcome encounter. At least he'd been spared from hearing such an unwarranted accusation. As I unlocked the car door, I felt the blood drain from my face, and my legs were starting to become very heavy. All I wanted to do was escape this moment in time, to rid myself of this person who had invaded my home.

"Please, just listen for a few minutes," Emily begged. "I'm so sorry I upset you. I remember how bad I felt when they told me about my son."

I paused with my hand on the door handle, then I released my grip and walked back to where she stood on the porch.

"Can you tell me why you think my daughter is retarded or autistic?" I asked.

Even as I asked, I told myself that nothing she said could possibly be true. But this woman had claimed that God had sent her, and I desperately needed to know why.

"It's the way her hands feel. And the look she has in her eyes. She doesn't make eye contact. Haven't you noticed?"

For what seemed like an eternity, I simply stared at Emily. Then I returned to my car. Without looking at her, I opened the door, hopped in, and turned the key in the ignition.

As I backed out of the driveway, I felt torn. Part of me felt sorry for this woman who must have thought she was doing the right thing by coming to me. But another part of me was outraged that she had said such things about my child. I had to prove her wrong! I couldn't let myself believe that such a terrible fate had been inflicted on my sweet, silent, strange little Farema.

In a matter of minutes, this stranger had exposed the secret fears I'd been hiding deep inside. She had forced me to publicly entertain, just for a moment, the heartbreaking possibility that my daughter might not be normal—to entertain it in a way I never did on my own, even in the library. And worst of all, she had invoked the name of God as a way to get my attention and make me wonder whether her theory might actually be true.

My eyes welled with tears as I glanced in the rearview mirror and saw Emily walking slowly toward her car. I noticed that more of her long, silvery hair had sprung loose from its communal bun and now flapped awkwardly in the breeze. She looked pitiful, but I was too emotionally distraught to care about her feelings.

As I drove toward the restaurant, images of Farema's strange reactions flashed through my mind in an endless stream. One scene in particular would repeat itself every time I came home from my waitressing job. After running around for six or seven hours straight, I'd burst through the front door, intent on getting my uniform off, especially my tight pantyhose. Baby Fee would run over to me, and I would reach out for her, a huge smile on my face, ready to sweep my little one into my arms and kiss her soft baby cheeks. But she would never look at my face. No matter how hard I tried to engage her eyes, she'd pull away and with open hands gesture excitedly toward my legs. I knew what she was waiting for, but I longed to hold her close instead, to feel any reciprocation on her part. It was not to be.

"Okay, baby. Come on with Mommy. I have to sit down to take them off."

As soon as I'd pull my nylons down over my knees and off my feet, she'd stare intently at the indentations the elastic had left on my skin, her little nose almost touching my leg. Then she'd reach out a tiny index finger and trace the lines.

"You know Mommy's nylons leave those marks, honey. See? Here are some on your tummy."

She would usually ignore me or glance for a moment at the marks I was pointing to around her waist. Then she'd go right back to studying the marks on my legs until she seemed satisfied. At that point, she would stop abruptly and walk away, as if a switch had been turned off.

I'd stare after her, confused and dismayed that my little one didn't seem to care that Mommy was home. I was just an object of curiosity. She had only needed to check the elastic marks on my skin, and as soon as that task was done, she was off to do whatever she'd been up to before I walked in. I had no reasonable explanation for such puzzling behavior, so I buried it in a secret place in my mind, along with all the other weird things she did that I couldn't understand.

But Emily's visit had blown the door off that secret place, and all the scary things I'd stashed there began floating to the surface of my consciousness. I tried to push the thoughts away, but they kept coming fast and furious. On an impulse, I turned down the street that led to Randee's house. Work would have to wait. The tears I'd been holding back began trickling down my face the closer I got to her home. My memory had opened up, and everything I hadn't wanted to see or acknowledge came gushing out.

I'd often wondered why Farema stared right through me as if I were a pane of glass. Why didn't she show any attachment to me? I was her mommy! Why didn't she look into my eyes like my other girls did? Why didn't she respond when I called and called her name? Why did she have such a weird, glazed-over expression most of the time? Why wasn't she talking yet? And why did she do that alien-baby thing, with her fingers twitching in front of her eyes and the vibrating and all?

I pulled my car up to the curb in front of Randee's house and hurried to the front door. Randee had been my best friend since childhood. We'd been together through our teenage years and had weathered the numerous youthful disasters that came with the territory. She'd been there when I'd gone through my divorce and when I married Cody, and she'd been there when all four of my children were born. I shared things with her that I never shared with Cody because I wanted to protect him from worry. Randee knew my secrets and fears, my heartaches and joys.

When she opened the door and smiled in surprise to see me, I burst into uncontrollable sobs. She could tell that something was terribly wrong, but she didn't ask what had reduced me to tears and incoherent phrases like "My baby!" and "How could she?" Instead, she led me to the couch and handed me a cold washcloth to hold over my face. She sat down beside me and lightly patted my back until the sobs began to subside and I was able to recount the incident that had just taken place.

After pouring out the story, I asked her if she thought there was something wrong with my toddler. This wasn't the first time I'd asked her opinion about Farema, though I tried not to let on that I had serious concerns. I'd asked Randee what she thought of the alien-baby antics, and she was convinced it was Farema's way of getting attention. I had also confided my concerns about Farema's slowness in reaching certain developmental milestones. But no matter how worried I was, my dear, level-headed friend always had a way of calming me down and offering words of comfort and hope. She always pointed out Farema's strengths, reminding me of the things that seemed normal about her.

"I think Farema is fine," Randee assured me once again as we sat together on the couch. "She's just a little slow, that's all. Remember, Einstein didn't talk until he was at least four years old. And little Fee is so smart! How many kids her age can remember the things she does? She never forgets where anything is, and she always finds her toys when no one else can!"

Randee was right. Farema had a great memory, though I often wondered if it was a way to compensate for her inability to speak or follow simple instructions. She certainly danced to a different drum. Unlike most little girls her age, she never played with her Barbies or My Little Pony dolls. Instead, she'd line them up or tear them apart and use the appendages to hammer things. And for some reason, her dolls had to be the same color. Whenever I let her pick one out at the store, she always chose the same color as the last four or five. I'd always wondered why. Still, my pediatrician had said, "No two children are the same," and that gave me some comfort too.

Thanks to Randee's encouragement and TLC, I began to feel a little better. I dried my face and reapplied my makeup while Randee called the restaurant and told them I would be arriving a little late. A few minutes later, I gave her a big hug and thanked her for letting me barge in.

As I drove to the restaurant, I silently thanked God for Randee. I decided I would reflect on my encounter with Emily when I had time to really give it some thought. I was relieved that I didn't work at Cody's restaurant. He would never have to know about what had happened that day. I could stash the event in the secret place in my mind, along with all my other concerns about Farema. And from now on, I would be more vigilant about guarding the door.

But Emily's words didn't leave me. A few days after her surprise visit, I walked over to Lois's house and knocked on the front door. I was embarrassed to let her see the panic in my eyes, but I had to know what she thought about Farema. For all I knew, Emily Watson was mentally unstable, but I trusted Lois.

"Have you noticed anything unusual about Farema?" I asked, bracing myself for her reply.

Lois hesitated a moment and then answered, "Well, I have noticed that little Fee doesn't look in our faces when we talk to her."

Lois always had such a gentle demeanor. Her words stung, but I knew they had been spoken with kindness and sympathy.

I thanked her and tried to hide how devastated I felt. As I walked back across the grass to my house, I fell apart, tears streaming down my cheeks.

Over the next couple of weeks, Emily tried to call me at work, but I told a coworker to say that I'd call her back later. I never did. Her calls to my house went unanswered as well. She must have called at least four times before giving up.

It was too threatening to me to talk to this woman again. With her scrutiny and her words, she had torn away the protective cloak I had wrapped around my youngest child. I couldn't let her destroy the defenses I'd worked so hard to build. For now, I wanted to pretend that Farema was normal. I knew she was a little different from most children her age, but I told myself that things couldn't possibly be as bad as I feared. Emily had to be wrong, and I was determined to prove it.

Chapter 7

A FEW LITTLE TESTS

mily Watson appeared on my doorstep around the end of September 1982,
but I waited almost two months before I made an appointment with our
pediatrician to discuss my concerns. During that time, I went over the
incident more than once with Randee. Besides offering me agreement that
Emily was out of line, she and other friends assured me that Farema was just
taking her sweet time to talk. Most of our family members blamed her silence
on too much attention or the fact that the last child is always "spoiled" by doting sisters and parents. I continued sneaking off to the library to read books
on child development, and I took every opportunity to question others I knew
who'd not be suspicious of why I was interested in what age their child had
talked, walked, and interacted with other small children. Farema was behind
in some things, but in walking she'd been early, like all her sisters before her.
Yet, despite all my investigations, I knew I needed expert advice.

I'd been careful not to bother with doctors if I could remedy any situation myself. With no health insurance to cover the costs, even in 1982 a visit
to a pediatrician was more than Cody and I could afford. I hoped before the
appointment came up that someone would talk me out of it, telling me it was
ludicrous or that I'd been overreacting and Farema was as normal as any child
her age. I had anticipated that Lois would be the first to talk me out of going
when I met her on the porch soon after Emily's visit, but she'd only reinforced
my decision to take Farema to the doctor. When I fell into a pool of tears and
poured out the whole story to Cody, there was no argument from him. I'd
wanted to keep the whole "church lady" story a secret from my husband, as I

was unwilling to hear Cody make derogatory comments about Christianity or church, and I didn't want to dissuade him from knowing Jesus one day— but my emotional dam unexpectedly burst, and he demanded to know why. I pulled myself together and told it all.

"Remember the woman who kept calling here, and I told you to tell her I wasn't home? During the time I covered the lunch shifts for Dee for a few days? Well, that same woman came by the restaurant to see me. I met her when I took Fee to the Vacation Bible School last summer. She was the teacher. I was too busy to talk to her, and I told the other waitress to tell her I couldn't take time out. But the truth was that I didn't want to talk to her after what she did."

Cody nodded in silence.

"She came here a few weeks ago to tell me she thought there was something wrong with Farema. She thinks she's retarded and that she has autism!"

I spat the last word out as if it were poison. But Cody remained as calm as ever and replied, "Well, she's wrong. There's nothing wrong with our Fee. The woman is mistaken, and that's all you need to say to her or anyone else."

Cody rose from his place beside me on the edge of our bed and continued to do his usual evening routine. He said it didn't matter what some old lady said, but I heard a hint of worry in his voice.

I tried to put the event out of my mind while waiting for the day I'd see the physician, but like a bothersome splinter, it refused to be ignored. When the appointment date finally came around, I was wound up and anxious. I wanted to hear Dr. Swank tell me what my heart wanted to hear. When he came smiling into the room and made a teasing gesture to Farema, then asked me why we'd come to see him, I blurted it out.

"There was a woman from a church nursery who thought Farema might be autistic or retarded like her son."

He listened without answering while I told him the whole story, word by word, the same as I'd told it to Cody. As I spoke I choked back the tears that tried to escape and kept my eyes averted so as not to give myself away as I explained that the woman had seen Farema only a few times and certainly wasn't a close friend who knew her well.

The doctor listened, then calmly dismissed Emily's hypothesis. He assured me that Emily Watson was probably trying to make herself feel better about her own son's problems and the decisions she'd made years before. He told me that in her day, the only option available to parents with a severely disabled son would have been to institutionalize him. The doctor reminded me that by the 1980s, there were other options and resources for parents with special-needs children.

He closed with a reassuring comment.

"Often, when someone has had to do something they regretted, they will try to relieve their own feelings of guilt by convincing others that they should take the same action."

I wanted to jump up off my chair in the office and kiss this medical professional who'd eased my qualms and given me back my peace of mind. Instead, I just agreed wholeheartedly and smiled back. To me, Dr. Swank's explanation made sense, and I accepted his word as proof that Emily had been misinformed. But in a hidden corner of my mind, I tucked away what she'd said about being sent by God. I could ignore her words for the time being, but I could never forget them.

After listening to Farema's heart with his stethoscope, thumping her back with his fingers, and looking in her mouth, the doctor smiled. Then he took a cartoon-decorated Band-Aid out of the pocket of his white lab jacket. He pulled the tabs off each end, and while she sat still, watching him, he put it on her knee. With a big smile for a thank-you, Farema "talked" away in her own special baby language. Dr. Swank leaned back against the wall and seemed to be surveying her, as if deep in thought, while tapping his pen lightly against his lips. I wondered what he was thinking as he watched little Farema babbling and kicking her feet until the white paper covering the exam table was in shreds. After a few seconds he stopped, pointed his pen at her, and said, "That's not normal. Wait here a minute."

The doctor turned and left the room, and I sat motionless, trying to understand what he meant. Hadn't he just finished easing my fears and assuring me that all was fine with my child? Within seconds he returned with a slip of paper in his hand.

"Farema's language doesn't appear to be at age level. She should be babbling, but this isn't necessarily how it should sound. It may be nothing to worry about, but just the same, I'd like you to take her to the Center on Human Development Language Preschool. If they think it's necessary, they may recommend early intervention therapy at the Child Development Clinic, located in the Clinical Services Building on the campus at the University of Oregon. After they test her language skills and her hearing, you'll find out whether she needs some extra help."

He went on to tell me that the CCD, the department he was referring her to, was a division of the Oregon Health Sciences University and would be the very best place to help Farema get her talking sorted out. He said his referral was all the insurance company would need to cover any expenses if she qualified for admission. The tests would determine whether or not she could attend the preschool, and the practicum students there would also watch her while she played with other kids, a mix of children with disabilities and the children of university students. The preschool might be full for the rest of the year and wouldn't start up again until the beginning of the fall term, but some pre-entrance exams could be done sooner. There was usually a long list of hopefuls to get in, but they would put those with the greater need at the top of the list. As he spoke, I couldn't help but hope my daughter wouldn't be given priority on that particular list.

With that, he gave me a kind smile and said good-bye to Farema before breezing out the door to see his next patient.

As my child and I walked out of the building, she held my hand and giggled at the leaves dancing on the wind. In my other hand, I grasped the referral slip as if it held the secret to solving the puzzle that had become my little girl. As new and exciting thoughts of actually getting some answers filled my head on our drive home, I recalled the last time I'd been to the OHSU.

I'd driven to the OHSU with my friend, heading to the huge clump of white hospital buildings atop a hill in the center of Portland, when she had taken her daughter to a clinic that specialized in children with Cystic Fibrosis. I didn't know then that the Oregon Health Sciences University was involved with anything on campus or that they worked with children who had language delays. I'd gone along to support a friend whose life had taken a terrible turn. At ten months old, her little Angie had been diagnosed with a disease that would one day take her life. And I had prayed that God would give her a miracle. Little did I know then that one day I too would need a God-given miracle for my own daughter.

That evening when Cody asked how the doctor's appointment had gone, I pretended not to hear him. I was afraid to bring too much attention to a problem that might be resolved before Farema actually went to get tested. I didn't want to alarm Cody when I was quite sure the tests would prove there was little, if anything, going on with our daughter.

"So she's fine, right?" he persisted.

"Of course," I said lightly. "The doctor wants her to take a few little tests at the University of Oregon, just in case she needs some speech therapy to get her talking. And she might even be able to go to a special preschool there."

I told Cody about the doctor's assuring me that the preschool was for perfectly normal children as well as those with disabilities. They would admit her even if they felt she didn't need "early intervention," which, I told Cody, was something I'd never heard of but which sounded good to me. I explained what the doctor had said about the help to get her talking, but the preschool was on a first-come, first-serve basis, and we might have to wait on a list for an opening. I told him that sending Farema there would help us know for sure if she had any hearing problems.

Cody was interested in the possibility of finding out what, if anything, might be wrong with our little girl's ears. One of the things we both agreed on was that sometimes she acted as if she were deaf.

I busied myself with the usual evening dinner prep and continued to tell him as much as I thought he needed to know.

"He said she'll love it. And she'll probably learn a lot too."

I didn't tell him what Dr. Swank had said about Farema's speech not being normal. The guilt I had carried with me from the moment I knew I was pregnant and felt reluctance to have another child was hovering overhead like a dark cloud, telling me that somehow I was the reason for her language delay. I told Cody how much fun the preschool would be, complete with new friends for Farema to play with. I assured him of how lucky we were, that there would be no cost, that insurance would cover any charges. None of our girls had gone to preschool; we'd never been able to afford such a luxury. I felt safe in convincing Cody that this was a fun thing first and a learning experience as a fringe benefit.

What I *didn't* want to talk about was the worry Cody's parents kept expressing when asking if the baby had started to talk yet. I would again be the calm over the storm—the compass of peaceful conditions on the horizon. Inside, I was unraveling.

The following day, I called the phone number on the paper the doctor had handed me to schedule an appointment for Farema. The woman I spoke with told me that the preschool followed regular University of Oregon class schedules, beginning in the fall, and that it kept the same closures for holidays. Although on-site instruction and testing were done primarily by practicum students at the university, the developmental team and an exam by the clinic's own pediatrician could be scheduled during the summer months prior to the fall of 1983.

I watched Farema like a hawk in the months that followed, hoping for any signs of improvement in her language skills, any indication that she was growing out of all her strange behaviors. But instead of saying complete words, she just kept babbling in her own language that no one could understand.

While I waited, I decided to give her a try in a normal preschool, and in the spring I enrolled my two-year-old in a church preschool I'd driven by many times. It wasn't far from our home. When I called the church office I was elated to find there was an opening in the half-day program. On the following Monday I took a smiling Farema, all decked out in one of her new dresses—with a big white collar over a soft blue and green empire-shaped skirt with white lace peeking out at the hem—to the preschool and signed her up. After a vague account of my daughter's "limited language skills," I hurried away to do all I could before it was time to retrieve her at 12:30. But after attending only a few days, when I arrived at 12:25 to retrieve my little girl, one of the teachers caught me before I could leave.

"Oh, do you mind waiting for a few moments while I get the children settled for the afternoon rest? I'd like to talk to you before you go," she said.

I waited with Farema on the large covered porch so as not to disturb the youngsters now assembling themselves for nap time on little mats in the middle of the classroom floor. The woman came outside a few minutes later and stood with her hands clasped in front of her, her head cocked sideways and downward, looking at Farema as she spoke.

"Thank you for waiting for me. I need to ask you to find another more appropriate place for your daughter, as this is not the type of preschool that can deal with children who have behavior issues."

I froze where I stood. I stared at the teacher, though she didn't look at me except to glance up nervously to make sure I was paying attention. I had no idea what kind of response to offer. Had I heard her right? Was this really happening—at a church preschool?

"I'm sure there are other good schools that will take her—schools that have the extra personnel to assist a child like her," she finished. With that, she ducked inside the door and shut it behind her.

I stood staring at the closed door for a long minute. Farema and I walked down the steps and to my car. As I pulled out of the parking lot onto the street, I fought the tears that were begging to fall down my face—hot, angry, defiant tears that finally won the argument as I turned onto the highway that led to our house.

Farema had many times sparked curious stares when her tantrums were out of control in public places. I'd make comments about her missing her nap, all the while knowing that the unexplained tantrums came with or without naps. I wondered if it had been a colossal tantrum that made the teacher at the preschool decide Farema couldn't stay—but didn't she know about the terrible twos and temper tantrums? And what did she mean about Farema's "behavior?"

I didn't tell Cody, as was my pattern, but not for the usual reasons. I had long been praying that he would one day know the Lord as his Savior and abandon his Moslem upbringing. The last thing I wanted was to turn him off to the idea of one day going with me to church.

When I told him we'd decided the church preschool just wasn't all that much fun for Farema, Cody shrugged and nodded, and I tried to ignore the fact that I'd not been completely honest. I would tuck this event in that secret place where I stored and concealed those things I wasn't ready to reveal, either to myself or anyone else. It would have plenty of company.

I didn't try any more preschools, and finally summer arrived. On the morning of July 21, I helped Farema dress for her first appointment for evaluation at the CCD on campus. I made sure we left the house with plenty of time to find the address they'd given me. It was about twenty minutes from home, and we arrived with time to spare. I pulled into the parking lot of the old brick and concrete building and unstrapped Farema from her car seat. We followed the walkway to where a small sign signaled the entrance:

Oregon Health Sciences University
CRIPPLED CHILDREN'S DIVISION

"Crippled children?" I said out loud. The last word I'd think of to describe my active, sometimes hyper, and amazingly dexterous little girl would be "crippled." I led Farema slowly toward the door, unable to make myself rush too quickly into the beginning of a new chapter in my daughter's life.

The building was old, and the smell of damp, musty concrete was the first thing I noticed as we stepped inside. I could hear happy voices and children laughing and talking in play. As I stood wondering which concrete path with yellow footprints to follow, I felt a comforting sense that I was going to love this place, even if it did threaten of things I didn't want to hear. I had come to understand in past years that life itself has a taste of the bittersweet; and I was exceptionally skilled at ignoring the bitter and emphasizing the sweet.

I led little Fee by the hand to the left and through an open doorway where I could see a brightly lit foyer with a desk and a young girl of college age sitting behind it, busily working and answering the telephone.

She smiled, beckoned for us to come closer, and asked our names, then said for us to sit "anywhere" and wait for someone to call for us. Still holding Farema's hand so she wouldn't wander off and get lost in the maze of hallways, I led her over to a row of benches along the yellow-painted concrete walls. I pulled Farema up next to me, where she remained transfixed by the newness of her surroundings. I was proud of how pretty she looked in her little blue and white spring dress, another choice of hers made according to color and frilliness, and one of many that my little one loved to put on. Most often she'd refuse to put clothes on unless I let her wear one of the dresses she'd demanded I purchase under threat of a tantrum. I told someone once that if I hadn't known better, I'd have thought she was starting a collection of blue and white dresses.

When I heard voices coming toward us, I turned to look through the doorway and saw a young woman coming down the hall pulling a red wagon. As she neared us, I saw that she had a child, a boy who appeared by his size to be a two- or three-year-old, seated inside the wagon and leaning forward with his head resting on a blanket. His eyes were looking ahead, but they didn't appear focused on any one thing. His head was way too large for his toddler-sized body to support, and I gathered he'd not been able to walk upright with his head atop his neck. It made me think of a horse's head somehow. Immediately I was ashamed for thinking that way, but it wasn't as if I could help it.

The young woman chatted happily to the group, who, except for the boy in the wagon, were hand-in-hand with her. One of her charges was a child with Down syndrome, and there was a pair of young girls who looked like sisters, both with vacant eyes that I took for telltale signs of severe mental retardation. I turned to look again at the beautiful little girl seated next to me, and I couldn't help the thought that came into my head.

Why am I here? My daughter doesn't have anything nearly as bad as these kids! I felt embarrassed to be taking up time and space where someone with a far more serious need should be. *How could I have been so upset?* I chided myself, realizing I would leave this place a far more grateful mother.

As I looked after the little parade disappearing down the hallway, I heard someone call Farema's name. I stood up, and Farema happily jumped down and took my hand as we followed the young woman to a small classroom.

"We will have a therapist come by and speak with you, and then you can watch from the two-way mirror if you like while she is tested in here." The young woman waved her hand in the direction of an open door.

Within a minute or two another young woman appeared, this one looking and talking like a teacher. She introduced herself and spoke sweetly to Farema. I was told again that I could watch from the window, or that if I wanted to, I could join them while Farema began her testing. I told her I would go ahead and leave for the observation room.

I walked over to the door that read "Observation Only" and in smaller print asked observers to remain quiet so as not to disturb those working in various classrooms. After my eyes became accustomed to the darkness in the large room dotted with small nightlight fixtures, I saw that windows circled the four walls, looking into classrooms where children and teachers chatted and played. I walked along the wall until I found the window looking into the room where my daughter was, and I pulled a stool under me. I put on the earphones that were lying on a small ledge and squinted to read the sign that pointed to the button to push for listening and observing. What an experience, I thought: finally, a chance to see how my little girl acted without cues from me—not to mention with an expert at finding out what kind of help Farema would need to be like other children. It was exciting, but for just an instant, a tinge of fear flashed into my consciousness like a warning—maybe I didn't want to know this much!

"Can you hand me the red block?" I heard the teacher say, and I watched as a smiling Farema looked all around the room and fidgeted in her chair. The teacher continued her test. "Farema, can you hand me the red one? Do you see a red block on the table?"

Farema looked up at the teacher for a split second and back to the colored blocks. The young lady continued to ask for a red block, and Farema acted as if she didn't understand. Then, while I watched, Farema picked up the red one and placed it in the open hand of the teacher.

It was hard to sit there watching my daughter, who seemed not to understand everything that was asked of her. I made mental notes as I watched and listened. *She can't understand what the girl wants her to do—she thinks this is a game; she doesn't know this is a test!*

The teacher continued to ask for objects of various sizes, colors, and shapes. Some Farema knew, but mostly she just smiled and moved in and out of the little chair. The teacher wrote notes on a clipboard lying near her on the table. After a little more than half an hour, Farema and the teacher exited the room into the hall, signaling it was time for me to leave the dark observation room and hurry around the corner to where they were waiting. Farema's next evaluation would be done after a fifteen-minute break, and then she could eat some lunch. In all, there would be evaluations done by the whole developmental team including a physical therapist, a speech pathologist, and an audiologist, in addition to an exam by the pediatrician.

After the clinic pediatrician had finished his routine exam, he told me he would suggest Farema be admitted to the Early Education Preschool and that he could probably make sure there was room for her due to her lack of speech. He told me about the wonderful clinicians and practicum students and the communications program they had developed. This, he said, was the perfect place for her to become verbal. He said he would also refer her to the Eugene Hearing and Speech Center for a hearing evaluation in addition to the test they would do at the clinic.

The last thing on our list for the day was the one thing I had wanted for so long: a hearing test. After we left the doctor, we were ushered into an elevator and taken to the bowels of the concrete and red brick building. It was an old basement such as the one I had played in under my grandparents' home in Portland when I was five. I smiled to myself as the familiar odor of damp concrete, much stronger here than upstairs, mixed with years and years of subterranean existence, struck my senses and took me back many years to a happier time. For me, childhood was a blessed memory—a place I wished I could go back to and start over, and maybe avoid the choices I'd made. Maybe I would listen to the still small voice of God that Mother had told me about when I was still listening to her biblical instruction. *Yes, Cody was right,* I thought. *I am a dreamer.*

When we stepped out of the elevator, we were taken into a large open area. A small corner had been decorated and furnished to look less like a corner in a gigantic basement and more like a doctor's office. I was told I could wait here while they tested Farema, who went willingly with the audiologist who came to retrieve her.

From where I sat waiting, I could see a small glass chamber in the center of the open space. I watched as the woman in charge tried to settle Farema atop a stool in the center of the glass cage. The next sounds I heard were a mix of screams and sobs from a traumatized two-and-a-half-year-old refusing to let anyone put earphones on her head.

Before long a woman appeared in front of me.

"Maybe she will feel more comfortable with you standing nearby where she can see you."

I followed her where she told me to stand, up close but outside the glass. I wanted this hearing test to happen, so I didn't tell them that this child had never allowed even the tiniest baby cap to be placed on her head since the day she was born. I'd been convinced that she had some kind of infant headache at the time; who'd ever heard of a newborn not allowing a soft, warm baby cap atop her head? But despite all the tireless efforts of the clinicians and my pleading through the window to try to get Farema to leave the earphones on her head, her shrieking only increased as she sat trembling and sobbing with a look of pure fright on her little face. They gave up, brought her out to me, and said we could try again another time.

It was nearly five o'clock by the end of the testing and evaluation. The staff was kind and told me we had another appointment for the hearing test and that they were going to refer Farema to the Eugene Hearing and Speech Center for better testing. We were to return in August for a test called the Gesell and one more pediatric evaluation. One of the staff members offered to show us the way out to the door where we'd come in.

"You know, I suppose it's difficult to know for sure if Farema needs any special attention," I said as we followed her through the narrow halls, "with her lack of talking and all."

The young lady stopped and turned around to face us. She just smiled warmly and bent down close to Farema's face, gently putting her finger under her chin and tilting her eyes up toward her own as she spoke. "Oh, I think we can help little Fee. Yes, I really believe we have a talker here!"

I grew a smile on my face that had been lost during the months since the church lady set me in the direction of discovering what was really affecting my daughter. I felt an instant devotion to this redheaded, angelic spirit who'd spoken the words I'd longed to hear. We said good-bye with another assurance that Farema would be in the preschool in September. The focus would be to get Farema talking, along with the social integration she would receive. There would be educational games for her to play, and one-on-one class instruction as well. The speech therapy would be constant, and the hearing test would be repeated until there was a clear answer to what might be wrong with her ears. They were covering every part of this child's development.

On the drive home I was glad that Fee would soon be attending the preschool, no waiting list necessary. She would be admitted as a child who needed treatment. She would also receive individual therapy, three times a week. I felt blessed by all the attention Farema would receive and relieved that much of the weight I'd carried would be lifted, thanks to so many experts helping our little girl. All in all, I told myself, before too long, Farema would be talking.

Chapter 8

EARLY INTERVENTION

FALL 1983

Farema's first week at the early intervention preschool was much more than I had anticipated. In addition to one-on-one instruction, our little girl had other kids her age to play with. Farema still didn't play the way most toddlers did, but I hoped that attending the preschool might stimulate her to engage in more normal interaction. I longed for her to be able to laugh and have fun with other children, making friends and experiencing all the things a little girl her age should enjoy. I was sure the only reason she refused to respond to other children her age was because she was surrounded by so many "mothers" at our house.

One day Cody came with me, and we sat together in the observation room and watched Farema's class through the two-way tinted windows. While we sat together in the darkened room, I became conscious of my husband's discomfort. Although I found it invigorating to see the new procedures they were using to bring my daughter out of her cocoon of silence, Cody would look away each time Farema failed to recognize or match the simple colors and shapes of the toys. Before the class was over I asked him if he wanted to go out. He couldn't get off the stool and out the door fast enough.

When the door was closed behind us and we started down the hallway to the waiting room, he stopped and turned to speak to me in a whisper.

"I hate that! I don't want to watch her like that ever again! She is having so much trouble doing what they want. Maybe this isn't a good idea."

I knew he wouldn't make her quit the preschool, but his heart was wrenched with concern for his little girl. I didn't ask Cody to come again, and he never again asked to join me. He was content with my keeping him updated, and I was perfectly happy to tell him the highlights of her preschool days and suppress the rest.

Cody was content to be the good guy—the ever-smiling and playful daddy who tossed his little girl up high in the air to make her laugh, who held out his arms for her to run into when she was excited over something wonderful, like a sunny afternoon on a swing, flying high up in the air and down again. I would be the other one—the serious one. The one who forced her to sit through sessions of trying to learn so she could one day catch up—could find *normal*.

Months into Farema's early education and play sessions, I read one of the regular assessments as it was recorded in the Social Casework Report. After reading it I could see they'd found me out early on:

> The mother seems to feel that, if her daughter receives the needed speech and language assistance, this will address all of her problems; she appears unaware that there are other difficulties with this child.
>
> Please refer to the other Team reports for a description of this child's problems and level of function . . .

There were other assessments too. Some, from classroom and playtime sessions, detailed Farema's slowness in other areas of development. Many times the tests were inconclusive due to her inability to answer, and when I met with her teachers, I was told how "difficult it is to test a nonverbal child." But instead of worrying me, these words became the ties that bound me to a firm belief that I knew my child. I believed that once the teachers and practicum students were able to decipher Farema's language, they would see that they were dealing with a very intelligent and normal little girl.

Farema attended the preschool four days a week. I continued telling Cody of my certainty that before long his youngest daughter would talk normally.

After some time, little Fee began to say words like "nai-nai" for *night-night* or "tu-tu" for *choo-choo*. She didn't use the words often, and no amount of coaxing would get her to repeat them. When I read the reports, I could see that those who worked with Farema were as stumped as I was in trying to understand what she was saying:

Farema's spontaneous speech was highly unintelligible, and although a formal articulation test was not administered, a pattern of final consonant deletion, regressive assimilation, and devoicing was noted.

At home, we all tried every possible way to entice Farema to say words. One morning, after our family's combined efforts over a period of months of offering her more bananas than I could count, she spoke one word clearly. She simply said, "ba-na-na," pronouncing each syllable distinctly. I later read in the report:

> . . . one three-syllable word was pronounced with perfect clarity—"banana."

Banana became the one and only properly pronounced word out of Farema's mouth. No one cared that she used it constantly, and for every possible reason—the fact that there was one good, intelligible word in her small vocabulary was reason to celebrate. Everyone who heard her say her perfect word made a big deal out of it as they congratulated her and waited for the next perfectly pronounced word to be spoken. I kept my secret about the Rice Krispie's song, telling no one, but in my heart I wondered why she didn't just stop messing around and talk. Then again, I'd remind myself, maybe it *had* been a figment of my hopeful imagination.

Cody joined with everyone else in great expectation of more words to come, and for a while he felt relief and a little optimism. My defenses relaxed after *banana,* but not so much that I wasn't hypervigilant in watching for anything strange that might come up. I was more optimistic than ever that Farema would come through with flying colors, but until she did, I didn't let down my guard on her odd behaviors. Especially at home, when Cody was there. I wanted to keep him believing that all would soon be well and in turn encouraging me to believe the same.

When he first saw Farema do her alien-baby routine a few times, Cody thought it was funny. It seemed at times that what looked most worrisome to me didn't faze him. But I didn't take any chances, and as Farema continued to do her unusual hand and finger flipping in front of her eyes, or to focus on elastic marks on everyone she could detain long enough to inspect, I watched and redirected her if possible. When she let her tongue hang out of her mouth until the drooling soaked the front of her dresses, I reminded her to keep her mouth closed. And when she sat staring and rocking back and forth, I'd pick her up or get her attention to stop her. Some behaviors left. Others remained, and I excused them to the public eye with ever-changing explanations for why she did them. She never stopped her "stimming," as the clinicians had called the finger-flipping in front of her eyes—short for self-stimulating behaviors—though I never gave up trying to redirect her when she started it. I kept the banana word forefront in my mind as a ray of hope as I read more assessments that indicated weaknesses in her daily functioning. The hardest part was that I was now reading what I'd tried so hard to ignore:

Farema has difficulty focusing on a task (visually) for more than a few seconds.

Farema is a cute child with dark hair who made inconsistent eye contact throughout the exam.

She engaged in solitary play and continued her activity when joined by other children.

The preschool and early education teachers became my dearest allies in the fight against the mystery ailment that affected my littlest girl. As the weeks and months passed, I made a habit of haunting the observation room to watch every move my child made or standing alongside the huge picture window surrounding the outdoor play area.

One day, during playtime in the game room, I noticed a little girl in a red sweater trying to push a tricycle, but her feet were too short to reach the ground. The teacher tried to show her how to lean from side to side, pushing with one foot and then the other to get some traction, but it wasn't working. The teacher went to help another child, leaving the girl to fend for herself. Then I saw Farema walk over to the tricycle, and without even looking at the girl sitting astride the seat, begin edging herself in to take her place. She didn't do it in an unkind way, but just gradually slid her bottom onto the tricycle seat as the other child slowly fell off. I looked around to see if the helper or the teacher might come to the little girl's rescue, but no one had noticed. I didn't know whether to intervene and run to the little girl's aid or just stay behind the thick glass in the hallway where we parents often stood to watch. I was embarrassed, but glad that I was the only parent watching.

The little girl gave up the tricycle without a fight and wandered off to play with something else. But instead of pedaling around the room, Farema just sat there as if she had no idea what to do next. After a few minutes a different teacher came over and tried to show her how to make the tricycle work by pushing the pedals with her feet, but Farema clearly didn't have any interest in moving. She just wanted to sit there. So the teacher left her with her little hands gripping the handlebars and her feet resting on the pedals, perfectly still and smiling. Other mothers came to stand nearby, and I left.

While the children were in their classes or at play, a support group for parents of kids with disabilities was in progress. I'd been invited by a woman whose son was in the class with Farema. The first time I went, a mother talked about the serious medical problems her daughter suffered. Once more I was embarrassed to be comparing myself to parents whose children had severe impediments or illnesses when my daughter appeared so normal. Farema just had a speech problem. I'd have dropped out gracefully if the group hadn't ended before I had the chance.

Every new class day for Farema was equally matched by a new learning experience for me. I studied the written reports as soon as I received them. I skimmed over the ones that told of deficits and memorized the positive reports about her progress. One of the tests had been done at the beginning, before Farema started at the preschool. She was two years and five months old at the time. The SEED Gross Motor Scale said Farema was functioning at age level in gross motor skills.

No recommendations for physical therapy were warranted, the report said. *That was good.*

No recommendations for fine motor were warranted.

But in the speech and language report, I couldn't deny the facts.

Farema's receptive language level was questionable and her expressive language was at the eighteen-month level. The mother reported that 'Farema understands everything we say' . . . but 'doesn't talk much' and 'we baby her too much.' The mother did feel she had been more vocal in the last three months.

I knew we did baby her, and because of her inability to be like other children, we were overly protective. I made a mental note—again—to try to encourage Farema to grow up. I had long ago added this to my protective list of reasons why my daughter was not talking at age level and why some tests showed her cognitive level to be so much lower than it should have been. And I found comfort in one of the notations made after the pediatrician suggested we send her for a "Gene and Chromosome count":

Clearly there is not an x-link pattern to mental retardation in this family.

He'd added that the test would show if there was a rare syndrome or genetic disorder that we hadn't noticed earlier. None was found.

There was never a shortage of tests to be scheduled, and when it came time to set up a second hearing test for Farema, I knew we would be in for trouble. The audiologist would have to place a heavy headset over her head and ears as before. When we arrived the day of the test, I was told to accompany my daughter in the elevator to the basement level and someone would meet us there. As soon as I stepped off the elevator, the now-familiar, musty, cold concrete smell brought back the recent memory of poor Farema and her fight for survival in the glass prison with the crown of terror. This time would be no better, I feared.

I stood outside the glass-encased soundproof room once more, watching as the audiologist tried unsuccessfully to get my screeching, squirming child to cooperate. Once more I was sent out to the hall, and I waited for what seemed like forever for them to wear Farema down enough to sit still even for a few minutes. When the specialist emerged from the room, leading a red-faced, exhausted Farema over to me, it was hard to tell which of them was the worse for wear. The woman's hair was a mess and her face was flushed, and with a tinge of exasperation in her voice and a semi-smile she said they had accomplished most of the test. But she added a comment about "how hard it is to get a reliable test from a nonverbal child." Then she turned on her heel and made her escape into an open elevator.

I looked down at Farema, clinging to my arm and shuddering. I thought of how like a defenseless animal she was, accepting what was happening to her but not understanding why. I reached down and scooped her up, and we left the way we'd come. This time, instead of the usual dead weight fidgeting to get away, she laid her head on my shoulder and cuddled close. Only in those few times when she was fearful or sick did Farema allow me to hold her like this, and I relished every moment as we left the place of her distress.

Having to stand helplessly nearby and listen to my youngest daughter scream in agony once more affected me greatly on that particular day. I'd been emotionally worn from the war of wills that had been going on in our home between Cody and the older girls since they'd reached their mid-teens. While Farema slept soundly in her car seat on our way home, I wondered what would be happening once we arrived home.

The rebellion against Cody's strict rules had escalated when the girls began to regularly go on dates and attend school functions that lasted late on weekend evenings. I felt caught in the middle as I remembered my own dismay as a girl of sixteen and how I'd not been allowed to join my friends at school dances and drive-in movies. I'd begged my parents to let me go and most often was refused. I now understood my parents' frustration.

I also understood that I'd married a man who came from a world where women and men are brought together by their parents for marriage, never free to go out alone with a person of the opposite sex without a chaperone. Cody couldn't understand the relationships of friends of both sexes where his daughters were concerned, and Lisa and Lainee could not forget that he was their stepfather—not their "real" dad as they so often cried out in frustration. There would be angry words and bitter tears, but somehow we managed to get through it all. Guilt weighed heavily on my heart, along with the full load that was already there for other reasons.

The discord in our home concluded in the summer of 1984 when Lisa was married in a lovely church wedding at the age of nineteen. I had wanted my girls to wait until they were older and not follow my example, but I was happy for her. Soon after, Lainee moved out of our house and eventually married her high school sweetheart. When the girls were married with homes of their own, the rift between them and their stepdad was peacefully resolved.

Chapter 9

ELUSIVE DIAGNOSIS

Since Farema was first seen at the Child Development Clinic on July 21, 1983, she'd received the best there was to offer four days a week in speech therapy and early education. After a few months, she learned to pronounce some one-syllable words, but for most people, it was still impossible to understand her. In hopes of giving her the best chance to learn how to speak while she was getting speech therapy, I decided to take her to see a well-known and much-respected ear, nose, and throat specialist.

Although the tests at the clinic had shown some hearing loss in her left ear, still, the specialist said, he was sure she wasn't hearing as she should. She didn't turn her head and respond to normal sounds like a candy wrapper being taken off behind her back or shaking rice in a glass bottle. He'd have to look inside her ears to be sure. He said he felt certain she had some sort of blockage and believed he could operate and repair it. The exploratory surgery would be invasive but safe, he told me, and I convinced Cody after much opposition to let Farema have a better chance at hearing properly.

After the day surgery, which lasted only a couple of hours, Farema was pampered awake with orange juice and Popsicles and released to Cody and me. When the specialist came to give us the results of the surgery, he appeared visibly shaken. He expressed deep regret as he told us how sure he'd been that he'd find some kind of birth defect or blockage—and yet, what he saw inside Farema's ears was perfect in every way. Cody came away angry, blaming the doctor for putting us all through so much, especially the unnecessary surgery and anesthetic to Farema. I left with more unanswered questions and deep sympathy for the doctor, whose look of bewilderment I completely understood. Farema was becoming an enigma.

That poor ENT would not be the last doctor during Farema's preschool years to suggest something be done for her hearing. Cody agreed to let me try one more thing that had been proven to help children with hearing problems. Although it would be necessary to keep my water-loving child from submerging her head for up to a year, three days before her fifth birthday another specialist put tiny tubes inside her ears. Problems from constantly recurring ear infections might have been preventing her from hearing perfectly. The tubes would help prevent infection.

Next on the list of doctors were psychologists. By mid-1986, Cody and I felt we'd tried all we could to help Farema learn to speak normally, and so when the day of our appointment with the pediatric psychologists came, we knew we'd done our part. That morning, while helping Farema get dressed and ready to go, I anxiously looked forward to the assurance that she would soon catch up with her peers and attend regular kindergarten the following year.

Early spring rain pelted the car windows as Cody and I and five-year-old Farema pulled into the parking lot at the OHSU Crippled Children's Division in the Clinical Services Building on the University of Oregon campus. Parent meetings were scheduled during spring break, and Farema's classes were not in session when students were on vacation.

We were ushered by the receptionist into a tiny office with two chairs against the wall facing a huge desk. Farema was all smiles and sparkle in her new pastel blue-and- pink dress when the practicum student popped her head in to say she would take Farema and entertain her while we had our meeting. She took our little one by the hand and led her away.

"Good morning!" A thin woman entered the room and held out her hand to Cody and me as she introduced herself. She wore a white lab coat with a very official badge on her pocket that spoke of her authority as the head of the Psychology Department. She was smiling as if there was nothing but good news to discuss as she seated herself on the edge of the desk with her thin high-heeled legs crossed partly at the calves. She looked older than the others I'd met, and I took that to mean she was the expert here. She would have all the answers and be the one person with the best knowledge of what Farema needed to talk fluently and becoming like every other five-year-old. After a couple minutes' worth of small talk, she said, "My associate will join us in just a moment, and then we will go over our test results and the various progress reports and tell you what we suggest for your daughter."

Her black hair was slicked back tight against her head and into a small bun at the base of her neck, which further enhanced her professionalism and air of importance. When she excused herself to see why the other person hadn't arrived yet, I turned to say something to Cody in case he was feeling tense.

"Cody, remember, even if the tests aren't good, we can still take her to a special school where she can get one-on-one attention, and then when she's all caught up we can put her back in regular school. It'll be okay."

My words were directed at my husband but were actually meant for my own reassurance. Then I prayed. *Please, Lord, don't let there be anything seriously wrong with her!*

My plea was silent, but in my heart it was a cry of desperation. The women came in together then, and the older one took her place on the side of the desk while the other stood next to her.

They both looked straight at the two of us sitting stiffly in our chairs, backs against the wall as if we were awaiting our own sentence. Their faces no longer smiled, but looked serious as the one I suspected was the director spoke up.

"First of all, we want you to know that nothing you have ever done, or could have done differently, would change the outcome of our evaluation of your daughter and what we are going to tell you," she said.

I didn't move a muscle, but at that moment I felt my heart tear loose from its place in my chest and fall deep into the pit where my stomach had been.

"Of course," the other woman quickly added, "it is difficult to get accurate test scores with a nonverbal child. We will continue with some testing until the end of the year and see if we can get better results."

There it was again, my lifeline. I grabbed onto the admission that the tests might not be accurate. The women took turns offering more painful information about our little girl and explaining their analysis:

"We can't be sure this early on, but we believe Farema has some sort of brain damage—something she was probably born with that happened when her brain was being formed. We seldom find out the real source of such a problem. Often it is genetic. But we have seen the chromosome count, and there is nothing genetic that we can attest to, so we have to assume we will never know the cause."

They continued to sum up what might or might not be the culprit in my little one's abnormal brain, but I was somewhere else by then, trying to think of what next, what new place or therapy we could find that would change the outlook of Farema's future and ours. My focus returned when the younger woman glanced over at her superior, half-perched like a big white-and-black bird on the corner of the desk, and said, "There is one more thing that is possible, however. Little Farema could have autism."

She might as well have picked up a brick and thrown it in my face. The dreaded "A" word had come at me again. My eyes zeroed in and stayed fixed on hers as the two continued speaking, more to each other than to us: "No, we can't really say that at this time," the older woman said with a frown aimed at her associate. "Tests for autism are so varied and hard to comprehend even when the child is able to speak. We really can't be sure."

As she spoke, she appeared flustered. As if to further exasperate her, the younger woman added, "Well, there are some definite characteristics that point to Farema's having autism, but there is no definitive way to be sure right now—we will know more after we get some better tests done. And you know, great advances are now being done in the study of autism!"

Red-faced, the older woman ignored the remark and changed the subject.

Other possibilities were mentioned. Maybe Farema was challenged mentally, though she seemed to excel, in some areas, more than others her age. There was some explanation of the speech and language evaluation, the cognitive assessment, and the fact that when the last hearing test was done, Farema was found to be hearing within the normal limits in her right ear with a mild conductive loss in the left.

We listened, silent and motionless like statues as they spoke. When they'd finished, both women walked toward the doorway, stopped at the spot where we were seated in the cold metal folding chairs, held out their hands in unison for a last handshake, and disappeared.

Cody and I remained where we were for a few more seconds, alone to wonder where we would go from here. All I could remember at that moment was that the dreaded word *autism* had cropped up once more. Cody didn't realize the full impact of what a diagnosis could mean, but he knew there had to be something wrong with his little girl who looked so normal. Neither of us knew what to do or where to begin again. Our blank looks to each other confirmed our uncertainty at a point when we had expected to know more. We'd gone in to the meeting with anticipation of answers given, hope restored. Now we were at a loss, and neither of us could help the other.

We walked down the hall toward the play area without speaking. Farema came out as we passed the big glass windows where the teacher saw us and brought her out to meet us. Someone said "Good-bye" and "Thanks," and with a smiling, bubbling little Farema between us holding our hands, we exited the cold stone building, our hopeful expectations shattered.

Chapter 10

"WHERE IS GOD"

1986

After Cody and I returned home, I avoided any mention of the meeting. I didn't want to talk to anyone for fear I might have to answer questions. I was too fragile after our meeting with the psychologists to come to grips with any new reality about my little girl. I wanted to pretend it hadn't happened, that we'd never heard she wasn't learning normally, and that the frightening word *autism* had not come up, once more, in the reports.

Although I tried to forget, after that February morning I found it impossible to block the "A" word from my memory. I couldn't help recalling the frightening stories I'd read in the library books and that thirty or forty years ago these same autistic children had been diagnosed with "childhood schizophrenia." I couldn't forget the "Refrigerator Mother" theory or my own sense of guilt. As if it were a dirty word that shouldn't be spoken in public, I kept *autism* and what the clinician had told us locked safely behind the closed doors of my mind.

Cody and I didn't talk about it except to tell each other that Farema was still very young and maybe she'd catch up eventually. While we agreed to keep a hopeful perspective for our daughter's future, we became our own support group, one assuring the other that everything would be fine. Still, I couldn't shake the truth of my not wanting this last baby—a constant source of guilt for me to cower under. Was I a refrigerator mother? I felt unable to be sure. Cody was the one who constantly played and danced with little Fee on his shoulders, ever-constant in pulling her to himself for a hug and making her smile and giggle. I was the one who watched— maybe too intently, sure—but my longing to cuddle or snuggle with a child who seemed indifferent to physical affection never ceased.

Now that I had heard the results of most of her evaluations and hearing tests, there was little to do but make the most of Farema's last few weeks at the preschool and education classes. I drove her in her first school day after spring break, and though I was still feeling wounded and worn, I appreciated the time left until the year's end to better prepare her for kindergarten. During that time, I would have much to think about. I needed to come to grips with the difference in what I had expected to hear from all I'd actually heard the experts say about my youngest daughter.

I was the one who had insisted we try every possible way to "make her normal." Now, I felt immense self-blame for all I'd put Farema and our family through. It hadn't just been in the testing—our home life had been marked by my attempts to normalize Farema too. More than anyone, Farah had carried the burden. Farema didn't communicate, and when children her age were playing outside in the neighborhood, Farema was an odd duck in their midst. After they'd try to include her in their games with no response, they'd give up and ignore her completely. Farema didn't mind, but I did. Thus, her big sister was obliged to drag her sister along to play dates, sleepovers, and birthday parties. I insisted on taking every possible opportunity to socialize Farema in any way possible.

At first, Farah accepted her fate like a champion—a personal guardian angel to her little sister. But as time passed and she felt embarrassed and sometimes shunned by friends who didn't have to include a younger sibling in their play, she begged me to not make her take Farema along. Farah had become her sister's keeper for sure. I blamed myself.

I imagine I blamed God too, for not rescuing us and making our daughter well. When alone at home, I pleaded my case to the heavens.

"And what about all those prayers?" I asked my Lord. "Didn't you hear me? Don't you care that she is so different? How can I do this? Haven't I been through enough? I've lost so much already, and now this?"

Somehow I felt betrayed, as if the God I had prayed to so earnestly had given me a spark of hope, and when I had reached for it, jerked it away just short of my grasp. Again I felt that this was some kind of punishment.

Without question, I knew I *deserved* punishment. I'd done things my way, ignored and even rejected the still small voice of my conscience asking me to wait, to have patience. Whether God did or not, I accused myself of withholding forgiveness when I'd given up on my first marriage and left with my two little daughters and then so thoughtlessly jumped feet first into the next. But no matter how I tried to understand it, I could not see why God would use a helpless child to inflict on me the consequences of my disobedience.

Now, a Scripture I had come across before while searching for what God might have to say came unexpectedly to mind. It was the story of Jesus healing a man born blind. "Rabbi, his disciples asked him, why was this man born blind? Was it because of his own sins or his parents' sins?" (John 9:2–3). I'd read and heard the verses over the years, but they had never impressed me as they did now—suddenly they had new meaning for me.

The answer Jesus gave was eye-opening. He said the blindness was not because of the man's or his parents' sin, but so the power of God could be seen in him. I asked myself, was there a plan? Did God have a reason for why my little one was slow—or worse than slow? And then came the part that really captured my attention: Jesus healed the man. Would he do the same for Farema? Was God speaking to me now, through Scripture once unremarkable but now impacting me as never before?

Why, I wondered, does this one Scripture return to me? I hadn't been reading my Bible much; how could I find the time? But this one story kept coming back to my mind. Maybe God really was trying to tell me something. I uttered a prayer, hoping to rectify my lack of understanding and ask for new insight. Possibly, I thought, this was what our pastor meant when he spoke of "hearing God's voice."

As the school year came to a close, the students were ready for finals at the college, and subsequently Farema's time at the preschool and all her tests ended. We never again met with the women who'd informed us of our daughter's developmental delays, but evaluations were recorded of all the final tests and class instruction, and when I received them, I looked them over to see if Farema would be referred to a regular kindergarten. It was the one thing I had left to hope for. They simply said she should continue with speech therapy and wrote suggestions for her continuing education.

Her speech is highly unintelligible . . . It is felt that Farema will need long-term therapy, extending into grade school years, and that her language development will be commensurate with her cognitive development; there are communication disorders classrooms within the system, which may be appropriate for Farema.

I felt it would be safe to admit Farema to kindergarten in September, and I decided I'd leave the how-to up to the teachers and supervisors. I was relieved that summer had finally arrived.

But that story from the Gospel of John kept haunting me. With new energy, I made a promise to myself that I would turn to my Bible more often. Somehow, I had a sense that God was trying to get through to me. This time, I would try harder to listen.

Chapter 11

PULLING OUT ALL THE STOPS

My prayers hadn't been answered in the way I'd anticipated at the CCD preschool, but I did have a new goal and a host of information to help me as I searched out the best therapies and helps for Farema when she would enter a new world in the fall—the public school system.

My goals hadn't changed. I wanted her to be normal like the others, to go to a regular kindergarten and continue on from there, but I worried about what would happen when the teacher realized how little she could communicate. I had covered for her in social settings, always filling in the blanks, always making excuses for her strange language. And I worried about another aspect of her entering a new environment where others might not have the patience to understand her lack of comprehension. I had blamed her faulty hearing for much of her behavior, but her sisters weren't so accommodating.

"Mom! She is such a brat! Look at her, she just ignores me when I call her in here to get ready to go, and you let her get away with it!" Lainee declared often. "If you would spank her once in a while she'd know she has to come when we call her, and listen to us!"

It seemed I was the only one who realized how little Farema understood, and that her behavior wasn't because she was being obstinate, but because she had no idea what was expected of her. When she was younger, I'd given her a spat on her little bottom many times over when she ignored me, but it only frightened her. I was never able to erase the look of terror in her eyes, as she looked up at me the first time with an expression of total shock and horror, from my memory. Everyone else believed her disobedience was because she was spoiled, a brat who had her parents wrapped around her finger. Family members were the first to complain, and I knew strangers wondered why I didn't deal with her tantrums and refusal to listen to me in public as if she were a normal child who had a behavioral issue. I had continually excused her to others with statements about her lack of hearing.

Now my concerns were what would happen when she started a new school. Would the teachers assume she was a kid who needed major discipline, or see her as I did? I hung my hopes on all the new information and test results I could offer as help to the new participants in Farema's future.

I was especially hopeful after what I had observed when tubes were placed in her ears shortly before the end of the preschool program. The day after they were put in, I noticed Farema staring at her record player as it played children's songs one afternoon. I'd made a habit of turning it on softly while she napped, and when she awoke that day, she got up out of bed, walked over, and stood staring at it. I felt a sense of relief and thankfulness that she appeared to hear clearly now what might have been muffled before. I made up my mind to be sure and tell the teachers that she could understand them, even if they didn't know what she was saying. My plans were in place. Still, I was glad there would be nearly three months before I'd have to register her for kindergarten. Hopefully that would be just the right amount of time for my daughter to catch up.

Summer that year came with relief from schedules and juggling school activities for Farah, but Lainee's wedding was coming up in July. It kept us busy making wedding plans and outfitting Farema and Farah to be flower girls. I was also busy keeping track of a five-and-a-half-year-old who'd well mastered the art of vanishing in an instant, though the first place I'd look was out in the pasture behind the house to see if she was riding the horse—minus saddle, bridle, or anyone's knowledge that she'd climbed up on an old tree trunk to board old Misty.

I spent many hot summer afternoons frantically searching the neighborhood as I ran door-to-door looking for my daughter, losing her a more fearsome prospect because I knew she could never tell anyone where she lived. They would never understand her. I'd tracked her down more than once visiting strangers who lived down the block from us. If they had a dog or a cat to lure her away from our yard, Farema would just take off and walk uninvited through the open screen door of anyone's house. Her sisters, frustrated with having to help me search, demanded that I "teach her to mind!" Eleven-year-old Farah would stop me while I was panic-stricken and dashing down the street yelling Farema's name and tell me to "do something."

"Mother! You have got to make her mind; she gets away with murder! You can't let her keep doing this. I am sick of knocking on doors, it's embarrassing!"

Farah was a shy girl and hated to confront the neighbors while looking for her little sister. I was always sorry that she had the burden of helping me keep track of her sister, and I wished I could do as she asked and "make Farema mind"—but I knew it wasn't possible. Farema couldn't help it.

Lainee's July wedding was beautiful. Her father, Larry, came too. That made her very happy, and I was too busy watching that I didn't lose Farema in the park to be overly shaken at the time. But I would have my own private meltdown later after Lainee and her new husband left for their honeymoon, as I had done more than a year before at Lisa's wedding. For me, seeing Larry was a bittersweet and emotionally draining experience. Losing my husband and family to divorce had left me broken and scarred, and still, after all those years, I was unable to shake the regrets that hung like an albatross of guilt around my already burdened heart.

As summer came to a close, a visit to her ear doctor brought the welcome release for Farema to put her head under water. The tubes had fallen out a few months short of the year they were supposed to remain inside her ears, meaning that no surgery to remove them would be required. For that I was thankful, and also that she could now begin swimming lessons, a necessary requirement for a child who couldn't resist water no matter how deep or dangerous it might be. Since the day she could walk, at less than a year old, I had seen how tempting it was for Farema to jump, fall, or walk into any body of water. The girls had to be reminded of the danger of leaving a tub full of water, as Farema would find it and be underwater in an instant. I'd caught her once on tiptoes, leaning over and ready to slide headfirst over the wet edge of the bathtub, looking like a white baby seal ready to take its first plunge.

The tub wasn't her only attraction. She'd walk right off the edge of any swimming pool into the water, deep end or not, with no hesitation. At first, she was just a baby doing baby things, unknowingly. Later, it was more than that. She went into any pool, anywhere, fully clothed. I'd jump in and pull her out, frantically at first for fear she'd drown. Later, by the time she was three, I took my time. She was a tadpole of sorts, heading straight into the depths and onward, with no fear of any sort. My nerves would be stressed to the limit, but I'd learned to control my reaction with the realization that this child knew how to swim, and always below the surface. But natural ability or no, she was still a small child and vulnerable to accidents. By the time she was signed up for lessons, I was certain that drowning, especially after the neighbors alerted me to incidents in their backyard pools, was too real a prospect.

Swimming soon became Farema's favorite pastime, and the teachers at the local community center and pool remarked on her bravery. Then they told me that although she'd passed each new level of swimming instruction with flying colors, from "Tadpole" to "Shark," she needed to be signed up for the beginner classes again.

"We feel like Farema has a unique affinity for water—obviously, she is learning easily because she has no fear of the water. In fact," the instructor said, "she has a very unusual lack of fear which can be a detriment for her. What I mean is, little Farema seems to lack comprehension of any kind that the water can be a dangerous place for her—as if she thinks she is really a fish!"

The head swim coach laughed at his own comment, but his eyes showed his very real concern. My daughter was a puzzlement to his staff. They'd not seen anything like her before, and they wanted to feel safe in letting her pass to the next level of instruction, which would be taught in the twelve-foot diving pool for the older kids and those who were brave enough to try the diving board. It wasn't more than a few more lessons when I heard about my daughter, not yet six years old and the size of the average three- or four-year-old, climbing the tall rungs to the top of the highest professional diving board and walking out onto the plank and into the air. She emerged safely from the water, with a throng of onlookers and startled teachers ready to dive in and save her. I was told when I arrived to pick her up that afternoon that no child had ever gone off the high dive, and in fact, she was under the age allowed to be on it—yet it would not be the last time she would sneak up to the top and show off by repeating the dangerous performance. By September, summer had nearly worn me out.

Chapter 12

MAINSTREAMED ... ALMOST

Fall 1986–87

The end of summer ushered in Farema's entrance to public school. She was one of the first to enroll in the Guy Lee Christian Kindergarten, and her first week was exciting with all the new class toys, a lot of attention, and recess, which was her favorite time of all. The Christian kindergarten had opened in the nearby elementary school because Springfield didn't yet have funding for a public kindergarten. Farema walked to school in the morning with the other children who were going, and I followed a little way behind in the car to see how they managed.

At our first meeting a couple of weeks after school started, I was told that Farema had a hard time following instruction, but the teachers were kind and made me feel that she was welcome. After she had attended for a few weeks, someone at the school told me that a new kindergarten program in Eugene had just started and was equipped with computers and extra learning helps for children like her. They said it would be a much more appropriate placement and that she could get continued speech therapy. I was told they had computers, and I was sold—Farema was amazingly adept at computer games, and everyone who'd witnessed her using one commented that she should spend more time on them. The school was only a few blocks away, and when I called to see if Farema would be allowed to enter the Eugene School District, I was told it would be no problem. I felt saddened to see her leave the school that had been all three of her sisters' introduction to school life, but if there was something that might better help her, I was more than ready to try it.

Farema was happy to go, no matter where the school was, as long as she could play on the jungle gym at recess and partake of all the physical education activities. She was there for fun. On that first Monday morning, I was told to take her to the classroom down the hall and to the right, the second door to the left. I saw the placard on the door before I opened it.

"*SPECIAL K CLASSROOM*," it read.

We went inside, and a smiling young woman welcomed us with a warm greeting and a ready place for Farema to sit. Before I quietly ducked out, I scanned the room and noticed the children seated at their desks. Most had the obvious physical signs of developmental disabilities. The reality of what "Special K" meant hit me suddenly. This was the special education kindergarten. I'd not given any thought to the possibility that my daughter would be in a special class, and I couldn't stop the tears that fell as I pulled out of the school parking lot and left. I had almost three hours to pull myself together till the end of the school day—or until they called me, as the woman in the office had said they would if Farema had any problems. As it turned out, I was the only one with a problem. I sat in the car knowing that Farema's school life would begin in a setting I'd never considered. What I couldn't have known then was that this would be a turning point for me and the direction of Farema's life from that day on.

Telling Cody about his daughter's new kindergarten was not the experience I expected. While I thought he'd be upset with the school officials for putting Farema in a special education class, he was calm as if it all made sense. He just asked a couple of questions and waited for me to pour my heart and soul out to him. I told him how disappointed I felt and how I was sure she should be in a regular class with the regular kids.

"So, what is wrong with that?" he responded upon hearing my obvious dismay at Farema's new school placement. "Did she have fun in the kindergarten? Did she play outside with the other kids?"

I stared at him in surprise as I tried to put words to how I was feeling; I needed to come to grips with what it was that had upset me so much earlier in the day. It took what seemed like minutes, then I said to him, "I can't believe this isn't bothering you too." I was pushing for time to think—to look deep into my heart and see what was really the issue.

"It's okay," I said. "I guess I was just surprised when I saw she wasn't in a regular class." I got up from the family room couch and left to be alone and analyze my reaction to Farema's new class.

That evening, while Farema and Farah were happily entertained outside on the backyard deck with some neighbor friends, I retreated into my bedroom to contemplate my true feelings. It was always hard for me to look into my own heart and find what was lurking there, especially when I was constantly hiding things under blankets of hopeful expectations that, if bared in the light of honesty, might bring painful consequences to someone—most often me. I sat on the edge of the bed and looked out the big window to the open pasture where I could see Misty, Farah's small pinto horse, grazing peacefully. I forced my mind to go over what had happened. My feeling when I'd realized that Farema was not in a regular kindergarten was strangely sad, as if I'd lost something. All I could think was that they should have seen there was nothing really wrong with my child—that she only had a really bad speech impediment. That was how I saw it, and I couldn't understand why the people in charge at the public school district didn't see it that way too. I mulled it over, pulling up memories of my daughter in past years, trying to see if I could put my finger on one other good solid reason why anyone would think her less than "normal."

In all the assessments at the CCD that required physical skills, Farema had tested above normal. Her gross motor and fine motor skills were average or higher, except for her handwriting because she held the pencil unlike anyone they'd seen before. I'd known Farema was exceptional at riding the horse. I had watched from my window before anyone else actually found out she was doing it. She'd just gone out into the back pasture one day before she was four, climbed up on the tree stump in the center of Misty's corral, and waited for Misty to trot over and nuzzle her for a treat. Then she leaned forward, grabbed two small fistfuls of the long mane, and pulled herself up and onto the mid-neck of the little pinto. She slid down to her seat just below the horse's withers.

"What a smart little girl!" I said to myself the first time I saw her do it. I decided not to rush out and rescue her but instead to stand at the kitchen window to watch. Falling off didn't deter her; she'd pull herself up onto her feet, climb back onto the stump, and do it all again. Upon being discovered and brought inside by me or one of her sisters, she would be cleaned up and told not to do that again. But she'd do it again the next day if she felt like it.

She was just as able-bodied when, on another occasion, she climbed up on one of her sisters' ten-speed bikes. With the porch rail to steady the bike while she boarded, she took off, leaning precariously from side to side to push each pedal down. She was much too small to ride it normally, but with her shifting, she could get it going at a good clip down the middle of the road. We kept tabs on her bike riding after that by making the girls put their bikes inside the garage.

I sat there on the bed a long time, mentally comparing Farema's physical prowess to other children her age. She was way ahead. Even her preschool had verified that in their reports.

"So she can't talk!" I said out loud. But there was one last thing I saw as I inspected my motives that I didn't want to spend too much time thinking about—the one thing that made me feel shame.

I didn't want a baby with a disability, certainly not one like she'd been accused of, the thing I couldn't bring myself to consider. Autism was not an option. Maybe a learning disability, but not more. I wasn't able to deal with it, and I wasn't about to give in and accept that I would be like those families I'd served in restaurants, whose grown son or daughter never grew up and moved away. When I helped out at lunchtime in Cody's restaurant, I came to know a family of three, the parents in their late seventies, who came often because it was easier to go out for meals than to prepare them at home due to their age. Their son, Martin, was disabled, though I never knew what was wrong with him. I'd laugh and visit and be as kind as I could to them, and my heart ached for what they'd confided to me about how they worried for their son when the time came that they would die or be too infirm to care for him any longer. He'd never be able to live alone, and he had no one but them. I'd be as kind and accommodating as I could when they came in to eat, all the while hearing the words echo in my head: *That will* never *happen to me!* More than anything, I wanted my fourth daughter to be like her sisters. I heard the girls come in the door, signaling that my private moments had come to an end. I'd have to hurry and get dinner going for them. But before I left my room, I faced that last thing. Was I embarrassed to have a child with a disability? Was that what bothered me so much? The answer was hazy, maybe because I couldn't face the truth about myself. Was I so shallow a person that I would be ashamed of a daughter who might be *retarded?*

As I rose to go out to the main part of the house and tend to the girls, the answer came back with clarity.

No, I was not that shallow.

For Farema, the Washington School Special K Kindergarten was a continuous fun day. She didn't care that no one knew what she was telling them, or that the teacher ordered and received special speech therapy for her. After the shock of seeing the sign on the classroom door that verified Farema's need for "special" help in her class, I felt we were blessed to have the extra support. I knew by the time first grade came that Farema would be in a regular first-grade classroom. I was sure of it.

Before the end of the year, I was told that Farema could return to her own district for first grade and that Guy Lee would have the same speech therapy for her three and a half days a week. Time flew by, and Farema grew a little taller, making her look more like a very small first grader instead of like a baby with very long hair. During the spring and summer she continued to ride Farah's ten-speed bike and climb on Misty the pinto whenever she felt like it. Lisa and Lainee came to see us when they were in town, and we all loved to play with the girls' babies. Farema was especially delighted to hold and kiss Lisa's little Ashley, and then Lainee had Jakey, and when they came to stay for a few days the house was filled with baby smells and diapers and love. And Farema found one more obsession—something to add to her list of cherished collectibles: diapers. Lisa was constantly asking what had happened to the stack of diapers she'd bought for the baby, and Farema's open-eyed and pure, innocent look of resolve to conceal their whereabouts no matter what was too funny and too precious for us to make her give them back. I'd run to the store and buy a new package.

I looked forward to Farema's entering first grade at Guy Lee for many reasons. One, it would be the beginning of my freedom for more than a couple of hours during the week. Farah and Farema would both be in school until after two every weekday, and they could walk to school and home, freeing me up even more. Second, I expected Farema to enter the regular first grade. I worried silently that her still-unintelligible speech could be a problem. Cody and I had been doing our best to prepare Farema for public school by following the advice and suggestions given to us at the CCD preschool and education program. We'd tried to force her to dress herself like they'd told us to do by pretending not to hear her whining and crying out of frustration as she put her clothes on in the morning. If she did get them all the way on, they were nearly always inside out or backwards or both. Tying her tennis shoes was very difficult; it seemed her fingers didn't work right, but Cody took on the job of teaching her.

"Someday she'll be doing it by herself," he assured me, and I was most appreciative of the help. Before first grade started up I bought Farema some shoes with Velcro, the miracle fabric for those who need a little edge. I was thankful Farema wouldn't have to ask for help when most of the other first graders would probably know how to tie their own shoes. I'd been told by one of the practicum students to let Farema use speaking to get things, rather than depend on the sign language she'd been taught during her time at the CCD preschool. I'd urge her to speak, to pronounce the words so I could understand with as little help as possible, until her frustration won the battle. Her screaming and tantrums would push me to give in until she was satisfied, still not using the proper words to ask for things. She preferred to use signing and then try broken two-word sentences as a last resort. On her first day of classes in first grade, I explained as much as I could about Farema's differences. I wanted to be sure the teacher would consider her probable hearing problems, her mostly frustration-induced meltdowns, and her preference for sign language. When I started to go, Farema barely noticed, having busied herself by removing every item from a box filled with toys and games. She still never cared if I stayed or left. I had gotten used to it, but the teacher was amazed at her confidence. I left feeling relieved about the teacher, who seemed to have all the patience in the world, and I prayed as I walked back home.

Farema was still in a special classroom, which didn't make me happy, but I had to deal with it. I would later learn the term "self-contained classroom," used for a classroom where children are removed from the general school population for all academic subjects. I would accept that for Farema to receive the one-on-one instruction and speech therapy she desperately needed, it would have to be that way. Her class would be for children with disabilities. I would not, however, forget my plans to eventually see my daughter in a regular classroom with kids who were able to talk and interact better than those who, like her, had trouble talking or knowing how to play together. I was sure there would be better days ahead, just around the corner, after a little more one-on-one instruction, another year of speech therapy, and the very special attention she was receiving in a classroom for kids with problems. She met friends there who had very minor issues like hers, and I was content to relax and look forward to the day she'd come out of her shell and talk so she could learn what she'd missed out on and catch up. That was my new goal.

Chapter 13

NEW BEGINNINGS

With the welcome freedom of Farema's entrance to first grade, I returned to a part-time job a few afternoons each week at El Kiosco. Farah's bus didn't get her home until after Farema was out of school, so I hired my sister, Dianna, to watch Farema until Farah came to pick her up. Dianna, Ramon, and their daughter Jennifer lived in our neighborhood only two blocks away; like us, just down the street from the school. Living within walking distance of each other was a plus when I went to help out at Cody's restaurant.

One afternoon while I was at work, Dianna asked Ramon to stop at the school and pick up Farema. When he pulled up to the curb where the kids stood waiting for rides, Farema saw him and started to walk toward the car, but then stopped and hesitated for a few seconds. She took a few more steps and slowly inched up to the car door that he'd pushed open for her. The teacher standing with the children reported that Farema seemed unsure about getting into the car, but after hearing Ramon call out her name, she finally got in and they went home to meet Dianna.

A few days later I received a call from the school secretary.

"Hello, is this Farema's mother, Lauri? Would you mind coming in tomorrow around noon for a short meeting with some of the school staff?" An uneasy wave hit my stomach as I responded that I would of course be there. I wondered what the meeting was about, but didn't ask. Had Farema worn out her welcome?

I'd never forgotten the first preschool that had virtually kicked her out when she was very young, presumably because of her tantrums. Had she done it again? I didn't know what to think, and sleep was difficult for me that night.

I arrived at the school early the next day so as not to keep anyone waiting. When I was ushered into the small, private meeting room near the main office, I said hello to the six people sitting in chairs around a circular table. They all smiled and said hello back. I began to feel off balance as I took my place at the table. I waited, and felt more than heard the uncomfortable silence that permeated the air. Then one of the women, who I recognized as the school nurse, spoke first.

"Something has come to our attention that has been cause for concern, and we need to talk to you about it before we make any further decisions. We don't look forward to this, but we have no other choice." As I listened to her speak, dread kicked back in—as if I couldn't bear to listen to the rest, but had no idea how to stop it. I just remained seated.

"We want to talk to you about the young man who came by Monday and picked up your daughter after school. Some teachers and staff were out front standing with the children, and apparently, a relative of yours came in a small red car and picked up your daughter. What concerned the staff was that he called to Farema to come to the car and she started toward him, and then stopped—almost as if she was afraid to go any further. We need to ask you about him first, of course, before we make any further assumptions or call in any outside participants."

My mind was beginning to whirl. As I processed their insinuation, I began to boil. Then I replied, "What exactly are you asking me? Or what are you trying to say?"

I suppose my face was pale, as one of the teachers I'd never met spoke up. "We had no intention of upsetting you, and we aren't really sure what we are inferring except that we can't figure out why your daughter hesitated to get into his car. Often that can be a sign of molestation. We are only thinking of little Freema's welfare."

I ignored the wrong pronunciation of Farema's name, which was an everyday happening. At the same time my brain seized the word "molestation," and I could hear nothing else even as the others spoke up with calming epithets to soothe my frayed nerves. I remained silent, looking down at my wringing hands and saying nothing for what seemed like a long time. *Ramon? Molest Farema?* I thought while they waited. Then I looked slowly from one person to the next as I quietly answered them.

"Ramon is my brother-in-law. He was sent by my sister to pick Farema up, and he only takes her one block away to their house, where my sister babysits three days a week after school. My sister doesn't work, she is never gone when Ramon is home, and I trust them completely. I am positive there is nothing wrong with him picking her up!"

Another person I didn't know responded. "Often those who abuse children are family members. And her teachers have reported that she makes sounds that are strange—like someone panting or breathing hard. Like this." The woman made panting sounds very much like those a happy puppy would make. The breathing also sounded like an animal, probably a dog—and then it came to me. She was imitating our dog—the little black puppy that Cody had brought home a few months before! I'd heard Farema mimic the puppy many times, but I'd always thought it was funny. She was so good at that one imitation.

I started to laugh, and they all stared at me as I said, "Yes! She does make those sounds, and sometimes she barks just like the dog—she does it all the time at home! She imitates our puppy, and she does a very job of it!"

They all looked at each other, then at me, and some chuckled or laughed as they agreed that was exactly what they'd been hearing. I told them about more animal sounds we'd heard out of Farema and how we considered her imitations a good sign that talking would clearly one day interest her and she'd master that too. While the faces on the teachers showed their embarrassment, I felt a surge of human nature well up inside of me, a tempting urge to retaliate—to ask what might be going on in minds such as theirs. Instead, I kept silent.

The meeting closed. The teachers all apologized as they thanked me profusely for coming in and for being "such a good sport" about something as potentially devastating as what I'd been confronted with that day. I assured them it was okay; no harm done. But as I walked out the front door and around the back of the school to the path that led to my house, I was anything but sure there had been no harm done.

Their words *had* hurt. I'd been injured to the core of my soul. How could they think such things about my family? And how long would it be before my little girl would stop doing such weird things, risking harm to herself or some other innocent person? I felt sorry for my sister and her husband too, who'd been nothing but wonderful with all the girls.

I told Cody about the meeting when he came home. He was angry at the school personnel as he agreed that, of course, Farema's sounds were her imitation of the dog and not brought on by anything anyone, especially Ramon, might have done to her. As for her hesitation to get into his car—well, who knew what she had been thinking? Later I remembered that one of the many ophthalmologists I'd taken Farema to had diagnosed her with keratoconus, a condition that causes thinning of the corneas, and had told me to have her eyes checked every year to be safe. I'd been happy about that too, thinking it the reason why my daughter never looked in my direction when I entered a room or ran to me when I picked her up at school like the other mothers' children. More than a decade later, we would find her to be legally blind, and she received cornea transplants in both eyes. Farema might not have recognized Ramon until he called her name.

Later I worried over the meeting again, but not in any way to do with my sister's Cuban husband, who'd been the one constant endearing influence besides Farema's daddy, the one relative who'd tickle and tease her and pull her out of her shell as a little girl, making her laugh and giggle like a normal kid. Instead, I questioned why my daughter emulated animal sounds like she did. It was funny—wasn't it? But why was she so ready to emulate animal sounds while she continued to avoid speech?

I never said anything more about the meeting to those I saw at the school, and they acted as if it had never happened. I did notice I got many more smiles and "hellos" from the teachers and staff that had been in attendance that day. I felt their accommodating kindness, but I couldn't shake the sense that something had been lost or damaged. I wasn't sure if I worried that people at the school might still believe that something had happened to Farema, or if I was just bothered because here was one more unexplained thing to add to the list of things I couldn't explain about my little girl.

I held no ill feelings toward the teachers and school officials because I knew they were truly considering my daughter's welfare, but when I heard about the benefits of moving her to a grade school in the Eugene District that offered more one-on-one instruction and computers for children in special ed classes, I was compelled to find out more. I had friends whose children were excelling because of the better funding in that district, but the one thing that really piqued my interest was that the school had something called "mainstreaming."

"Mainstreaming" was a term used to describe an organized (and successful) method of offering specialized instruction for students like Farema in some academic studies while at the same time including those students in a regular homeroom class and others where they could keep up.

Finally, I thought, here was a program that would not only focus on Farema's deficits but would also give her important interaction with regular children so she could emulate their actions and speech. I was sure it was important for Farema to see and hear other children who had no disabilities or speech problems so they could be examples for her. I had proof of her adeptness at imitating, and long before her public school years had begun, I'd been told by the CCD clinicians that it was imperative Farema be around others who could pull her up in her social and language skills.

The student teacher's words rang in my mind each time I discussed school placement with the officials in the school system. "You will always have to hold your ground when little Farema starts to go to school. The best placement will be where she is the one in the class who is at the bottom—she has to be where she must strive to pull herself up to the standards of the class in academics and social situations. If she is at the bottom of the class, she will get better. This will be a kind of battle for you in the public school system because it's easier for them to put her where it is easier for her—and for them." I was overawed by her words at the time, and I didn't think it would be that bad, but in the coming years I remembered what she'd said and could see exactly what she meant.

I began to compare the differences in school districts and came to the conclusion that I wanted more. Before the end of the school year I'd checked out the other school, and when they told me about the availability of computers for all the kids, even the ones in special education, I was sold. Farema had amazed us with her ability to speed along in video and computer games, and I knew this would be one area where she could excel. Cody was easily convinced, and Farema was enrolled.

As it had been in kindergarten, transferring to the new school in the Eugene District was easy—but Farema would have to repeat second grade to help her catch up. The special ed teacher said that since Farema was so small, it wouldn't be an issue what grade she was in. She would spend up to two and a half hours each day with the regular kids in opening activities, PE, music, recess, lunch, and special events. The rest of the time she would receive one-on-one speech therapy and small-group instruction within the Educable Mentally Retarded classroom, called the EMR.

I would have to take Farema to school and pick her up, but I felt we'd have a new start. Maybe now I would find the perfect mix of teachers and programs to help my daughter learn to talk so that someone besides Farah could understand her. I held high hopes that she could learn enough to eventually drop her special ed classes and completely integrate into the regular school day with kids who could talk normally.

To add to my hopeful expectations, just before school was to start in September, Cody and I found a house in Eugene with a perfect neighborhood where there were children Farema's age. Across the street from the house was a small neighborhood park. We purchased the house, and I envisioned lots of young girls and boys coming to play with our daughter in what would soon be referred to as "Farema's park."

My instincts were right. The first weekend in our new house with a picture-perfect park as an extension of our front yard brought multitudes of blessings in the form of girlfriends for Farema. Though her language was mostly indistinguishable to the other children, she managed to find an immediate friend in Whitney, a girl her age who lived across the street to the left of the park. Whitney's parents became our friends just as quickly, and my heart soared when I looked out my kitchen window on a sunny day to see Farema on the park swings laughing and interacting with Whitney and others who came to play. I felt secure in my dream of finding the answer to her differences by continuing with constant inclusion in social situations where she would learn to be like the others. I thanked God every day for the house I was sure he'd placed in that particular spot just for us.

But after a few months of attendance at the new school, I was approached by the regular homeroom teacher and asked if I would check with our doctor about putting Farema on medication. The suggestion rang with hints that we might lose the mainstreaming placement if Farema didn't settle down. I called her pediatrician, and Farema was given a drug called Ritalin to help her be less hyperactive and disruptive in class and focus better on the classroom instruction. I'd never heard of giving drugs to children, but the doctor said it was done quite often. I knew it was hard to have a child like Farema in a quiet place, especially when she was always in motion. Soon after she started taking Ritalin, the teacher said she was doing much better, even reading short words and sitting quietly in class.

I was glad the drug helped her learn better, but I didn't like the changes I saw in Farema. Something had affected her personality, and I knew it was the medication. Each day since she'd started taking the drug, she would come in after the bus let her off, go straight to her room, and fall asleep on her bed. When she awoke she would be incoherent and angry at the same time, a personality change that coincided with the drug wearing off.

I wouldn't have to worry about it for long, however. Cody came home from the restaurant early one day, and when Farema climbed off the bus and came in the front door, she met her father just inside as he waited with a big smile and outstretched arms for a welcome hug. She blankly looked at him, and without a smile or a word, stomped past him to go to her room.

"Where is the bottle that stuff comes in?" Cody asked me after watching Farema flop on top of her bed and fall asleep. "Go get it; I want to see what it is."

When I returned with the small amber pill bottle and handed it over, he immediately walked past me and down the hall to the bathroom where he flushed the pills down the toilet.

"I never want to see her take drugs again, is that clear?" he said.

I wholeheartedly agreed, and before Farema woke up, he went back to the restaurant for the dinner hour. The day her father saw her come in was the last day she'd be on medication for many years. I didn't inform the teachers about the flushing of the pills, and I prayed they would find ways to help Farema pay attention and that she would be allowed to remain in the regular classroom for part of the day. I wondered if this was just the beginning of the real battle the clinician had warned me would come my way.

That year brought other new beginnings and adjustments as we got used to a whole new environment. I missed the home of sixteen years where I'd raised all four daughters. It was hard to leave the place where all the neighbors and their children knew about Farema and her unusual talent for disappearing, where most of the kids and some of the parents had been involved in at least one house-to-house search for her. I told myself it would take time to adjust, but it would be a welcome new adventure for all of us.

It took time to get moved in and put things where we all could find them, but soon enough the new house felt like home. It was much bigger than our old house and had a wonderful family room with natural cedar walls surrounding a plush carpet for the kids to lie on and watch television in the evenings. The smell of fresh cedar was soothing while offering a warm, woodsy feeling. I especially loved the glass-encased solarium that jutted out from the room into the backyard where Cody and I could sit in the morning and enjoy the sunshine all around us from the small table where we sipped our breakfast coffee or tea, or in the winter months, where we could watch the rain fall all around us while we sat warm and cozily inside.

I didn't know that I was about to face another change—a whole new way of looking at Farema.

Cody was able to take time off a couple evenings a week now that the restaurant was established enough, and we took one of those evenings to see a new movie starring one of my favorite actors, Dustin Hoffman. It was called *Rain Man,* and it was playing at the theater in the mall nearby. I'd heard it was a great new film and had won the Academy Award for Best Movie in March. Cody loved a good movie, and when Farah offered to stay home with Farema, we made it a date and went to see it.

I'd heard a little about the story and that Dustin Hoffman's performance was more than the usual actor doing a part—he was supposedly able to capture the real characteristics and personality of a person who was seriously disabled. I hadn't heard what the disability was.

Cody and I seldom got away alone without the girls, or at least without Farema. But when Farah was home she was happy to let us go out. Our absence meant she was free to talk on the phone without interruption even if it meant watching her little sister. The deal worked for us!

The theater was packed, and the film started with immediate indications of living up to its rave reviews. Tom Cruise was talented as usual in his portrayal of a fast-talking dealer of expensive automobiles with a chip on his shoulder. He hadn't met his brother, Hoffman's character, because he didn't know he existed. The brother, it turned out, had been born with a developmental disability that made his parents afraid to leave the boys together in case the disabled older brother put the baby at risk. Raymond was sent to live in an institution before the brothers had a chance to know each other.

Sometime during the movie the disabling condition that affected the institutionalized brother was revealed—he was afflicted with autism.

The movie was, as we'd heard, excellent. And Cody and I might have spent an enjoyable hour or more discussing how so-and-so played this or that, or how true to life Dustin Hoffman's character was on the screen. But when the final credits displayed across the screen and the audience rose to exit the theater, neither of us had words to speak.

Anyone familiar with our daughter's peculiar behaviors could have identified similarities between her and the character of Raymond; even with his special abilities as a savant, Dustin Hoffman's portrayal showed behaviors that were everyday happenings in our home.

I recognized too well the sudden outburst, the tantrum that happened frequently at our house and in public places. As with Farema, there was no reasonable explanation for the character's intense reaction, expressed in loud, high-pitched screams, over something as insignificant as not getting to watch his favorite program on time. I'd seen Farema react just as vocally when she didn't receive the immediate response she expected, much to the dismay and confusion of everyone within earshot.

Another familiar behavior was the way Raymond seemed to lack any sense of attachment to his brother. He understood his brother's place of belonging in the same family, but was obviously unresponsive emotionally—almost detached—from the young man he remembered as the baby brother he'd apparently loved. It was a sad story, yet disturbingly real to life as I watched my own feelings and questions depicted before me on the screen.

I walked a couple steps behind my husband as we left the dark theater so he wouldn't see the devastation I knew was plastered over my face. I kept my eyes down and followed the multicolored carpet of the foyer to the doors and the front parking lot. I waited at the passenger door for Cody to unlock it from inside, and when I sat down and pulled the door shut, I kept my eyes glued to the window. Neither of us spoke on the way home. I knew what I'd seen. I knew he knew, though I prayed silently that he was just lost in thought and not really silent due to the pain of realization—the pain of seeing the connection between Farema and this movie character; the pain of recognizing autism in our child and seeing the uncertain future ahead for our Farema and for us.

It was an awakening—a time of profound reflection for me as I began to acknowledge, deep in my heart, that all the suggestions from the experts at the preschool, the words offered by doctors, the stares from strangers, and even the message from the church lady might actually be true. How long, I asked myself as I lay awake in my bed that night, would I hold onto hope that this would pass? How long would I wait for that one blessed morning when I'd awake and find my youngest daughter to be like all the others—normal? I had no answer, and the feeling that followed was as if something deep inside of me was beginning to crumble, maybe even to break.

Chapter 14

SEARCHING FOR GOD

Cody and I barely spoke to each other after we arrived home from the theater that evening, except to agree that *Rain Man* was one of the best movies we'd ever seen.

"Wasn't he good? That Dustin Hoffman is an amazing actor!" I said as I changed into my nightgown and retreated into the bathroom to wash my face. I heard Cody answer with the same kind of remarks, and we both said we didn't know Tom Cruise was such a good actor. Cody thought it was a little far-fetched to believe anyone would be able to see toothpicks fall on the floor, as Raymond had in one scene, and know in seconds how many there were. He reminded me, too, that later on in the film someone had supposed Raymond knew because he saw the number of toothpicks written on the box. I agreed with him, and we said good night and crawled into bed.

I lay beside Cody quietly, and when I heard the familiar, even breathing that meant he was asleep, I took a deep breath, turned over, and let the details of the film replay in my memory. Then I let the warm tears of acceptance and sadness fall to the pillow beneath my head. I kept quiet, not willing to wake my husband and feel his grief add weight to my own.

I fell asleep finally after lying awake praying that God would show me how to continue and how to help Farema as best as I could. I prayed for knowledge of the disorder I was afraid might be afflicting my child, and I prayed for our family, already invisibly separated by the differences in our cultures and beliefs. If Farema was not going to be able to grow out of whatever was affecting her, it would certainly take a toll on our marriage. Our relationship had

had barely stood intact when decisions needed to be made, about Farema first of all, and about other things that came up between two people who couldn't have been more different.

"Now this?" I asked God point-blank in my prayer between tears of anguish. The answer I heard was, "Why not?"

I didn't know if the answer came from my own guilt-filled mind or from the Lord as I begged him for answers. I felt lost, more than ever before. Even more, if it were possible, than I'd felt with my oldest two girls when I'd walked out on my marriage to Larry and held back all forgiveness, running off after my own understanding rather than waiting and praying for God's will.

In the days following the movie, I prayed more than I remembered praying in many years. Sometimes I felt consumed with guilt and shame. How had I been able to ignore something so obvious? But I hadn't been the only one ignoring it, I told myself. The girls, and my parents, were sure Farema was just spoiled. My mother had complained to me about Cody allowing her to get away with bad behavior. I'd covered for him, because I was letting her get away with her terrible tantrums too. The only way to have peace, I'd decided long before, was to give her whatever would quiet her down. Spanking had never worked, and I was sure if we'd continued to do it she would still have won the battle, no matter the cost.

As I went over and over the scenes in the movie that had brought so many of my daughter's behaviors back for scrutiny in my mind, I wondered one thing. Had God intended for us to see this film to show us that Farema had something far more serious than we'd imagined? And had he tried to open my eyes to it long before through Emily Watson, the woman who'd come to see me from my neighbor's church? I had no clear answer, but I wasn't sure I'd have listened if God had stood in front of me and screamed it in my face. Was God dealing with me over my hardheadedness and denial of Farema's illness?

I could now see more clearly the enormity of my falling away from the Lord of my youth. Now I needed him again, to help me understand what I was facing with my daughter and her unusual differences. And I wondered if his plans were even deeper than dealing with me now. Could it be possible that my fourth pregnancy wasn't the accident I'd always believed—that for some reason, unknown to me, I was destined to have this last, unplanned, unwanted baby?

My fear of what the future might hold collided with my guilt over deserving the trials I'd been handed, and I suddenly wanted nothing more than to know God and what his plans were for me.

I turned to my Bible and searched for the Scripture for the story of the blind man Jesus healed. I read it slowly, savoring the truth of Jesus' words. I pondered how this Scripture might have some meaning in my own life. I couldn't imagine how it could, though the Scripture had returned to me over the years, from the long hours of my sleepless nights with Farema in her infancy to the day when exhaustion from chasing and consoling a screaming two-year-old whose tantrums had increased in volume and intensity threatened to make me want to give up.

Perhaps that story did mean something for me. I already knew that my life would not be what I'd hoped for: certain freedoms were already beginning to look more remote than I'd expected. One thing I didn't know, however, even as I grappled with the possibility of autism—grappled, but still didn't completely accept—was that on my own, I would not be able to withstand a diagnosis of autism as I'd seen it portrayed in *Rain Man*. I could not have foreseen how this small but rising gale would one day turn into a tempest of unbearable proportions.

Chapter 15

KEEPING FAREMA ENGAGED

When Farema entered the public school system, the teachers agreed with the clinicians at the CCD preschool that she needed to be with others who behaved appropriately and used correctly pronounced language. One of the clinicians had told me that as babies, children learn to first make sounds and then later talk by imitation. I'd seen that in full bloom with Farema, but why she imitated bizarre sounds like panting, barking, and other animal sounds instead of people, I had no idea. I sometimes thought it was because the animals interested her more than anything or anyone else. Farema was definitely different. I could only wait and hope that the intense speech therapy she continued to receive every school day would help her learn to talk coherently. I clung like a drowning person to all the encouraging moments and blocked out of my mind as best I could those things that would try to discourage me as I read each progress report. *Rain Man* had startled and upset me, but I wasn't yet ready to let go of my dreams.

In one of her first reports, the second-grade homeroom teacher in Farema's mainstream classroom wrote that she was functioning at kindergarten to early first-grade levels. The reports from the special education classes were the same. When Farema was in the preschool program, her development and language delay had been measured in months, but as she entered second grade for the second time, it was measured in years. To add to her more-than-two-year delay in most areas, she was still having problems with making eye contact.

After receiving forms of therapy and education for her language and academic progress for more than five years, Farema was coming out very low on the learning scale, and as she fell further behind the pattern of normal development, her ties to the girls in the neighborhood and with friends who had come to her birthday parties and play dates started to unravel. Farema was not able to communicate and interact with the other girls, so to them she was more like a bothersome little sister than a peer. She needed to find a place to be around others who could fill in as the old friends fell away. She also needed to find something she could do without much academic aptitude.

Then I saw something from my own front yard that got me thinking.

During the spring and summer months, I loved to sit on a small bench inside the wrought-iron-enclosed area in front of our house and sip my coffee. From there I had a bird's eye view of all that was going on at the park across the street. One such morning, while enjoying the sunshine and munching on a crisp, warm croissant, I found myself intent on a baseball practice in full swing at the side of the park, where the well-mowed grass was the perfect place for such things. Suddenly it came to me—sports!

My mind raced back and recalled some interesting aspects of Farema's physical history. Since the day she had stood and started walking at eleven months, Farema had been able to move very fast. She had a knack for getting out of my sight in the twinkling of an eye, and later, her agile boarding of the horse out in our pasture and learning to ride the girls' ten-speed all by herself proved she had remarkable physical ability. After recalling her other talents— like the swimming lessons with their diving board escapade; the way she'd managed to climb onto nearly anything in her path that looked interesting, in the house or out; and her seemingly devil-may-care lack of fear—it only made sense to believe she would do well in sports.

By the time I swallowed the last of the croissant and tossed the dregs of my coffee onto the shrub at the side of the porch steps, I knew what I'd do next. I would try to find a sports team for her, a way to channel her energies into something she might be better at than math and spelling. I had watched Farema and Whitney run around in the park, and I'd seen Whitney trying to teach Farema how to bat a softball. Whitney's mother had mentioned to me that her daughter played softball, and now I wondered if Farema could do the same.

The team Whitney played on was managed by an organization called Kid's Sports. I looked the number up in the phone book, called the Kid's Sports information line, and found out they offered all kinds of sports teams for kids in the schools. Parents and other interested persons who volunteered to serve as coaches and organize the teams were credited for the overall success of the organization, which charged a minimal fee for joining. Kid's Sports never discriminated against kids who had a disability, and they said they'd find a team for Farema. Softball practice had just begun for the season, and though she would be a week or two behind, I signed Farema up over the phone and we rushed out to buy new tennis shoes and shorts for the first practice, which would take place across the street in our very own neighborhood park. Better yet, I could sit and watch the whole thing from my own porch bench!

Saturday came, and when the kids began to arrive I went across the street with Farema and introduced myself to the woman who wore the coach's hat.

"Hi there!" I said happily.

"Well, hi to you! Who do we have here?" she responded.

"This is Farema. She's new to this, and she may need a little extra help." I did my usual face, my way of dropping a hint with a half-wink and a silly grin while making sure Farema wasn't looking at me. I didn't want to embarrass my daughter by asking for special attention. The woman, whose name I forgot instantly, replied with a bigger smile and a nod that implied she'd caught my meaning.

"Oh, yes, we all need a little extra help with the game when we're new to this!" she replied.

I felt a sense of relief, along with a feeling of immense joy, at the prospect that this new team might be the very thing we needed. Maybe now Farema could do something well and make friends at the same time. I walked back across the street to my house and watched Farema follow the coach to where the other girls on the team were waiting to begin.

After a little more than an hour, the coach gathered the girls at the picnic table under the big oak tree near the swing set, and they all sat for juice and a snack. Parents began pulling up along the street to pick up their children, others walked home, and I stood at the edge of our lawn and watched for oncoming cars as Farema crossed over. She looked happy enough, but of course, she didn't have much to say no matter how much I prompted her to fill me in on how the game had gone and how much she liked it. I'd have to find out some other way.

My hopes were still high, but they were not to be fulfilled. The girls were nice to her, but after the second practice I knew softball wasn't going to last.

Farema just stood in the outfield and fluttered her fingers in front of her face like she did when she was excited, and when the ball came close to her and all the other teammates hollered for her to "Throw it back!", she just ran over to each of them without touching the ball, as if she'd never seen it. I finally felt it was only fair to approach the coach and tell her I had a feeling my daughter was a detriment to the team. The coach said it was fine, no problem, that Farema had just as much right to play as anyone else. I didn't want to make the girls suffer and maybe dislike Farema for helping them lose when she played on their side, so I promised we wouldn't sign up for the next season. But I didn't give up on my quest to find something Farema could do.

Not long after the softball team wrapped up for the season, I ran into my old friend Peggy, and when I told her about Farema's unsuccessful attempt to play softball, she informed me that her husband, Brittany's father, would be coaching a Kid's Sports soccer team for girls. I didn't know a thing about soccer, but Cody had played in Iran, and how perfect, I thought, to have Farema's father help her learn the game! I waited until Willie, Peggy's husband, was home from work that evening, and when I called their house Peggy answered and quickly called him to the phone.

"Hi there, Willie! Peggy tells me you're coaching the girls' soccer team! If there's room for her, I think Farema would love to try it. She is very athletic, you know, but she has never played soccer, though she should catch on okay. I think she'll understand if you just explain the game and give her some time to figure it out. I'm sure she'll get it soon enough." I held my breath until I heard his reassuring reply that Farema would be a welcome member of the team. I thanked him, but the truth was, I wasn't sure my daughter would even walk out on the field, let alone try to kick a soccer ball.

With a prayer and an optimistic outlook, I took Farema to the practice meets. This time I prayed for her to keep up, and I especially prayed for Willie. I knew it wouldn't be easy to teach Farema the ins and outs of soccer. He would need a whole lot of patience.

I went to the games and watched as Farema, the smallest girl on the team, stood among her teammates and glowed—silent and motionless—as the game ensued around her. She stimmed happily, doing her finger flipping in front of her face. Her little fingers twitched at hummingbird speed close to her nose in front of her eyes, and then there was the flick of her hair that she always included just before grasping her hands together tightly and slapping them down at her side. Farema was very happy to be there with the girls she considered her friends, most especially with Brittany, but she had not an inkling of what was going on around her. I knew it, and the kids and the coach knew it too. But Willie, true friend that he was, only offered words of encouragement.

"She'll catch on—sometimes it takes a while to learn the game and how to play!"

Cody tried to help her in the park when he was home, and Farema continued to join in a few more games and play with her team, but I knew she would never catch on. During her last game, I stood watching her excitement in bittersweet awe. Happy she was, but I would have to swallow my yearning to see her accomplish a sport for the sake of being included and give the other girls a break. Farema loved the pizza party and the group picture that showed she was on a real soccer team, and then, one more time I put a smile on my face and thanked my friend for his wonderful efforts on behalf of my child.

"Thanks so much for trying, Willie, but she just can't see the ball well enough. I think we can find something she likes better, anyway." With one more sincere thank-you to seal my appreciation, I turned and left. As he waved back, I could see the relief on his face.

My disappointment was real, but my resolve was strong. I kept my ears open and researched anything that looked like an opportunity for Farema to join with other kids her own age, especially if it involved action. We still had the neighbor friends, and as Farema continued to be mainstreamed at school, she acquired other friends who were especially nice to the kids from the special ed class. Meanwhile, I invited and enticed any child to my house for play times and parties to keep Farema involved in social interaction. I wanted desperately for her to have permanent friendships, but I feared they would all be fleeting.

When we celebrated her ninth birthday, I made sure all the girls she had come to know in her mainstream classroom were invited, along with her friends from the special ed classroom. Much to my amazement, nearly all of them came. I knew they were mostly interested in Farema because she was close to Whitney, but I never cared about the reason—only that they came and were kind to Farema. Socialization, I was learning, could be a mixed blessing. I realized that the more friends she had within the mainstreaming track, the less chance there was that I'd see a repeat of the experience that introduced me to the downside of inclusion with the regular student population.

It had begun with a dental appointment. Early one afternoon, I'd arrived at the school to pick up Farema and take her to a regular checkup with our dentist. When I went to her classroom, the teacher said I could find her outside on the playground. I walked to the end of the hall and stepped out the doors that led to the outdoor playground. Just as I started toward the play area, a group of six young girls caught my attention. They were sitting in a huddle giggling and pointing. One girl was making circles around her ear with her index finger to signify that someone or something was "crazy."

My eyes followed the pointing fingers to the one who was being laughed at. They were pointing straight at Farema, who was alone at the top of the jungle gym. Farema hadn't seen them; even if she had, she'd never have caught on to what they were doing. I was instantly infuriated and crushed, but these were children, and I knew they didn't realize how cruel they were. I plastered a big phony smile on my face and walked straight over to them. Then when they all stopped to look at me, I said, "Hey, do you girls know her name? The one you're pointing and laughing at?" Before anyone could answer, I went on. "Her name is Fa-ree-ma." I pronounced it slowly and phonetically so they would understand, and I went on to teach my lesson in manners.

"She is in the special ed class here because she can't talk very well. But she loves to make friends, and there is nothing she would rather do than be your friend. And if you want to, you could help her learn to talk too. You see, when she was born her brain wasn't formed perfectly, like yours. Something happened to her when she was a tiny baby inside my tummy, and because of that she didn't learn how to talk well like you girls. And she could really use your help!"

I was one who learned a lesson that day, whether the girls did or not. Without hesitation, and to my surprise, one of them spoke up: "Hey! We could teach her to talk! We would like to do that, wouldn't we?" Her compatriots responded with a quick and healthy response of "Yes!"

As I thanked them all and told them what a wonderful idea they'd come up with, I called for Farema to come, and we left the schoolyard. As we left, the girls walked up to Farema one by one and took turns speaking to her, each saying her own name very slowly as if it were the first installment of many lessons to come. I'd been holding back tears of anger and frustration when I'd first arrived on the scene, but when we left I was holding back tears of thankfulness and relief. I hadn't expected such a response from girls I'd initially believed to be thoughtless brats. Instead, they wanted to help her; they wanted to be her friends. Without any intention on her part, Farema had acquired a clutch of friends and blessed my heart at the same time. I'd find out soon enough that it would not be the last of such miracles in her young life.

Chapter 16

NEAR DROWNING

T he girls on the playground were true to their word. I made it a point to show up unannounced and sneak around outside at recess to see what was up with Farema. What I saw was a happy girl playing two-square with another girl, and a few others waiting their turns. I was again over-whelmed by how readily the normal second and third graders had accepted my odd child without any further intervention on my part. I didn't know how long it would last, but any attention from friends was precious to her and would give her more opportunity to hear words spoken correctly.

As Farema continued into the third grade, there was little change from the previous year. Most of the students were the same ones she already knew. Grade school had become a good place for Farema and a welcome relief for me, although the progress she made was minimal. When I asked her special ed teacher why she was so slow in learning, I was told that as children with a developmental delay grow older, the "gap" between what they can learn and others without disabilities becomes wider. When they are babies, the gap is barely visible because less is expected of them—but when they are older the expectations raise, and the child who is slow falls behind on the learning scale. I could see exactly the pattern she was explaining in the last few years. It was hard for me to hear her refer to my daughter as "developmentally delayed," but I had to get used to it. It was the truth.

Parent-teacher progress reports verified Farema's deficit. I'd skim the notes written in the little boxes for teacher's suggestions and goals and then toss them in a drawer in the dining room where they would stay. I didn't go back and read them again, but what I read I remembered, and no matter how I tried to forget it, the statements I read on the Individual Education Placement—the IEP—told me the unwelcome gap was ever widening.

I didn't know if she would ever meet the goals set up for her, but even so, these years were amazingly good in other ways. So good, in fact, that I became relaxed about letting her play outside when she was with other kids her age and didn't go into a panic if she wasn't in my sight. I was pleased to see that all the years I had spent inviting—and with treats and toys, often enticing—children to come play in our house and yard had succeeded. Farema had learned to love interacting and joining in play with other children. I hoped it would never end.

To help Farema with acceptance in social gatherings, I devised a way to help her control those unusual behaviors that were more exaggerated in public places or when she was very excited about something going on. The tantrums that had once rocked entire stores in volume were replaced by new behaviors that sometimes invited open-mouthed stares from strangers, but were easier on the ears and somewhat more acceptable. If she began to flip her fingers and giggle and make weird guttural sounds in her throat while stiffening up from head to feet, I'd tap her lightly on the shoulder. When she turned her attention toward me, I'd say, "Do you see the people looking? Shall we relax?" Farema would instantly smile back and force her arms down to her side. Eventually it became a habit, something we both did without thinking: I'd cue her with a tap and a look, and her twitching would stop as she brought both hands down, slapping them to her sides. Her habit of stopping when cued led to stopping her stims when she was with friends at home or at the park. I was happy to see that she had some control over the odd gestures she'd exhibited for so long.

The new park across the street offered more than I'd first imagined: it was a place of refuge for Farema, and when she was alone, she could go there and swing and be in the company of other kids, even if they weren't her friends. As she grew older, retaining friendships became harder for her, and when she began to tell me she didn't want to grow up, I understood why. As birthdays came each year, her excitement and joy were great, mainly because the event was all about her—one thing I had learned early on was the highlight of her existence—but the concept of growing up was another story. References to getting older were disconcerting to Farema. She often said she didn't want to get older; she wanted to stay the same.

Many years later, I would reflect on her defiant resolve to remain a little girl, at her balking at the mention that one day she too would grow up as her sisters had before her, and I'd wonder if she had an insight that I did not. Growing older, Cody and I were to eventually understand, would be the most damaging threat to Farema's welfare.

During the time she learned to turn off her finger flipping, Farema's hyperactivity level decreased just a little. The change came after I resolved to follow the advice of Dr. Ben F. Feingold in his diet, eliminating sugary breakfast cereals and all foods with dyes and certain additives. She never minded not getting wieners or bologna, colored cereals or packaged foods—all she wanted was macaroni and cheese. Her behavior was calmer than before, and her eye contact was getting better. I was sure that eliminating sugar and chemicals couldn't help but be healthier for Farema, and I accepted that it did in fact increase her ability to focus a little better.

Some changes were for the better; others, like her gradual loss of companions who would join her in the active outdoor things she could do well, such as riding bikes and running or climbing trees, were a noticeable disappointment. Farema still didn't communicate in the second and third grades well enough to sustain a relationship with girls her own age who loved to chatter about all the things preteen girls love to talk about. But there was one sustaining relationship I thanked God for, and until she no longer lived in our neighborhood, Mandy and Farema were the best of friends. I never forgot the first time I laid eyes on Mandy and her little sister, Christie.

Summer had come in our new home, and Farema was spending every day that the weather was good (and many others that weren't so good) in her park across the street. It was mid-morning, and I was getting my shoes on and searching for my purse to head out to the grocery store. Farah was home with Farema, and both girls were still in their nightgowns. I ran down the hall, stuck my head into Farah's room, and told her I would be back soon. As I opened our front door to head out, I was surprised to see a young girl standing on the porch smiling back at me.

"I was just about to knock!" the girl said in a lovely Australian accent. She went on to introduce herself and her little sister and bless my heart in a way that I will not live long enough to forget.

"My name is Mandy—Mandy Bubb. And this is my sister, Christine. We call her Christie. We met your daughter in the park on Saturday, and we wondered if she could come join us there today!"

At first sight of Mandy, I was in love. I loved the smiles and the accent, I loved the ease and the friendliness of this girl who'd miraculously appeared, no less than a gift from God, at a time when I needed her—when Farema needed her—the most.

"Well, come in, and I'll get Farema to find her shoes!" I said back, as thrilled as if I'd won a lottery. The girls stepped inside, and I called again.

"Farema! Come meet a new friend!" I yelled a bit louder, and when Farema came down the hall from her room, she saw the two girls standing beside me. Her eyes lit up, and from that moment on Mandy and Farema would be constant companions.

Mandy was mature beyond her years, though she was less than a year older than Farema, who had always looked much younger than others her age. Mandy had grown up in a family of high achievers: her father had worked with the Australian Police Department, and her mother was a teacher. She came to be thought of as nothing less than an earthbound angel by Cody and me.

She didn't mind being spokesman for Farema, whose language was still nearly impossible for new acquaintances to understand. Even with her accent, Mandy understood most of what Farema wanted to say, and when she didn't, she'd wait patiently until she did. I often wondered how she could comprehend many of the words that even I could not. Their friendship was a heavenly gift. Mandy kept returning, and when she had other friends over at her house, she'd come anyway and bring them along. If something was going on at her house, Farema was always invited.

And then there came the day it came too close to ending—in tragedy.

Mandy, her sister, and another girl came by to get Farema for a Saturday bike ride. As always, Farema was ecstatic and aboard her bike in a flash. It was in the month of October, and the day was gray and overcast as was common for that time of year in the Willamette Valley. I hollered at Farema to get a warm sweatshirt over her T-shirt in case it rained. I watched as the foursome rode up the street on their bikes to explore the safe, kid-friendly neighborhood, then went in and reminded Farah, now a sixteen-year-old who appreciated Mandy's visits as much as we did, not to forget that her sister was outside and should be in the house before dark. I grabbed my purse, got into my car, and left for Cody's restaurant where huge weekend crowds were now a common occurrence, necessitating my help on Saturdays. Farah was a capable sitter for her sister, and I never worried for a minute.

The night was fast and furious, and when I heard the phone ringing off the wall I knew it was just another take-out order that would have to be patient until one of the waitresses could free her hands to write it up. I had been working on the cash register, taking money and seating the dinner patrons as they came in. Not until late in the evening did I see that the phone had been laid on the counter and forgotten in the rush of customers and phone orders. For a brief moment I was perturbed that someone on the other end might have been forgotten or that we could have lost a lot of business with only a busy signal coming from our end. Never did it occur to me that the phone was also a lifeline to my daughters at home. With the dinner rush over, Cody told me to go on home; he would be late after closing and waiting for the last of the dinner patrons to leave.

I pulled into the garage, and with nylon feet that had shed my all-day high heels went into the house through the door that led through the family room. As I stepped up into the kitchen and passed the little laundry room, just barely big enough for a washer and dryer, I saw it on the floor.

A huge, clear plastic garbage bag was bulging at all sides and tied at the top. I stopped to look at it and flipped on the light to get a better look. I could make out some filthy, muddy water mixed with what looked like seaweed, sticks, and rocks—and what was that? A small, white tennis shoe, a red sock, something that resembled a white sweatshirt, now dark and muddy, and a trace of blue—blue jeans. They were so small, like the ones Farema was wearing last time I saw her on her bike!

My heart throbbed in my throat, and I held my breath as I ran on shaky legs through the kitchen to the back of the house where the girls' bedrooms were. I saw a light shining out of Farema's room. As I rounded the doorway I almost ran over Farah, who was on her way out of the room to call for me after hearing my gasp from the hallway.

"Mom!" Farah yelled. "You won't believe what she did this time! I tried to call you a million times, but no one answered and then there was a busy signal, and, oh Mom, you won't believe it . . ."

Talking fast and furious, my older daughter tried to explode all the pertinent information on me in a single moment of impact, but I was focusing with all my senses on the red-faced, perfectly silent child lying in the bed with all the bedcovers and a quilt tucked right up under her chin, only her head sticking out atop two pillows.

"Farema! What happened?" I asked with what little breath I had left for speaking.

Farema didn't respond but kept a steady, wide-eyed stare on my face. Farah didn't pause at my interruption but continued her discourse of the night's terrors.

She told me about the frightful look on Mandy's mother's face when she and Mandy brought Farema home wearing some of Mandy's clothes. She expressed the panic she'd heard in Mrs. Bubb's voice when she appeared at the front door lugging a huge dirty plastic bag full of Farema's river-soaked clothes and muddy water. I heard about Mandy's traumatic tirade of tears as she stood next to her mother. Then I heard how we, as parents, had no business leaving Farah in charge of a kid who would "do anything and probably kill herself" if we didn't do something with her! Farah was obviously traumatized herself, and my heart ached for what she'd been through.

Finally, with only my blank stare to calm her as she continued, Farah told me how Farema and her friends had ridden their bikes down to the river. The Willamette River, only a little more than a mile from our neighborhood, is one of two rivers that run through our city. The Willamette winds its way through the Willamette Valley, rippling and gushing with deep undercurrents and treacherous undertows right where the highway and the Ferry Street Bridge pass overhead. The girls had ridden down to the park and stopped under the bridge alongside the river to play.

"The kids were all throwing rocks into the river and there was this huge tree that had fallen into the river and was bouncing up and down with the current, and of course, *Farema* had to be the one to jump up on it and started running back and forth—"

Farah had a way of accenting her little sister's name when she was telling of an incident where she had suffered embarrassment or anxiety. I sat there feeling terribly sorry for Farah who, more than any of the other girls, had sacrificed a great deal of personal comfort to help protect and oversee her little sister.

"Mom, you know how she is in the water. Any water. She just jumps in!" And you know this isn't the last time; she'll do something just as bad, and maybe she won't be so lucky!"

I wanted to cry, but I had to be calm for both their sakes. Farah kept going.

"Mom, Mandy just cried so hard she couldn't tell me everything, but her mom said the girls were teasing each other and someone dared her to jump in."

My daughter's big, round blue eyes now gazed back at me with a solemn expression. "Farema was jumping up and down, the tree was bobbing around on the water, and the next thing they knew she had walked off the log and into the river. She said they started to laugh because they thought she knew what she was doing, but the river pulled her under and she started to go into the rapids and they got scared. No one knew what to do, and they ran along the bank calling to her to come over so they could pull her up, but they didn't think she could ever get out and she was swimming as hard as she could but the river kept pulling her down!"

I imagined my little girl, smaller than most much younger kids, trying to fight the grip of a raging river that had claimed many lives over the years. I'd not yet had the chance to wrap my mind around how heavily the water-drenched sweatshirt and jeans would weigh down so small a frame.

While her sister talked on about the harrowing details of her sister's near drowning, Farema lay motionless, peering over the bedcovers clutched with cold pink hands up to her chin, as if she was taking in for the first time the reality of how perilous a night she'd endured.

Farah said she couldn't stand to look at the bag of river-drenched clothing or even to imagine what fear must have overwhelmed her poor little sister. Finally, exhausted with the evening's disastrous events, Farah decided she needed to go to bed herself and gave me one last warning.

"I don't know what you're gonna do with her, Mom, but you and Dad have to do something! Next time she probably won't be so lucky!" With one last look of fear and frustration, Farah turned and stomped out of the room.

I sat momentarily looking at Farema, my own imaginary fears running helter-skelter in my head. Then suddenly I was exhausted and could barely stand up to leave. I felt old and worn.

"Good night, honey; don't you worry. It will all be okay tomorrow," I whispered as I leaned over and kissed Farema and pulled the comforter up closer to her chin. She slid down deeper into the blankets as I turned off the light and pulled the door partly shut.

My legs felt like poles of lead as I stepped onto the first stair that led up to my bedroom. My mind felt dark and blank as I turned the light on and sat on the edge of the bed to remove my skirt and pantyhose, thinking that a hot shower would wash away the feeling of hopelessness that was starting to come over me.

But I wasn't able to make it that far. With no warning, my mind succumbed to the reality of what had taken place while I was running around serving people, worrying about customers' needs while my child—my unusual, strange, uncommon little girl—came so close to losing her life. What if she hadn't made her way to the bank—hadn't survived? My mind raced back through time, and the old guilt of believing that I'd somehow caused my child's infirmity, added to the even older guilt I'd lugged around in my soul before she was born—guilt that made me feel I deserved all this—burdened me to the breaking point. I felt my eyes begin to tear and then to flood. The tears came so fast that they were down my cheeks before my sobs were audible. I sank to the floor beside my bed and buried my face in the quilt to silence the sounds of my grief. I knew that I could not continue any longer as if all was okay. Life would never again be okay again.

Chapter 17

NIGHT TERRORS

Cody came home from the restaurant late on the evening we nearly lost our youngest daughter to the river. When he came in, I was asleep. Mentally and emotionally exhausted, I had given way to the peace that finally came—a welcome escape to the nothingness of sleep.

That night after Farema's life was given back to us, I sobbed until I had no more tears. I was so exhausted I could only kneel and pray with tearful expressions of gratitude and promises to stop ignoring the obvious about my child.

I crawled into bed, and before falling asleep, I pulled the dusty Bible off my nightstand and began to read from the first place my eyes fell: the 139th Psalm.

As I read, a feeling came over me that God had directed me to that particular Scripture. As if he'd whispered it in my ear, I felt peace: he was using the words of Psalm 139 to assure me that it was not my fault Farema had been born with a serious disorder—of some kind. Despite everything, I wasn't ready to completely accept that it was autism. But I knew now that she wasn't likely to grow out of it. I thought back to the church lady, and to all the suggestions and inferences over the years. If we did find out Farema had autism, I told myself, I would be the first to admit it. Even so, the words of Psalm 139 were a major breakthrough for me. *I had not caused Farema's disorder.* For the first time in my life, I knew it clearly. God was the Creator; God was in charge of every detail of my life—and of Farema's.

But before I fell asleep, I asked God to give me courage for one more task. As much as I dreaded it, come morning, I would have to explain the whole frightening story to Farema's father.

Still in my nightgown and robe the next morning, I came downstairs and sat sipping my morning cup of coffee. Cody came in and sat next to me on a stool at the breakfast counter between the kitchen and dining room. I customarily held back information about Farema's encounters with danger because Cody would become angry and make me feel inept in protecting her, and because he always blamed me when she was injured or might have been—as if I could stop her from doing the daring things that caused us great concern. Now I knew I was incapable of dealing with Farema by myself. I decided to just lay it all out on the table. I took a big gulp of coffee and looked over at him.

"Cody, I have to tell you what happened last night." I started out calm, but when he abruptly turned his head to look at me, I began to feel unsettled—as if I might have been able to prevent what had happened to Farema, and that he would think so too. I continued anyway.

"Remember the phone lying on the counter last night at the restaurant when we asked the girls who had forgotten to hang it up? Well, you know it was there a long time before we caught it, and Farah had been trying to call us. She wanted to tell us that Farema wasn't home yet and it was after dark. Then she tried a few more times to tell me to come home, but the line was busy. Cody," I said softly, still searching for the gentlest way of disclosing the truth and finding no answer but to tell it like it was, "Farema jumped into the river."

I waited for his so-far-expressionless face to tell me he'd processed my words. He stared back at me without answering for a long moment, and then, without taking his eyes away, put his hands on the table as if he were about to jump up and run down the hall to Farema's bedroom and see if she was all right. I spoke as fast as I could: she was asleep, she was fine, but I was sure she was very tired. I added that I was positive God had sent angels to keep her above water and had pulled her to safety. Cody only nodded in agreement and sat back down on the stool, too stunned to respond. When he did speak, he told me we would have to be very careful. Then, as I watched his face to see if he might crumble like I had, the reality of what had happened to Farema hit him. But where I'd fallen apart, Cody remained stoic and ready to activate a game plan.

"You stay home with her from now on," he said. "We will find someone to help out at the restaurant. Or we can tell Farah that if you have to come in, she can't let Farema out of her sight. No matter what she wants to do, she has to stay inside the house."

I nodded my head in agreement. I was beginning to see another side of my husband, and it came as a welcome comfort. Instead of the angry blame he often hurled at me whenever I allowed Farema to take off with the older girls and she got lost or came home with scrapes and bruises, my husband was showing his gentle and protective side. It was as if he'd expected something earth-shattering to come our way concerning Farema, and now that it had, he was taking full control of the situation.

Cody and I talked about how frightened Farah had been and how unfair it was that she be put through so much strain; about how we needed to find a way to assure Farema's safety. We talked over the times she'd turned up missing, how we'd phoned down to the nearby neighbors' homes to ask if she was there, and how much we'd worried because she was always looking for the girls who lived there to come play with her—girls who both had swimming pools in their backyards. Farema wouldn't think twice about jumping in if the mood hit her, no matter if someone was at home or not. The fact that she was an excellent swimmer did not remedy the wave of nausea I felt as I sat remembering how many times I'd searched for her.

Cody was very gentle with Farema when she finally got up and wandered out to find us still sitting at the counter. We smiled at her and spoke softly, as if she had just returned to us from a perilous journey. In a sense, she had. I asked her how she felt, and she smiled and murmured something I took for "Fine." Cody pulled her onto his lap and hugged and kissed her as long as she would sit there, which was longer than the few seconds she'd allowed any of us to cuddle her in the past. Neither of us mentioned her river affair. It was much too soon to know how to approach it. I knew it was no laughing matter, so I didn't want to mistakenly make light of the incident lest she ever do something like that again. On the other hand, Cody and I had agreed that when we talked about it with her, we would be careful not to bring more trauma to her than she might have already suffered. But it was always hard to know for sure what Farema was feeling or thinking.

Cody spent time with Farema while she ate breakfast, and acting like everything was as it should be, he went upstairs to get dressed for work. Farah had gotten up and come out to say good morning, and I noticed a long glance at her sister before she disappeared to her room to get ready for the day. As for me, besides the great sense of relief and gratitude for Farema's safe return to her family, I felt different somehow. Something had been revealed and now lay open for viewing. The near-disaster had been the first time since Farema's birth that I hadn't made excuses for her or blamed some outside factor for why she'd attempted something no normal ten-year-old would do.

Before my day went on, I thanked God with deep sincerity and asked him to have a serious talk with Farema's guardian angel. I asked him to make sure he or she stayed very, very close to Farema every minute and never let her out of sight.

For a long while no one mentioned the river incident, and life carried on as usual. Cody and I both delved into getting better acquainted with our close neighbors. Our agreement was unspoken, but we knew we had to do all we could to make our street an even safer place for Farema to live.

The first year that we lived in our new house across from the park, we had been invited to the yearly potluck that took place there. We hadn't gone. Cody and I were both used to missing everything that happened on weekends, a downside of being restaurant people. But this year, we were going no matter what. It was the perfect opportunity for our neighbors to see where Farema lived in case she ever got lost. And, I thought to myself, the best possible avenue for introducing everyone to our daughter's unusual lack of discernible language should she need someone to recognize her as a child with less power than most to care for—or defend—herself. I wanted everyone to know my daughter and what she was all about. Uncharacteristically, I wanted to be close to my neighbors, a real first-name kind of close. I wanted them to help me in any small way they could to watch out for Farema. My whole mindset was beginning to change.

Cody prepared a large casserole dish of the famous enchiladas that were a big hit at his restaurant, and with plenty of his excellent homemade salsa and chips at hand, those who attended became fast admirers of his cooking talents. Many asked about his excellent cuisine, and news spread fast as many, including Whitney's parents, became not only friends in the neighborhood but also returning customers to El Kiosco. Any and all who came to eat in our restaurant after meeting us at the picnic were special in my book, and I wanted to bond with them all.

Life pretty much revolved around the busyness we had running the restaurant, but after the river incident, I only went to work on the days that Cody or Farah could be home with Farema. When school was out for the summer,

I traded places with Farah, and she helped in the restaurant while I stayed home with Farema. It was a good change for me, and Farah liked having a job with tips to boot.

Farema continued to love her teachers in special education and to do the best she could in the mainstream classroom. She hardly noticed the change in grades, since the combined age groups of the third and fourth grades were together; then the fourth and fifth. Friends remained the same, though only Farema stayed close to the same academically.

I kept up my aerobics classes, my favorite outlet, and did other typical housewife things. I had close friends in the neighborhood to stop and visit with if they came by, and sometimes I joined Farema out at the picnic table with my cup of coffee, watching her while she flew as high as the swings would go or climbed up as far as she could in the big old oak tree smack in the middle of the play area. If mothers brought small children to play in the oversized sandbox, Farema would join them, scooping up the sand with her hands and filling their buckets and pails while she talked and giggled. The little ones adored her, as if she were a big sister paying them complete attention.

Yet, despite the fun she was having and the adoration lavished on her by toddlers, it was times like these that I clearly saw the profound deficits in my daughter.

The summer of her last year in elementary school, I worried that after the girls who were her mainstay continued on to middle school they would all but cease to exist in Farema's life. The possibility kept me on alert, wondering what might better prepare her for the new school year and changes she might not be able to deal with. While she was eight or nine years older than the little ones she played with in the sand, it appeared she sometimes understood less than they. When their mothers spoke to them, they turned their heads in recognition. Farema had never done that as a toddler, and now as a ten-year-old she hadn't changed much. I worried that she might not grow up and mature.

While I worried about Farema, Farah was growing up fast. A busy teenager, she wanted to be home less and go out with her friends more, especially if being home meant babysitting her sister. Both her father and I understood that Farah had been burdened with more than her fair share since Farema had come along. Farah had become my backup. She helped with the crying baby, sitting in the rocker and holding her just like I told her to, rocking fast to keep the baby in motion. Sometimes I asked her to entertain Farema, show her some toys, and talk to her so I could take a fast bath. It seemed time had slipped away while I'd been too overwhelmed to notice. Now Farah was growing up, and soon she would be gone too.

A few weeks after our little girl's most frightful experience, it looked as if everything was going smoothly and life had returned to normal. But it would only be a matter of months before what we considered normal would vaporize, disappearing during the night hours when most people are safe in bed..

Weeknights were busy at the restaurant, but Cody came home at least an hour or two earlier than on the weekends. We could lie in our bed upstairs and watch TV and talk about the business and what had happened at the restaurant. Then came the night when we entered a new phase of bewildering behavior from Farema.

Cody and I often watched the Late Show, but on this night we were too tired to stay awake. I switched it off, lay back, and pulled the covers around me. I had said good night to Farah and Farema hours earlier. Cody rolled over and was asleep in seconds. I lay there listening to him snoring and wished I'd gone to sleep first. I had only been asleep a few moments before I heard the shrill wail and felt my eyes fly open at the approaching sound that was penetrating my brain. It was at first unrecognizable.

"Maaaaaaa! Oooh! Momaaaaaaa!" I heard the footsteps lunging up the oak stairs to our bedroom, and for an instant the hairs on the back of my neck and arms stood up with eerie dread. The moon shining in the big open window near the door gave me a slight hope that maybe I could at least see what was happening. But just as I was attempting to sit up, what I suddenly recognized as my screeching and crying child lunged at me and knocked me down into the pillow again.

"Farema! What is the matter?" I couldn't see her face in the dark, but I knew her eyes were wide with fear and terror from the sound of her screams, as she bellowed like a wounded wild animal searching for help but finding none.

"What happened, what is it?" came Cody's half-dazed, panicked question as I scrambled to find the switch on the lamp beside my bed and get a better picture of what was going on with my daughter.

"My weins! My weins!" Farema screamed over and over, but I couldn't understand her. After a few more tearful screams of "my weins" between huge sobs that made understanding her words harder than it would have been anyway,

I found the light and realized what she was saying about her "veins" when I looked down at both arms. She held them close to my face with her wrists turned up to me, screeching about something going on with the veins in her arms.

"Farema, nothing is wrong with your veins!" I yelled back. "You're fine, you're okay now— "

"No! The blood—*the blood*!"

I was more than a little startled, and I didn't know how to calm her. So we sat there, Cody on the bed at our feet patting her back while I tried to put my arms around the squirming, shrieking child and hold her while she forced her wrists up close to my eyes and screamed about her veins and the blood.

It must have been fifteen minutes or more before I got her calmed down enough that I could understand her fear. She said she could hear the blood rushing through her veins, and it was waking her up and she was afraid of the sound. When I tried to explain that everyone has blood passing through their veins, and that it is necessary for life and how the heart pumps the blood, I realized there was no good way to solve this dilemma. My explanation about her heart stopped her screams only long enough for her to understand before she became even more hysterical. Blood was rushing through her heart, and now that was scaring her more. There seemed no way to calm her. Still weeping as if she'd suffered some terrifying assault, she allowed me to lead her back to her bed and sit with her for more than an hour while she sobbed herself to sleep. Before the sun came up, very early in the morning, the whole scene replayed itself once more. I gave up on getting my usual seven and a half hours of sleep.

The night of "the veins" was only the beginning. The onslaught of screams in the night and early morning hours would steal away our peace and lead to almost a year of sleeplessness in our home.

Fear of things she couldn't understand, like the way her body was made and some of its functions, was understandable. Farema had no concept of the abstract. Her special ed teachers had tried to tell me why she had so much trouble understanding time, and why equations of money, including checking accounts and other things that could not be explained in simple terms, were extremely hard for her to follow. But how in the world could it be that she could "hear" the blood in her veins? It was impossible.

Farah, who was once more left in the background of her sister's all-consuming behaviors, became exasperated and angry at the constant interruption of her night's sleep. Her room was next to her sister's, and she was the first to awaken when the "terrors of the veins" began in the middle of what became every night. Though I hurried down the stairs to Farema's room at the first whimper I'd hear, it was always too late to keep Farema's cries from waking everyone. My frustration grew as I anticipated the possibility that our daughter's nightly screams would never cease.

I'd never forgotten the first years of her life that had kept me from sleep and drained my energy for so long. I was distraught at the prospect of doing it again: so distraught that I began reading whatever the books said about the dreaded specter. I was beginning to read on the basis that Farema did, in fact, suffer from the thing called autism.

The only change in the nights was the time it took for Farema to awake. I'd appease her cries by talking about how she could hear things most people ignore; it was nothing that could hurt her; everyone had the same thing.

I'd sit in the living room in the dark for a long while just in case it started up again right away to save myself a second fast run down the stairs. Always, while I sat on the little loveseat under the big window that framed the moonlight, I'd pray for strength and energy to keep going during the coming day. Usually I had plenty of time while I sat there listening for an encore to think back and recall the past years.

One night, I sat remembering the long nights when she hadn't slept as a baby and how finally, the crying did stop. I smiled while remembering the uniqueness of her physical agility in almost any situation. Laughing aloud at how shocked I was to see her, I remembered the tinier-than-average toddler bouncing up and down atop that pinto mare when no one had a clue how she'd gotten up there. Soon enough, I let my mind creep down into the recesses where I tried to hide things I didn't want to face. Now I let them seep up to my consciousness.

A few months before this night, I'd taken Farema to see our pediatrician for a recheck after one more bad ear infection, and I'd asked him, out of the blue, what he thought would become of her. I summarized the results of the psychology reports for him, and the meeting Cody and I had had with the women at the preschool just before the end of the year. I didn't say anything about the possibility of autism. I wanted to leave that open for him to bring up on his own; there was no sense in putting words or ideas in his mouth.

His response was not something I would ever relay to another person, and there in the dark, I remembered verbatim what he'd said.

He had read her records from the preschool. He told me how happy he was to see that she'd made progress with her speech, but he predicted she would need daily speech therapy right up to the point of graduation. He'd looked in her eyes and ears and checked her over much like he'd done each time he'd seen her, reminding me to be sure she wore her ear plugs when she was in the pool. When he was finished, he told me to bring her out into the hall after she was dressed and he'd meet us out there. I helped Farema put on her shorts and shirt to hurry her along, and I watched as she proudly tied her own tennis shoes. Cody had prevailed in teaching her to tie her shoes just before her first day in the first grade, and she loved to show how well she did it. When we walked out into the foyer, I could see the office staff getting ready to go to lunch, and I wasn't surprised when the doctor came from his office up the hall without his white lab coat, looking more like a kind, bespectacled businessman. He said he'd walk out to the elevator with us.

The doctor chatted with us on the way out as we exited the lobby and walked down the long hall to the elevators. I wondered when he would offer some suggestions or at least his professional take on what was going on with our daughter's unusual fear in the night. I hoped he would offer a ray of hope. Once more I asked about his thoughts on Farema's behavior, and he stopped and turned to face me squarely. As he looked down at Farema and then back at me he said, "Of course, I can't be sure, but I do believe I have a pretty good grasp of what is in the future for Farema."

I could see compassion in his eyes as he hesitated momentarily, as if he wasn't exactly sure how to say it. Then he looked at me and quietly said, "Worse-case scenario, a facility that cares for developmentally delayed adults, something like an institution. Best-case scenario, a group home for mentally or developmentally disabled adults—but that's not a decision you need to consider until much later down the road."

I couldn't process his suggestions. I calmly asked a couple of questions about why he believed these would be her options. He didn't answer me, really, but offered some comforting words that he hoped he would one day learn that he was totally off-base. He said he understood this was a very hard prognosis for any parent to hear. Still calm, as though I was in shock, I thanked him and smiled, and we stepped into the open elevator. I pushed the button and looked down at the perfectly formed, beautiful, baby-faced girl standing next to me. By the time the elevator stopped and the doors opened, I'd resolved to prove the doctor wrong. I drove home and made a pact with myself that "Someday, maybe many years from now, I will take her to see him again, and he will be embarrassed and very, very sorry for what he said!"

Now, sitting in the darkness of my living room, I still could hear my promise. I'd spoken the words aloud as if to convince myself they held some truth. But if the truth were told, it was I who was irreparably broken. I could see that in Farema's future, nothing would stay the same. She had already changed so many times in ten years.

I closed my eyes and leaned back. At least we could hope for another transformation to come along soon, with less noise and a lot more sleep.

Chapter 18

WITHDRAWAL

W hile the "vein invasion" continued at night, days were normal. Farema never mentioned the veins in her arms or her heart beating. Night was a whole different story, and I began to wonder if she could really hear the blood moving through her body after dark. It sounded crazy, but a lot of things were unexplainable with Farema.

Hearing tests had been done at the request of Farema's speech teacher, tests that were far less traumatic and more conclusive than those done when she was a toddler. She was not, as I had so long believed, deaf. Far from it. The testers said she had hyper-acoustic hearing. She could hear very well, sort of like a dog. Dogs have a heightened ability to hear sounds, and I'd read somewhere that they couldn't discriminate between them. Many nights I lay awake listening to her sobbing herself to sleep, imagining what it would be like to hear such things. Maybe she really could. Then again, maybe she'd just heard about the body's functions at school and her imagination had run amuck. I was never sure what to think.

I began to wonder if Farema's lack of close relationships was taking a toll on her. I worried more about her loneliness than anything else, and I knew why.

As a child, my life had been a series of new schools and trying to make new friends. Dianna and I attended three different schools one year as my father traveled up and down the west coast, Mom and two kids in the backseat, looking for work as a salesman. After trying to reestablish myself in ten new school settings, I cherished the friends I made in high school when my father finally settled us in Springfield, where my sister and I went to the same high school for three consecutive years. It was the beginning of my stability, and when I had children, all I wanted was for them to have lasting and long friendships such as I'd longed for as a girl. When Farema was at home with no one to interact with except me, I focused all my energy on how to rectify a situation that, I felt, was nearly unbearable.

Farema still had Whitney two doors down from us, and until Mandy's family returned to Australia, Farema had someone to be with on the weekends if her friends weren't gone somewhere with their families. But during the winter months the rain kept children indoors, and Farema's lack of interest and comprehension of things other preteens found exciting left her alone at home more than I felt was safe. She would disappear somewhere in the house, doing I didn't know what. I felt like I was watching her fade—almost undetectably—ever-so-slightly slipping away from my reach. Then one damp, gray afternoon, I saw where she'd been going.

"Farema—where are you?" I called.

When I got no answer, I walked to the end of the long hallway to Farema's room. I heard laughing and talking behind a nearly closed door. First I put my ear to the door, and I heard the sound of two young girls chattering happily. My curiosity overcame me, and after listening for a few minutes trying to recognize the voice and figure out who had come over to play with Farema, I quietly pushed the door open just enough to peek in without disturbing the play that was in progress.

I saw Farema sitting alone on the edge of her bed. There was no one with her. She sat facing a small lamp table that held an array of birthday and valentine cards she'd saved, propped up carefully with folded letters, notes, and all the small school pictures she'd acquired over the years. Alone in her room, she had created a small shrine to her grade school and middle school acquaintances and childhood friends.

In her hand she held a well-worn page torn from a fifth-grade paper yearbook album, where her "friends," some of whom she barely knew but who had said hi to her in passing, had signed their names. They'd written short-and-sweet but loving words to the special ed kid.

Farema often held onto the pages in precious adoration, and she had nearly worn them out by reading and rereading them over and over. When she'd bring them to me and hold them in front of my face to signify she wanted me to read them to her again, I'd read slowly, with more than enough emphasis on the nice words directed to her and as much dramatic intonation as it was possible to interject in a one- or two-sentence statement.

I knew she was lonely—this child who seldom talked unless she had to. I'd seen a whole new side of my daughter as she grew older, a side of her that longed to be like the others, a girl who knew what having a friend meant. She was around eleven, nearing the age when young girls begin to identify with their peers, and her childhood friends were gradually moving on to the things that come with maturity. Farema was not like them. She didn't know what the attraction was with boys, and she'd never been able to spend time talking to friends on the phone. They couldn't have understood her if she had. Her inarticulate way of speaking was difficult for kids to understand, and I'd see their faces change after a few first words of introduction. She was becoming the "odd kid that no one understood," and because she attended the special education classroom, it was easy to label her as retarded.

I pulled the door shut without making a sound and turned quietly away. With my back against the wall, I slid down to the floor, letting the tears fall as I buried my face against my knees. I didn't know what to do to help her. I'd worn myself out with worry about this day, when those children who'd played with her would tire of her oddness and be gone.

When I finally got up to find some tissue to blow my nose, I reran the scene in my mind. Farema was happy—laughing, giggling, even talking in her own disjointed sentences. It sounded as if she was conversing with the pictures and letters she'd enshrined before her. Though I had a hard time understanding exactly what she'd said, I could tell she was pretending to have a regular friend-to-friend interaction. But her friends, this time, were made of paper.

"Is she that lonely?" I asked in a whisper to no one but myself. "So desperate for someone to play with that she has to talk to pictures?"

❧

"I'm retard, aren't I?" Farema said to me one day after school. I was startled. How could she have known the meaning of that word? We'd not ever used it in our home. And how was she able to apply it to herself? Was it possible that Farema understood far more than I had given her credit for? I tried to act nonchalant as I pulled up a chair to look into her face and convince her that the charge was absolutely unfounded.

"Where did you hear that?" I tried to sound calm, with no hint that the word she was hearing from some unkind student was a bad thing. "Some people have trouble speaking clearly, some have other problems, and you have some speech problems, but there is nothing wrong with that."

She continued to avoid my gaze as was her style, and I pretended to be going about the business of picking up lint off the breakfast-nook table while I spoke, all the while watching her response out of the corner of my eye. She smiled, turned, and walked away. She'd accepted my explanation and that was that, but deep down in my heart I knew there would be more disappointing moments in her life to come, and I whispered a prayer that once more, God would send his guardian angels to hover near her, to protect her as much as they dared from pain and loneliness. I knew things were changing. She knew now that she was different. I had hoped her inability to understand some things would protect her, but I didn't know how to keep her protected from the truth of real life forever.

I found myself longing for the old days when all four girls were home and Farema had three sisters at her beck and call. Time had taken her sisters; they all had their own lives and were not around to include her in their plans. Lisa and Lainee had moved far from us and were raising their own children. Farah loved her job working for a dentist who had hired her right after graduation, and she had a steady boyfriend who would later become her husband. Cody was busier than he had ever imagined possible with his restaurant as word spread of his excellent cuisine. He was obligated to put in more hours at work than ever before. Farema and I were on our own.

I continued to research ways to help my youngest daughter become interested and involved in life, whether with others she could imitate or on her own in a constant state of motion, riding her bike or walking the dog we'd found in the parking lot of Cody's restaurant. I started writing things down that I wanted to look up at the library, and I began to notice that many of the behaviors Farema exhibited, either short-lived behaviors from years before or those that had become regular habits, I'd read about in those books full of strange childhood syndromes and disabilities.

Because of her nighttime terrors, I came to learn the importance of perseverance. There were times when I was so tired from lack of sleep that I wanted to scream my sorrows to the ceiling. I dared not. I sometimes wanted to run away, go far away from this life that had become mine. Cody was able to leave for the restaurant where he spent more and more time. I had to stay. I wanted sometimes to just escape, never to return, to disappear and let someone else deal with this disability that was no one's fault—certainly it wasn't Farema's. And yet there she was, and there we were. No way out. I had to persevere. I had to teach myself to learn patience where she was concerned, and I had to extend that patience to my family and especially to Cody. I had to find enough strength to carry the both of us. And I began to pray in earnest for God to grant me the ability to overcome my urge to run.

Chapter 19

THE "A" WORD

Nearly a year passed, and Farema was still afraid of the blood rushing through her heart and veins. We knew we had to find help. I had spent the first five years of her life walking and rocking her back to sleep two or more times each night, and I had learned to go on and excuse her distress as indigestion or something that would end eventually. This time, I knew that whatever was going on in her psyche, I was powerless to resolve it. My prayers were repetitious in begging God's help to find an answer and let us get some sleep, but sometimes I wondered if this was how it might always be.

Once in a while, almost weekly, Farema would succumb to exhaustion herself, only waking up once and then sleeping till morning, and I would feel like there was a break in the storm that was clouding my nights. Days held no trace of the craziness that went on during the nighttime hours. I was thankful for that. Yet, when I let myself believe the worst was over, I would find the worst hadn't even begun. I'd find myself near total exhaustion after a long night of no rest whatsoever, back to wondering how I would survive if things didn't change. Finally, I had no other option than to search for answers outside our home.

Cody and I weren't superhuman or experienced in dealing with a child whose needs were beyond anything we'd ever witnessed or even heard of, and we were unable to begin to know what to do to help her. I turned again to my only source of information: the city library. There I read up on all sorts of childhood disabilities, but I couldn't find anything like what we were experiencing in our home at night.

One afternoon in mid-September, as I stood watching Cody from the kitchen window while he trimmed a few branches off the two small willow trees that graced our front yard, I breathed a big sigh of regret for what I was about to say to him.

I stepped outside, walked up behind Cody, and waited for him to feel me standing there. When he turned around, looking tired as usual from the little sleep from the night before, I spoke up.

"You know, I don't think we can go on like this much longer. I think we need to find a place for Farema—so we can get some sleep. We're going to crack if we don't. At least I am. I know I can't take much more."

Cody turned back and went on to cut some more branches. I stood silent behind him with my head down, searching for something, some words I might add to make it better.

"I've heard there are places where people take a kid who has disabilities; it's called 'respite,' I think. Like a place where they'll watch over her, and then when the parents can handle it again, they can pick her up. I heard about it at the preschool, and I can call and find out if they take older kids too."

Cody just looked at me as if he couldn't bring himself to admit I might be right. I turned and went back into the house with a decision to ask around at the school. Maybe some teachers or parents in the special ed class would have some information. I was willing to try anything.

But before the opportunity rose for me to ask at the school, I came across a book at the library that changed everything. Written by the mother of an autistic girl and published in 1991, it was called *The Sound of a Miracle*.

The Sound of a Miracle is the story of Georgie, a girl whose parents in the beginning had no idea what was wrong with her. I recognized familiar instances in the life of this young girl—once again, I silently applied autism to Farema. The mother, Annabelle Stehli, had heard of a French doctor who'd invented and successfully used an instrument for treating children with autism. The doctor had invented the device for himself, hopeful that it might prevent his own deafness. By listening to different frequencies of music, he was successful in retaining his own ability to hear. After that, for twenty years a large part of his practice was dedicated to treating children with "hyper audition." In the book, Georgie's mother gave so much credit to the therapy her daughter had received from the procedure that I wondered if maybe it could help us.

I made calls and spoke to everyone I could find for advice on who might know something about Auditory Intervention Therapy. I called the Autism Society of America in Los Angeles, where I found information about a study taking place in the Portland, Oregon, area. I was willing to try anything to help my daughter and our family, and especially to find a way to get a good night's sleep. There was another reason I was anxious to attend the auditory training sessions with Farema and meet the personnel at the Center for the Study of Autism—I'd learned in my numerous treks to the library that the founder of the center was Bernard Rimland, the same psychologist who in 1964 produced the book *Infantile Autism: The Syndrome and Its Implications for a Neural Theory of Behavior,* which attacked the "Refrigerator Mother" idea. Mr. Rimland set out to dispel the belief that the mother was to blame, believing that autism actually had a biological connection. The new information was the continuation of my personal pardon, a pardon spelled out more beautifully and powerfully in Psalm 139, which continued to speak to me. In David's words, I saw that God already knew Farema, saw her, and loved her before she was born. Her design was his doing.

Another phone call to the Center for the Study of Autism in Newburg answered my questions: the center was in the process of collecting names for their own experimental study using the French inventor's method. I couldn't wait to tell Cody. But if I did mention the center and the possibility of it helping us with Farema, I would not tell him that the criteria, the one thing they stressed above all else for being accepted to the study, was that it was only for children already diagnosed with autism. My plan was that I would explain to them why I wanted to come, then see if they would accept her after they met her and began the first stages of processing her application for treatment. These were the experts. They would know for certain if what so many had suspected—if what now, even I suspected—was true. I'd wait until I was comfortable and then I'd simply ask for their opinion. I'd let the professionals decide if my daughter met the criteria. And if those with expertise and knowledge deduced that my daughter did have autism—well, I told myself, I'd cross that bridge when and if I came to it, and I'd accept it too.

Dr. Stephen Edelson would be the psychologist directing the sessions of auditory training, and when I called them, the receptionist at the center told me once more that the sessions were exclusively for children with autism.

"Yes, I understand," I said. "And there will be autism experts there to work with her?"

In my heart, I knew she would be accepted.

The woman on the phone said the study would include a fourteen-day, two-hundred-and-forty-mile round trip for us without any breaks. It was imperative that the days be successive. It would cost a lot, around $1250 in cash, required at the time of registration. The procedure was not covered by insurance. But no cost was too much for us at that point. We needed sleep. After we'd sent in the money, with the preliminary registration forms promising to show up on time, I was excited about the sessions coming up. And deep in my heart, I wanted to ask these experts point-blank if they believed she really did have autism. It was time for me to learn the truth.

Though I'd never wanted to speak the possibility aloud to another living soul, in my heart I'd long known the doctors and therapists who'd suggested autism might very well be right. I'd researched it over the years. Farema had exhibited every one of the classic behaviors written in the many books I'd read, since the day of her birth and before. I'd always tried to ignore and explain away what a more courageous person would have long ago accepted. The noises she made whenever water was running or the vacuum cleaner was on or the lawn mower engine was going outside; the laundry list of "autistic behaviors"; the sleeplessness and the screaming in the night—they all added up to something I'd read about many times.

After calling and signing her up for the study, I knew I would soon hear what these experts had to say, and though I told myself I was ready for the truth and that I could handle it, my heart held onto a thread of hope that there was something else, something more acceptable, wrong with Farema. Something curable.

Our appointment date came on October 4, 1992, and at 7:00 in the morning we set out on our road trip for two weeks of therapy. I drove Farema to the Center for the Study of Autism where she would undergo a series of auditory training treatments first used on people with auditory processing problems by Dr. Guy Berard in Annecy, France.

When we arrived that first morning, experts in autism tested Farema. The desperation I'd felt when I signed my daughter up for the program eased when, after days of intense testing and observation, I was invited to sit down with one of the clinicians. We talked about Farema, and I told her the whole story of how I'd come to the center suspecting that my daughter was in fact autistic. I was honest with her, explaining that whenever a suggestion had been made by psychologists in the school district or medical professionals that I accept a diagnosis of autism, I had refused to consider it.

I realized I was talking fast and furiously, almost ready to excuse myself. With a compassionate smile and a voice soft with sincerity, she replied, "I understand."

I knew that she did.

And then she told me the truth.

"Farema has classic autism," she said. "She is high functioning, which doesn't necessarily mean she is academically high functioning, but that she is able to talk and interact in social situations, where many others with autism do not."

I swallowed and listened quietly.

"There are those with a form of autism called Asperger's Syndrome who are high functioning and able to learn languages and attend college, but who are usually a lot less social. That is not what Farema is like. And Farema will likely have it a lot easier because she is able to adapt to most social situations."

She also explained the Autistic Savant, individuals with unique and superior intelligence in one area but severe lack in most all other abilities. Some could solve mathematical equations with the expertise of a Harvard professor, yet be unable to dress or brush their own teeth. This was nothing like my child, and I silently thanked God that Farema was as capable as she was.

After what seemed like fewer than a couple of hours but was actually more than three, I left with a small, four-track tape with our afternoon discussion recorded on it. I had put it in my purse with a promise to listen to it again when I had plenty of time.

I appreciated the woman's honesty and the compassion of the staff at the Center for the Study of Autism, but my heart had hurt as I listened to the conclusive words that confirmed my worst fears. According to their analysis, Farema had probably been born with it. It was as simple as that.

Farema was autistic.

Pretending not to know had protected me for a while. But hearing it from someone who had read all the previous testing in addition to doing in-depth testing of her own, someone who was an authority in diagnosing the disorder, sealed our fate. I cried silent tears as I drove the two hours back to Eugene. Something in me was crumbling, and I felt I was experiencing a true grieving for the child I'd hoped would prove one day to be normal. I heard the words replay in my head as I tried to accept her diagnosis. This was not just a suspicion gleaned from a library book or a movie; it was far more substantial than that. Now that the verdict was in, I couldn't kid myself into believing that one day I would wake up and everything would be just fine. The daughter I wanted, the one I planned to take shopping for her prom dress, the one who would one day follow her sisters in marriage to a great man to raise a family of her own no longer existed. She was gone.

The dream I'd clung to from the early days, the one that expected to wake up one morning and find that Farema was like all the other kids her age, had to be replaced with reality. In place of the dream was a little girl who would never know the normal things of life. This girl was different. This little girl was not now, nor would she ever be, normal.

Finally, in my heart, I bade farewell to the daughter who would never be. And I prayed for God's strength for the years ahead.

When we arrived home that night, I went straight upstairs and dropped the day's recording in a small dresser drawer. Ten years would pass, and we would move twice, and that tape would remain in the drawer, right where I'd left it.

Chapter 20

TURNING POINT

1992–93

Cody didn't say much after I told him about Farema's diagnosis. He hadn't read about it like I had, only hearing things I said about the disorder when someone brought it up or there was mention of autism in the newspaper. In the early '90s, autism was only beginning to be noticed and talked about, and most believed the interest was borne out of the success of the movie that had opened our eyes, *Rain Man*. Cody said his usual. "Doesn't matter anyway; she's fine the way she is."

After we'd seen the movie and I'd recovered from the initial shock, I'd mentioned little things to my husband, hoping he'd respond with a good reason why Farema couldn't have the same disorder. But Cody had never found enough interest in autism to say anything at all. He supported his child and loved her no matter what. I knew he had the healthier attitude.

I found myself bonding instantly with the other mothers while we sat waiting our turn for the soundproof room where the auditory sessions took place. Farema made some friends too, older and younger, some her age, all with strange behaviors that were fascinating to me. One boy spent a lot of time reading the phone book, and while I visited with his mother, she told me he'd already read every atlas he could get his hands on. She'd been told he was a "Rain Man," although she didn't know much about autism. Another child made all sorts of strange animal sounds. And then there was Jonathan.

Jonathan didn't sleep. He had come to the center with his grandmother, who told me she often helped her daughter with transportation and to give her a little break some afternoons. She said he had to be locked inside his bedroom at night so the rest of the family could get some sleep, but still it was difficult for them. Jonathan made all kinds of noise all night; he'd scream and bang, and no matter what kind of medications they tried, nothing worked for long. Their psychiatrist had decided to finally take him off everything for fear the damage to his liver would be too great.

Farema and I accepted the grandmother's invitation for lunch and tea at her home not far from the center. While we enjoyed a sandwich in her modest mobile home, she told me more of how their family managed with Jonathan's bizarre sleeping habits. Her story was deeply moving, and I found myself praying for her and her family while she continued.

After we ate, we sat sipping a cup of tea at the kitchen table, and Farema and Jonathan played together in the big yard outside. When I realized it was nearing time for us to get back for Farema's afternoon session, I stuck my head out the door to tell Farema to come and get in the car. She didn't come. After a few minutes we both went outside, called, and looked around the large property. We found nothing. No kids—anywhere. I began to panic. Only moments before I would have called 911 on my cell phone, the trunk of my car sprung up suddenly, and a wide-eyed, panicky Farema jumped—no, flew— out. I stood staring at the sight.

Farema, still a tiny girl at the age of eleven, with her long, light brown ponytail all tangled and tousled about her head and shoulders as if she'd been in a fight, was obviously traumatized. Jonathan was laughing hysterically as he uncurled his long, skinny frame from the back of the trunk. Once out, he jumped and ran all around, as if it was the greatest trick he'd ever pulled. Farema was scared stiff. I held her close for a few minutes, feeling her heart pounding. We said our shaky good-byes and drove off, but not without my silent resolve to never let my daughter out of my sight in strange surroundings again.

At the end of the two-week hearing sessions, Farema slept without waking. The therapy, which consisted of hours of either continuous or intermittent listening to various levels of music and unusual sounds through special headphones, seemed like an unlikely way to help autistic children learn to cope with their environment. But although I was skeptical at first, I watched as our daughter exhibited every one of the changes the literature warned us might be evident during the procedure. I didn't try to figure it out. On the third day of the treatment, Farema ate less and appeared to lose her appetite. A few days later, she became irritable. Later in the week, she seemed more withdrawn, and even acted very nervous and edgy.

For her relaxation during the breaks in therapy, Farema was able to try the "Squeeze Machine," invented by an autistic woman named Temple Grandin. It did exactly what Temple designed it to do. She had created the machine with insight from another invention, one that made her famous in the cattle industry—a much larger machine designed to gently squeeze animals as they stood or walked between the sides while they were loaded into trucks. I'd seen the invention on a TV program about ranching, but I'd never dreamed my child would benefit from something created for animals! I was amazed when I saw a smile come across Farema's face while she knelt on her hands and knees in the strange contraption, using the handle to control the length of time she wanted to be inside and the firmness of the squeeze.

After the fifteen full days of traveling the two-hour round trip to Portland, Cody and I were blessed with the luxury of sleeping all night uninterrupted. I couldn't question the necessity of the past two weeks. We were grateful and feeling a magnitude of physical and emotional relief. After what had seemed like forever, our sleepless nights were indeed over.

As if the very memory of Farema's all-night fear had vanished, we never again heard the screams or ran to defend her from "the blood!" I would never know for sure if the auditory therapy had miraculously resolved Farema's night terrors, but it didn't matter. Farema—the "changeling"—was now sleeping soundly, as were we.

One night after Farema and Cody were fast asleep, I lay awake in the darkness of my room and remembered the many times Farema had exhibited a sudden transformation. It was becoming a pattern, a paradigm for what this child would do many times over in the years to come.

While I thought about the recent past, the changes I'd witnessed, and what still was to come, I thanked God for coming to our rescue just when I'd thought there was no hope. I thanked Him for keeping us safe on the many trips up and down the freeway and for giving me a child who was now opening my eyes and heart to what really mattered in life. Not money, not worldly treasures, but the peace of knowing that the God of the universe was on my side. Somehow, I could feel the peace that surpasses understanding as I forced myself to begin putting aside my dreams of a normal life for my youngest child and focus on the companionship and activities that would enhance the life she would now live as a girl with autism.

I would need far more help than I'd ever imagined while I was unable to accept what was wrong. Before I let myself fall asleep in the quiet, peace-filled house that night, I asked God to please, please, watch over us all and now, finally, change me. I had no idea how, in my weakness and uncertainty, I'd ever be able to raise this most peculiar child.

Coming to grips with the firm diagnosis from the experts, of whom there were so few in those days, was going to be a day-to-day process for me. First, I knew I had to made amends where my stubborn resolve to ignore any insinuation of Farema's differentness had hurt others.

The first apology, I knew, would have to be to the church lady who'd tried to point me in the right direction when Farema was so little.

I'd never again heard from Emily Watson, the woman whose frightening words had forced me to seek out answers that finally led to Farema's diagnosis. But I decided that, although it would be hard, I would go to her and explain that when she had surprised me at my door, I hadn't been ready to face something so devastating as having a child with autism. I seldom saw my old neighbor, Lois, but now, with Farema's new diagnosis, I couldn't shake the shame I felt for having been so abrupt and rude to her friend.

Hoping to run into my friend at the department store where she was working, I wrote a note of apology and explanation on a blank card with a pretty bouquet of blue flowers pictured on the front and kept it in my purse. Then my opportunity arrived, in the middle of a busy lunch hour at the restaurant when I was filling in for a sick waitress. I saw a couple who'd been close friends of Lois and who also attended her church. I knew they'd probably see her before long.

When I was sure they'd finished their lunch, I smiled and waved, then ducked into the storage closet to retrieve the card from my purse. I went straight over to the booth where they sat and said "Hello." They responded with smiles and asked how our family was doing, and after a few words of the same, I laid the envelope with the card on the table between them.

"I'm so glad to see you both here today, and I'd like to ask a favor of you! I know you go to the same church as Lois and her family, and I wonder if you know a woman named Emily Watson?" They looked up at me, standing there with a big smile on my face, thinking I would soon be free of the burden I'd carried ever since the day nine years earlier when I'd treated the older woman on my porch with so little compassion. I'd known then how hard it must have been for her to tell a mother what she'd felt compelled by God to convey. I continued, "I'm not sure you know what took place long ago when Farema was little, and I went to talk to Lois about it, after Emily Watson came to my door . . ."

I stammered out a few more words about how I needed to apologize, about how badly I'd felt all these years, and then I saw the look on their faces that told me they already knew. Lois had probably confided the whole story to them—that's what friends do. When the woman responded, I knew instantly I was on the verge of learning a great lesson.

"Lauri, that is so good of you to want to say how sorry you are . . . and to tell Mrs. Watson why you were so hard on her then—but I'm so sorry to tell you, she passed away a month ago."

I looked from her to her husband and tried to hold back the escaping tears of shame and regret as I tucked the card back into my apron pocket and said "thank you." I turned and walked into the back storage room. I was saddened to the depth of my soul. God himself had sent Emily to me those many years ago. I had not wanted to hear her, though she'd tried to express that hers was a message from God. I'd treated her horribly. Now I could never rectify what I'd done to her; could never make right how I'd rejected God's attempt to intervene and speak to me so long ago. I asked God for forgiveness then and there, before hanging up my apron and scurrying out the back door, hoping it appeared I had an important appointment. I didn't want to talk to anyone, but just to be alone.

My only real appointment that afternoon was to go home, get down on my knees, and tell God I would never, never again take lightly a message that he was trying to give me, even if I didn't want to hear it. And while I was there, with tears of sincere remorse, I asked him to pass the message of my deep regret and heartfelt apology on to Emily Watson.

Chapter 21

"I LIKE ICE"

K eeping Farema socially engaged was becoming more of a challenge as both of us grew older. After her friend Mandy moved away and other friends left her behind developmentally, more of the burden of finding interesting things to occupy her time fell on me. It hurt me terribly to see the way other kids ignored and excluded her, and I was determined to make sure that Farema's life was filled with fun and friends, just like any other child her age. That was easier said than done.

Now that I was in my mid-forties, I longed to spend time with friends my own age, doing things that grown-up women do, like going on shopping sprees, attending Bible studies or workshops, or chatting over lunch or tea. Instead, life for me at forty-five was from start to finish a new mental list under the heading of "What to Do About Farema?"

Early intervention specialists at Farema's preschool had told me that she needed constant interaction with children her own age to stimulate her and help her develop social and communication skills. Without frequent interaction, she risked withdrawing into her own world as autistic children so often do. In recent months, she had done precisely that, and my biggest fear was losing her behind a glass wall where I wouldn't be able to reach her. So it became my daily quest to make sure my youngest daughter was involved in some kind of shared activity, even if it only involved the two of us.

Nothing in my life had prepared me for the role of social coordinator, but bowing out wasn't an option. I had to set aside my own apprehensions and actively seek out opportunities for my little girl to interact socially. That meant lots of trial and error, learning what worked and what didn't. Sedentary activities like making crafts, assembling puzzles, or playing board games had never captured Farema's interest. She could never sit still long enough. Team sports like soccer and basketball had proved unsuccessful as well. Like her mother, she didn't have the ability or the attention span necessary for ball sports, and even though she liked to swim, I knew she wouldn't be allowed to join a swim team because of her disability.

In spite of these failed attempts, I knew I had to keep trying. But by the winter of 1992, I had run out of ideas. I dreaded getting out of bed on weekend mornings because I would have to find something fun for us to do that day. But what?

I was certain of one thing: Farema loved to move. From birth she had been in constant motion, except for those moments when she would become catatonic and stare vacantly into space. (I had wondered at the time whether she was having seizures, a hunch that was later confirmed as I learned more about autism.)

Other than that, Farema had always had boundless energy, and it was rare to see her sit quietly. She squirmed and wriggled and twirled and spun through childhood . . . and practically wore me out in the process. I had hoped she'd slow down as she approached her teenage years and perhaps develop a few sedentary interests. But she showed no signs of that. I had to keep coming up with creative ideas that would fuel her love of motion.

One morning, Farema wandered into the kitchen, still groggy from sleep, her tousled hair sticking out every which way.

"So where do you want to go today?" I asked her. "Got any ideas?"

She looked at me expectantly but didn't say a word in reply. Farema was still living in the silent world she'd retreated into months before. In spite of my efforts to draw her out, she seemed content to let me do all the talking.

"I have to do some cleaning first, and then we can go see what we can find, okay?" I smiled at her as I fixed her some breakfast.

Farema gave me a little half-smile that signaled her agreement.

After breakfast, she retreated to her bedroom to entertain herself until I finished my chores. A couple of hours later, I poked my head around the doorway to Farema's room.

"Want to go on a bike ride?" I asked.

Farema looked at me with a sparkle in her eyes that told me she liked the idea. Any outdoor activity would have made her happy as long as it was physical.

As I grabbed my jacket, I glanced out the window and realized that the clouds overhead would soon open up, sending a cold drizzle down on top of us. Bad weather never stopped Farema. She would have been just as content riding in the rain as in the sunshine. But I wasn't. So I suggested we take a rain check on the bike ride and find something else to do instead.

"Farema, can *you* think of something new that we can do?" I asked. But she just smiled.

"Okay, honey, I'll just whip us up some grilled cheese sandwiches, and then we can drive around for a while. And if something looks fun, that's what we'll do!"

I turned my head so she wouldn't see the pain in my eyes. I knew that she was happy to be going somewhere, but it upset me that she didn't have any friends of her own to play with. She wanted friends so badly, and I wanted just as badly for her to have them. As the months passed and her loneliness deepened, I feared that her isolation would only get worse with time. I felt desperate to help her.

As we drove through town, I racked my brain trying to think of something we could do. As we turned onto Thirteenth Street and drove past the city ice arena, a wonderful idea came to me. I remembered drawing her attention to the figure skaters on television during the Winter Olympics earlier that year.

"Look at those skaters spin, Freem!" I had said as I gestured toward the TV screen.

It was a challenge to capture her attention even for a split second, but she paused to see what I was pointing at. Her eyes glowed with excitement when she saw how fast the skaters could spin on the ice. For one magic moment she was entranced—but as soon as the spinning stopped, she was off to do something else.

I remembered her affinity for things that could spin, prompting Cody and I to buy every kind of spinning toy we could find. Even as a baby, she had loved to watch the fast whirling of her many spinning tops, mesmerized by the speed and the motion. Spinning was the one activity that could hold her attention for hours. We could spend the afternoon watching the skaters twirl and spin gracefully across the ice. What a great idea! Farema would love it.

As I pulled into the arena parking lot, I shared my plan with Farema, who smiled as if she was going on a new adventure.

"Honey, we can just watch the others skate. You don't have to try it if you don't want to," I said.

She didn't answer, but the joyful grin she flashed told me she was looking forward to this experience. I just hoped it would be a positive one. When Farema was a toddler, we'd gone skating as a family after the ice arena first opened, but Cody had been so worried that Farema might hurt herself that we'd stopped after one or two visits. I wondered whether Farema remembered that now.

As we entered the arena, I glanced around, hoping to spot one of Farema's friends from school. Every outing was a potential opportunity for her to enjoy companionship with her peers, even if only for a short time. I always encouraged her to mix with kids her own age whenever she could because I knew it was the best way to draw her out of her silent world. My heart sank when I didn't see anyone she knew.

We walked over to the front counter, and I told the attendant we only wanted to watch the skating for a while. While I was still speaking, Farema wandered over to the big plate-glass windows that overlooked the rink. Below, skaters circled the huge arena, some holding hands and others holding on to their partners so they wouldn't fall. Younger children and some of the more inexperienced skaters made their way around the perimeter of the rink, holding on to the railing as others glided past them. Some skaters ventured farther out toward the middle with choppy, awkward strides, only to land on their backsides. Music and laughter filled the air. Everyone seemed to be having fun.

Farema's face lit up as she watched some of the more experienced skaters glide and spin and jump in the center of the rink. I knew she wanted to try it.

I walked over to stand beside her. "Freem, do you want me to skate with you for a while? Do you want to try it?" I figured she wouldn't be out there very long, but I was willing to give it a whirl. And by the look on her face, I knew the answer was yes.

I returned to the front counter to pay for the two of us, but a little voice inside me asked, *What if you break your leg—or worse? What good will you be to Farema then? Let her go by herself; God will hold her hand.*

I decided to listen to that intuitive whisper and told the attendant that I wanted just one admission ticket. Then I asked her about the chances of my daughter getting injured. She assured me that serious injuries were rare and that children younger than Farema skated by themselves all the time. Her assurance calmed my fears for the moment, so I led Farema to the skate rental window and handed a young girl the ticket for a pair of skates.

"We need a size—oh, I'm not sure—maybe a three?"

The girl realized I was new to this and asked to see one of Farema's shoes. "The skates need to fit tight," she said. "Not like shoes, though. Just big enough to fit, without any extra toe room."

I was glad to have her help. It made me feel better knowing I didn't have to figure all this out on my own. When I mentioned my concern about sending Farema onto the ice alone, the girl said, "Just tell her to stay close to the wall, and if she thinks she's going to fall, tell her to tuck her arms close into her body, bend forward, and roll." Then she demonstrated the move for Farema.

I helped Farema put on her skates, and then I demonstrated the tuck-and-roll maneuver once more so she wouldn't get hurt if she did fall. This kid had the balance of a cat, but she also seemed immune to pain and would never let me know if she was hurt. Whether she didn't feel pain the way most people did or was just unable to tell me that she was hurt I was never quite sure. But I had learned to check her over carefully for any kind of injury instead of expecting her to complain.

"Honey, Mom is going to sit here and watch while you skate, so you be careful and go slow, okay? No going out into the middle for now. You just stay by the wall like the lady said, and if you don't want to skate anymore, just come back to the door and get off the ice. Do you understand?"

Farema's eyes darted toward me for a split second and then away. It was her usual signal that she understood what I was saying; one that I'd miss if I wasn't watching closely. I hoped she really did understand; I could never be sure.

I double-checked Farema's skates to make sure the laces were tied securely and any loose ends were tucked into the top of each skate. Then we walked down a flight of concrete steps to the rink, passing a sign that warned in big black letters, "ICE-SKATING IS A DANGEROUS SPORT. SKATE WITH CAUTION. SKATE AT YOUR OWN RISK."

Farema made her way past the sign and onto the ice without any hesitation. But I was beginning to have serious doubts again. Cody would never have agreed to this. If I had told him we were coming to the rink, he would have demanded we do something else.

I stared after my daughter as she put one blade in front of the other and began to glide across the ice. She seemed to have all the confidence in the world and never once looked back to see if I was nearby. Even so, I breathed a silent prayer for her safety.

After watching her for a few minutes, I knew she was going to be fine, so I headed upstairs to watch through the plate-glass windows and escape the cold. I took a seat on the bench by the window and waved each time Farema passed by, her spindly legs covering the ice as fast as anyone out there—if not faster. Around and around she flew, her face lit up in a smile of pure satisfaction.

She looked beautiful—and happy.

I felt certain a miracle was unfolding before me. Skating was awakening something in Farema that she had never experienced before. It was no accident that we had stumbled across the ice arena. I had run out of ideas, but God hadn't. He had known all along what would make her heart sing, and I was certain that he had orchestrated this incredible experience for her at just this moment in time.

As I watched my autistic daughter move effortlessly across the ice, my heart overflowed with awe and gratitude to God. I waved at her as she passed, and she looked up at me, a huge grin on her face.

"She's very good! Has she been skating long?"

A voice from behind caught me off guard, and I quickly tried to wipe away the tears that were streaming down my cheeks. I knew I would be at a loss to explain why I was crying.

"She just started today," I said quietly, not expecting an answer.

I was so full of joy, I could barely breathe. Before my eyes, my little girl was emerging from her cocoon of autism and spreading her wings to fly. Out there on the ice was my Farema, the girl who never cared how cold the temperature might be outside and never noticed the chill of a rainy Oregon winter. She was finally in her own element. She was home.

When we walked out of the arena later that afternoon, Farema's face was glowing, and I couldn't have been more pleased. What an amazing day it had been. Then out of the blue, something even more amazing happened. Farema broke her silence, and for the first time in her life, without prompting or persuasion, she spoke a clear, perfectly formed sentence: "I like ice!"

Chapter 22

SKATING LESSONS

1993–97

The Saturday Farema came alive on the ice was the first in a string of weekends we would spend at the city ice rink. The more we went the better she talked. In a matter of weeks I was able to understand a lot more of what she said, and more importantly, she volunteered more verbal communication than ever before in her life. No longer did I ask question after question with not so much as a peep out of her. She was beginning to be a serious talker. Soon enough, she would become a virtual chatterbox.

Farema looked forward to every skating session. I'd sit watching her out on the ice, circling girls about her age who were obviously accomplished skaters. She would try hard to imitate them, looking over at them, then at her own feet, then back again. And sometimes, while I watched from the bench behind the big picture window, I'd see those same girls approaching her and then showing her how to move her feet, hold out her arms, and turn her body to accomplish the moves they were practicing. She mimicked them well, with one strange aberration—she did everything backwards, as though she was watching them in a mirror. I blessed them in silent prayers while thanking God for bringing us to this wonderful place.

"Watch! Watch, ma'm!" Farema had a way of crashing through the swinging double doors after ascending the four thick concrete steps from the ice rink to the viewing floor and then rushing over to me, demanding my absolute, undivided attention. It was always a surprise to see her so animated and excited, and her many words were a miracle: the broken and incomplete sentences we'd heard before she began skating were now spoken more clearly as she initiated communication on her own.

Watching Farema skate brought to mind a scene where the pearly gates of heaven swung wide open, dropping gifts of happiness and delight on top of my child and me. I never tired of watching this youngest daughter of mine bask in the attention she received from the other girls who practiced skating, some with hopes of Olympic futures.

Of course, I knew this too would pass. Farema had not been able to keep up with the girls in our neighborhood as childhood merged into the preteen years, and these girls wouldn't stay forever either. But I would bask in her joy as long as they did stay with her, and she loved gliding over the slippery frozen surface that somehow mirrored her own glacial affliction called autism. With her quick and easy aptitude for ice-skating, there was no doubt this would be a lifetime pursuit—her happiness and her joy.

Weeks passed, and we were faithful to go to the rink so Farema could skate every weekend possible. Then one Saturday afternoon, something I'd secretly longed for but didn't think possible happened.

I'd spent many afternoons drifting around the foyer at the skating rink, looking at the information about figure skating lessons and the pictures of the coaches who taught them. Private lessons were offered, but I knew I would never dare ask anyone to try to teach my autistic child, sometimes absent and in her own world, unable to communicate effectively. I still remembered the coaches of Farema's old baseball and soccer teams. On one such day, I started to head for the snack bar for a cup of coffee before I would return to my usual place on the bench and watch Farema, circling happily around in her icy realm.

"Oh, hi there!"

I stopped and turned to face the beautiful blonde woman who had spoken to me, younger than I was and looking like a poster for beautiful skin and blue eyes. I recognized her from her portrait on the wall. She was the head coach and girls' ice-skating coordinator, Lucinda Jensen.

With her captivating smile that seemed to express a true gentleness and peaceful spirit, she said to me, "I was just watching your little girl, let's see, how do you say her name? Freema?" I smiled back and told her how to pronounce the name, all the while wondering how she'd even come to know my daughter or have any interest in her name.

"I've seen how well she does out there, and she seems to have a great interest in skating—and she really does quite well at imitating the other girls! And they tell me she is so sweet!"

"Yes, she really loves the ice. You know, she is autistic." I forced myself to blurt it out, to face the inevitable and tell it like it was. I held out little hope that anyone would continue to have interest in my child after knowing the truth about her. I wasn't ready for what came next. Without missing a beat, as if my admission of Farema's autism made no difference at all, she said, "Oh, yes, and I would love to work with her in a private setting. I think it would be more beneficial for her instead of the group classes. She would probably pick it up faster with one-on-one lessons."

My heart flew out of its place in my chest and soared up to the clouds where dreams that come true are harbored. I told her I would love to see Farema have lessons. When she said she would be Farema's teacher, I felt as if there was no end to the goodness to come from this place.

Later that day I tried to express to Farema how fabulous it was that she would be starting private lessons, but she was happy with anything that went on in the ice rink. Cody was as surprised as I had been when I told him about the encounter with Lucinda. He was relieved and very glad that his daughter would be getting some solid instruction for the sake of her safety.

I registered Farema for private lessons with Cindy, as she liked to be called, and as God had planned it, the lessons began. Farema went on to make friends with girls who were regulars at the rink. Within a few months I felt so comfortable with her skating that I stopped being her constant shadow and started leaving her at the rink for her private lesson, and usually she stayed for the public ice session that followed. Then one day when I dropped Farema off, Cindy came up to me.

"I wanted to talk to you about Farema joining the Ice-Skating Institute, a recreational skating club for all ages that does competitions. She can win some medals and ribbons for her room!" she said. "We have a place that is perfect for her. It's called the Special Skaters Program, and it's a safe place for Farema to start in competition. She will only compete with others who, like her, have challenges to overcome and are comparable in ability. It's a great place for her to gain confidence." Cindy said that if Farema did well, she could always go on to compete with others her age in the regular ISI competitions.

That was all I needed to hear. Something deep inside told me that Farema's future on the ice was sealed. She would be grouped with others who, like her, had to work harder and practice longer to conquer their specific disabilities and achieve their goals.

I was overjoyed and said yes, that would be wonderful. But later, when Cody came home and I rushed excitedly to tell him about Farema joining a skating club for the purpose of competing and winning ribbons and medals, he asked me what I was thinking.

"Don't you know she isn't like other kids? That will be too hard on her. What if she does terrible and all the others win a prize and she is the only one left out? That is probably the way it will go!"

After hearing his concerns, I was afraid he might be right. I promised him I would pull her out the moment she appeared to be stressed or upset. I was concerned that instead of giving her a feeling of accomplishment, the competitive side of all this might cause her to retreat into her own world after I'd worked so hard to pull her out. That night, I prayed for guidance, for insight, and for Farema's protection.

As Farema proceeded to attend her private lessons with Cindy and practice every time she was on the ice, I waited and watched, wondering if I could detect any kind of hesitation about her upcoming performance. I saw none.

I'd read many books about autism, before and after Farema's diagnosis, and I'd read that though kids with autism do things that attract all kinds of attention, they do not especially enjoy being the one everyone is looking at. Farema often shied away from letting family members or others show up at the rink to see her skate. With careful consideration, I'd figured out a way for them to see her on the ice. I told them to go to the rink when she was in the middle of her lesson and then peek around from behind the thick beams that separated the windows so she wouldn't see anyone watching her. If Farema caught someone other than me focusing on her, she would immediately stop skating and come up the stairs to inquire about what was going on.

Farema continued to take her private lessons and practice as often as there were open sessions of ice. Later, when her skills improved so that she would not be a hazard to the other skaters who practiced jumps and spins, she was allowed to skate the freestyle sessions reserved for the better skaters who had the ability to avoid accidents. The sessions were only for those under the instruction of a private coach. Farema was fast becoming one of the regulars at the rink. With the Christmas season coming up soon after she'd realized "our" dream, Farema joined her classmates in preparing for her first performance on the ice in the Christmas Program.

Cody and I watched with the other parents, and none were more proud than we were that evening. I held my breath as I sat wondering if the noise, the music, or the bright lights would bring on a behavior that might disrupt the hard work Cindy and all the ice rink staff and skaters had worked so hard to perfect. With Farema, there was no predicting what might happen. But to our amazement and most thankful surprise, Farema skated with her group and looked as normal as any other child out there showing off her stuff. I was relieved to see her with a myriad of other skaters, younger and older, who unwittingly offered support to the girl who'd never before encountered something so exciting and wonderful. This time, as part of the team, she belonged!

One day when I was free to stay and watch her skate, Farema happily ran up to me ahead of her coach.

"Mom! I'm gonna be in the com-tition!" Farema had a difficult time speaking words she hadn't used before.

"You are?" I acted surprised, but I'd already heard about a home-based competition and that Farema would be one of the competitors.

"Don't you worry about a thing! Farema will do just great!" Cindy responded when I smiled and glanced over at her. "She is learning her program, and we will be sure she isn't competing with anyone too much higher in skill level. She will probably win a medal!" My heart soared at Cindy's confident prediction. I felt as if I was the one about to win the prize—though I knew I already had.

My greatest worry for Farema was that she would see the crowds of spectators, mostly parents and friends of the contestants who came from all over the state and others, and freeze up. She'd be performing—*alone*—there would be no large group this time! I wasn't at all sure that she wouldn't take one look at the filled bleachers, complete with noise, chatter, overhead music, and the bright lights that enhanced the whiteness of the ice, and simply walk off, never to return again. But Cindy assured me she would be there to remedy any problems, even joining Farema on the ice if need be.

February at the skating rink meant that everyone involved in figure skating lessons would be practicing and perfecting the routines they'd perform in the yearly Love to Skate Competition. The rink was a maze of Valentine décor, complete with big red paper hearts, red ribbons, and decorations of pink and red. The lobby was chock-full of vendors who came with ice-skating jewelry, cellophane-wrapped flowers to hand out to competitors after their programs, adorable stuffed animals, and people taking videos of participants for sale after the event. It was a cheerful and fun event that brought out all the smiles and happiness that had become Farema's life.

Cindy had worked closely with Farema to prepare her so there would be no surprises or worries, and when her name was called, Farema skated out into the center, waited for the music to start, and proceeded as if she'd done this a million times. Cody had decided not to come, unable to face his daughter's tears if she happened to fall, but he needn't have worried.

Farema won the blue ribbon, signifying first place. She was proud, and the smile that enveloped her face for the entire day proved it. The girls and boys who'd now become her circle of friends hugged and congratulated her. Farema would never know that with only two entrants in her age group and skill level, she would have won first or second no matter how well she skated. It was the accomplishment she felt that mattered. After she took her bows, Farema climbed up on the first-place platform with her blue ribbon pinned to her shoulder for photos. I purchased the biggest one from the photographer to show everyone we knew.

When Farema went to practice with Cindy, she was complete. Her love of skating and the friends she'd made only made her more social and able to interact. I watched as the girl who at one time hadn't cared if anyone paid attention to her or spoke to her or noticed if she was in the room emerged from her shell. "Chameleon" was a word that often came to my mind as I stood back and watched Farema simply blend in with her surroundings at the skating rink.

At school, in the last years of middle school and on into high school, Farema found the same acceptance that she'd found at the rink. Many of the kids in her mainstream classes had been with her in elementary school and had heard of her prowess on the ice, and before long they became her friends too. She told me stories of who came and sat with her at lunch and who gave her their pictures to keep. Cody finally confessed how happy he was that I'd helped her so much and that now she did indeed have a life all her own. My definition of happiness had become one three-letter word—*ice.*

One early afternoon while I dropped Farema at the rink for her weekly lesson, Cindy approached me as I lugged in Farema's skate bag, following behind my daughter like a dutiful skate-bag caddy.

"I was wondering if you would mind if I incorporate another assistant in Farema's lessons. I think it will help her improve her skills so much," she said. Cindy was the type of person who sparkled from the inside out, and all her suggestions could be trusted to contain the flavor of happiness for Farema. I was all for it.

Cindy continued. "Farema seems to be a visual learner, but I've noticed one interesting thing about her—you may have seen it too. When I show her how to move and maneuver on the ice, she mirrors me. When I turn in one direction, she goes the opposite way! I've thought about that, and since jumps are to be performed in one particular direction, I found someone who will work with her who can do them in both directions. That way Farema can still mirror her as she takes off, does the jump, and lands in the wrong direction, and Farema will go in the right direction. Her name is Gillian. She is Farema's age and could be a wonderful influence on her."

I didn't hesitate to accept. I felt once more that this was another miracle from God, one more comrade for my daughter's delight, and I was ecstatic. The next time Farema had a lesson, I went inside to watch how she worked with her new assistant.

"Mom! This is Gillian!" Farema couldn't wait to introduce me to her new companion, coach, and friend. "She can go in my direction!"

"Yes! That is what I hear! Isn't that wonderful?" I responded. Another friend for Farema meant another means of companionship, communication, and great happiness for her. My cup was running over.

Chapter 23

A LIFE OF HER OWN

Farema found her niche, her forte, and her happiness in her world of white and cold, and I found freedom. With my daughter happily entertained in a place where she could thrive, I found myself free from spending every waking moment concentrating on what I could pull out of my hat for her to do next. Her first and only choice when her free time coincided with the public sessions at the rink was to go there and skate.

At first, every possible weekend was spent at the rink while I waited, watching from my perch on the bench while she skated around and around. Later, I'd drop her off an hour before each practice session and pick her up when she called me from her cell phone. She spent as much time as she could just hanging out and being around the other skaters. She was often tired—healthily tired from exerting great volumes of energy on the ice, trying all sorts of new maneuvers and jumps to keep up with her friends.

I thanked the Lord every morning before I rose out of bed for sending us to the ice rink that first Saturday. Just when I was sure there was no hope—when it looked like I might be my youngest daughter's only friend for the rest of her life—God stepped in and saved me once more. My heart was overflowing with thankfulness. In the past I had viewed Farema's autism as a judgment on me. Now I was beginning to see God's abundant grace in her life—and in mine.

Life began to take on new meaning for me and for Cody. I went so far as to think that one day, life might be normal—maybe I would be able to plan something that didn't begin with the question of what I'd have to do with Farema.

I was living the dream, as they say, but still there were issues to work on. Our home was not a place of tranquility, and Farah had begun to reach her breaking point after growing up and recognizing how abnormal our household dynamics actually were.

Farah had played with and watched out for Farema since the day of her birth. When they were children, Farah toted her little sister around on the back of her bike and helped her learn to ride the horse safely so she wouldn't keep falling off when doing it on her own. She helped me by searching the neighbors' houses up and down the street, time and time again. Farah had been our interpreter, and she had been her sister's personal attendant when I was rushed to get her dressed for school. She had filled in when friends were scarce, and when she was older, she took her sister with her to movies and to the mall. Farah babysat Farema whenever I helped out at the restaurant; Farah had been like another mother in many ways. But finally, even Farah—tireless supporter and true friend—reached her breaking point.

After a traumatic evening, Farah announced she would be looking for an apartment so she could move out. Farema had wandered in, uninvited, to the family room where Farah sat next to her boyfriend, Brett, on the couch. As Farema walked through the doorway she caught them sneaking a young lovers' kiss. The scene had ensued before, and we'd warned her that it must never happen again—but it did. She ran over and hit at them, flailing her arms uncontrollably and screaming at the top of her lungs. Her intention was to halt the kissing she'd decided was not allowed—and most certainly not in our house.

Cody and I later discussed the outburst, and I came to the conclusion that this had to be Farema's autistic way of trying to prevent the loss of her closest friend. She must have figured out that when each of her sisters started to kiss boys, it was only a matter of time before they'd be leaving her. She'd watched it happen twice before.

Lisa and Lainee were more than fifteen years older than Farema, and while she was still a little girl, they'd grown up, fallen in love, and married. Within a couple of years after their weddings, both had newborns that kept them too busy to continue being the doting and adoring big sisters to Farema. Imagining how it looked through Farema's eyes, I could understand her loss as her beloved sisters moved out one by one. Farema had always had their constant attention—until their own babies came along. She knew history would repeat itself. And it was only a matter of time before she did, from her point of view, lose her last and closest sibling.

Farah had been Farema's best friend, her confidant and pal. She'd translated for Farema from the first babblings that made no sense to anyone else. When she left our home, we knew it was under great and unfair pressure, and Cody and I hoped she would recover and one day find common ground with Farema. True to her gentle and loving heart, within a couple of weeks Farah had Farema hanging out with her in her apartment, racing each other on the pair of treadmills in the complex's rec room near the pool until Farema turned up the speed so high it sent her flying into the wall. Both laughed until they cried. Farema had learned to be like Farah, a giggling, happy, and observant young girl who never missed a chance to sock her sis in the arm when driving along at the sight of a "bug" Volkswagen while blurting out, "Saw one!"

Cody and I didn't try to stop Farah. A few weeks later she'd rented a small apartment and moved out. But by then, Farema's life was already revolving entirely around the ice rink and her competitions, her friends, and all the parties and skating groups who would include her. I suspected she wouldn't be as upset as she'd been in the past. I was right.

The skating rink and its never-ending supply of friends took credit for Farema's ability to accept her last sister's moving on. (Two years later, at Farah's wedding, I would recall the disastrous incident with the poor boyfriend who on that fateful night was educated in the idiosyncrasies of autism at its worst. His love for Farah was ultimately proven true when, after witnessing the bizarre family dynamics in our home, he became a member of the family himself. For his bravery—among his many other attributes—Brett fast became a special and beloved member of our family.)

The ice rink was Farema's home away from home, and her birthdays were celebrated there with all her skating friends in attendance. The first time we had a party at the rink, I invited her friends from the special ed class too, hoping they might experience some of the same joy and acceptance in the sport of ice-skating that Farema had known. I brought in a huge cake and offered it to others who were there, whether they were regulars Farema knew or not. She especially enjoyed running around delivering big squares of frosting-laden cake to her friends who were working as cashiers and skate guards.

My knowledge of how to entice friendships and keep them flourishing was put into practice as I stood back and saw the thankful expressions on the faces of the working young people relishing the tasty surprise. One more idea caught my attention as I stood back, taking in the scene of how accepted and adored Farema was in this place of her awakening. One day in the future, Farema could get a job here too.

❧

I stood next to Cody in front of the stove where he was preparing the evenings' meal, an established routine he'd implemented soon after we were married and one that I greatly appreciated. After catching up on each other's day, I approached the subject that had been swimming around in my head since Farema's last birthday party at the rink.

"You know, I think someday Farema could get a real job. I think if she keeps up the skating like she does now—she is so happy there—and doesn't get bored, which I'm sure she won't, that she could someday get a job as a skate guard!" My excitement was palpable. "What do you think?"

"Don't get your hopes up that she will ever work *any* kind of job!" Cody shot back. My aspirations were meeting with full-scale revolt. "She will never be able to get a job; she isn't normal, and I wouldn't want her to ever be put in a place where she might not be able to keep up with the others. That would be terrible for her!"

Cody and I were worlds apart in many ways, and the most profound was how we perceived our youngest daughter's future. I uttered some combative remarks as I left the kitchen and retreated to find a quiet place to calm down. I had become accustomed to slamming into my husband's opposition concerning Farema. He'd balked at my starting her in skating competitions, and until he saw the utter joy on her face when she held up her blue and yellow ribbons and gold-colored medals, he'd tried to discourage my supporting her in it.

I would ignore his negativity and go it alone, as I'd done so many times in the past, just to keep the peace. I'd had to bury my hopes and dreams many times before, and this time was not unlike the others. Meanwhile, Farema continued to excel on the ice and learn little by little to speak more clearly in her one-on-one speech therapy sessions at school.

All in all, Farema's life was taking shape and going along on an even keel as she spent every possible free moment ice-skating. If nothing else, Farema and I knew beyond the shadow of a doubt that ice-skating and the ice rink were the best thing that had ever happened in her young life.

At the rink, Farema eventually learned how to restrain her visible autistic behaviors, and when her friends were with her, the twitching and flipping fingers decreased until they were almost nonexistent. But when she got home, as soon as she relaxed and felt safe enough to let her autism surface, the lifelong routine of stiffening, squeezing her eyes shut, and flipping her fingers up and over her face resumed. I knew from my reading that the stimming gestures were probably going to be around a long time, but I wished she could overcome them indefinitely for her own sake.

Farema was eligible for services that would help her greatly since she was listed with the school district as having autism. Tests by psychologists were reported, with *Autism* as her primary category of disability, and *Cognitive/Developmental Disability* as a secondary category. This second expert opinion benefited me as well, lest I try to revert to my stubborn belief that Farema would one day be normal.

Going to the Lord in prayer was my only recourse when I had bouts of thinking that way. It had been nearly impossible for me to say the "A" word for so long, and now I knew that only by God's grace had I been able to accept what to me was a life- shattering verdict. Things had turned around full circle, and thanks to God, I was more the optimist than I'd thought possible.

At no time since her birth had life looked so good, so hopeful, than these years when Farema was enjoying—no, loving—her skating lessons, complete with friends, her school, and her park across the street. Two or three competitions a year gave her something to look forward to. She performed in every Christmas show at the rink, and most exciting for her were the trips to enter competitions as far south as San Jose, California, and north to rinks located near Seattle, Washington. Farema was one of the regulars, entering in her age group and hoping to "get first!"

With all the excitement of ISI competitions out of town, complete with my being the head taxi driver and skate stage mom, Farema's last middle school years flew by. On Friday and Saturday nights she preferred to hang out at the rink, skating and talking to the girls who worked at the front desk. While other girls her age liked to go to the school dances, Farema had no interest in dancing with boys. I was happy with that; I'd often wondered how I would approach the dating thing if she ever showed an interest. She never did.

Farema's transition from middle school to Sheldon High School was easier than I expected since she knew many of the kids from years before, and they knew who she was. New to us was that she was no longer in a special ed classroom. She was in a regular high school setting as she learned to go from class to class as any other student would, within what they called "the Life Skills Program." I loved the new name by which Farema's education would be titled, and it was exactly what I'd expected would be greatly needed for her future. Life skills might make the difference between her success as an adult and possible disaster. My secret fears echoed those of most mothers I'd met who were raising children with a serious developmental disability—what would happen to the children when we, the parents, were gone?

I'd barely had time to process the good that would be coming in her new Life Skills classes before I was told by one of the counselors in the office about the Community Living Program. It was a successful and rather new program set within a complex of nearby apartments where the Life Skills students who qualified could walk to receive hands-on instruction and training in how to live as an adult and become independent in their own apartment, just like every other normal graduate!

I was immediately fascinated by the possibilities. The first chance I had to tell Cody, I blurted it out with all the potential for what it could mean to us as Farema's parents. Cody listened to all I said without interruption.

"The CLP program is actually taught at the apartments near the school. They teach the kids how to cook, clean, ride the bus, shop for themselves with a list, keep a checkbook; everything they need to learn to live on their own. When they are near to graduation, which isn't until they are twenty-one years old, they receive help to find a job! Can you imagine that one day she might actually move out on her own and be independent? We might one day be like everyone else—empty nesters!"

My excitement was pervasive, but Cody's sense of reality prevailed as he calmly reminded me that Farema was only fifteen. No one could be sure what the future might hold, and we would have to be realistic about our hope of ever living the child-free lives other couples we knew were already enjoying. I knew he was right. Cody was always the even keel when my hopes and dreams were in danger of reckless abandon and taking off on an uncharted course.

Farah had her own ideas after hearing me relay the information I'd gotten at the school about the endless possibilities within the CLP program at Sheldon.

"She can't even remember to do some little thing around the house, let alone learn to cook and clean for herself, and you and dad have made her a big baby. I think—it's too late to change her now!"

One thing about Farah's summary was absolutely correct. We had been guilty of enabling our child with autism to use the disorder to its full potential. She was so attached to us, even now as a teenager, that though her skating kept her involved at the rink and made it possible for her to partake of activities afforded to the completely "normal" young teen, she needed her mom and dad for rides to and from skating activities and to help her be aware of each time change when classes ended for Spring Break, holidays, and regular vacations. She needed special reminders for all her activities in competitive skating. Even in her newly social and active life, she needed our constant help.

⁂

In addition to on-ice instruction with two wonderful coaches, Farema joined off-ice groups to learn grace and endurance that were beneficial to her skating skill. Farema was a busy girl, but of course, so was I.

Life was getting better than I'd dare dream it would be. Farah married Brett, and all of her sisters stood with her as bridesmaids—including Farema. Apart from her uncontrollable giggling and a few interesting faces made while Farah and Brett took their vows, the ceremony was no less than heavenly.

Three of our girls were married and happily pursuing their futures with their own families. Farema was the only one left at home, but I had a feeling it wouldn't be long before she too would find a life on her own. Whenever I attended the CLP meetings, I heard stories of success where young adults had ventured out on their own and moved into apartments. The more I heard, the more I longed to be part of this new group of parents whose children had *all* grown—and gone.

Farema's young teenage years brought her a new life, one that nearly erased the memory of the past lonely years and the trying times while I searched and tried everything to make my child fit somewhere. Still, there were hard times, the tragically sad realities that are inevitable in the real world. A childhood friend, whose daughter Angie was one of those unique people in Farema's life who accepted her as a peer, a true friend in every sense, and who I had accompanied to the hospital more than once, called to say that her daughter had died of Cystic Fibrosis. Farah's wedding was the last time we saw Angie.

Farema's heart was broken, and the abstract concept of death brought a noticeable change in her demeanor. At Angie's funeral, with words of hope and of heaven, where we would one day see Angie again, Farema began to smile and be comforted by a faith unseen by most while the song "Angel" by Sarah McLachlan played softly. Farema *knew* that one day she would again play and laugh with her dear friend.

Chapter 24

"THERE'S A MAN IN MY ROOM"

The phone rang in the middle of the night.

"Mom!" I heard the whisper, barely audible, when I picked up the phone in the dark of my room. I'd been asleep at least three or four hours. I knew it had to be Farema, but the realization that something was wrong hadn't sunk in. My brain was still semi-locked in deep sleep.

"There's a man in my room!"

Suddenly I was awake, and I sat straight up in bed.

"Farema? Are you dreaming?" I didn't know what else to say, and with a long history of nightmares under her belt, I wasn't immediately as alarmed as I would become moments later. Farema often heard noises at night, and I'd been able to talk her through so she could go back to sleep. She'd done exceptionally well since beginning her new life—on her own.

Farema's decision to move out was made with great enthusiasm, with all the exuberance of someone at the door with packed bags in hand—but the actual move was done in baby steps. The move into her own apartment was made gradually, with teachers and advocates at hand ready to assist and maneuver her into a more independent mindset. She needed, first, to learn to care for herself and accept responsibility for her own safety and welfare. Without hesitation, Farema happily began to look forward to the day she would be on her own like her peers.

After starting high school and the Life Skills program, Farema had continued on so even a keel that Cody and I and the girls no longer noticed a great difference in our family from any other. Farema, against all odds, came to nearly replicate a normal young teen. Along with the regular senior high school class, Farema walked up and accepted her diploma at the graduation ceremonies at the Hilton Hotel theater auditorium in June of 1999. She was already attending the Community Living Program at the Fountain Villa Apartment Complex, where she'd learned how to cook simple meals in a microwave in addition to what she'd learned at home with Cody's help on how to use a stove.

Before too long she began the overnight program on weekends, which meant sharing an apartment with two other girls, with adults checking in and out at all hours. Just before her nineteenth birthday, Farema moved into an apartment above one of the CLP training apartments where she and two other roommates began their first chance at being independent.

I wasn't surprised when Farema decided to move out and into her own one-bedroom just across the walkway from the CLP teacher's classroom. The noises and music of her roommates bothered her intensely, and I was sure her autistic hums and screams and uncontrollable insistence on doing things her way, no matter what, bothered them as much or more. Eventually, all the girls would find that they lacked the coping skills required to live together, and they all moved into separate apartments within the same complex, which was so like a home to them but still under the watchful guidance of the Community Living Program teachers working at four different locations dotted all around the complex.

When Farema first asked to move out of our house and live on her own, Cody and I were shocked, especially after we'd moved across town to a hillside home with a locked security gate at the entrance. I'd worried that with Farema's sometimes inaudible communication skills and innocent trust in anyone who'd befriend her, she might be whisked away by someone who had ulterior motives, such as I'd heard about recently on news programs. Like her sisters, Farema was a beautiful young girl, but unlike the others, she would have no idea how to protect herself in a dangerous situation. Our new home had an extraordinary view and deer in the yard.

Way sooner than expected, after all the years of sleepless nights, the endless worries about how our youngest daughter would survive without us one day, and our coming to realize that eventually she would be on her own when old age or death would separate us, suddenly, the day I'd feared might never come was here. She simply announced it one afternoon after coming home from her CLP classes: "I'm gonna move out! In a 'partment of my own! With my friends!"

I was speechless, Cody quietly hesitant, but hopeful. A meeting with the program's teachers comforted us with the knowledge that while Farema was learning independent living in an apartment, she was still within the public school system, complete with ongoing cooking and life skills classes.

We happily took her bed, a small dresser, and her TV to the new three-bedroom apartment and moved her in. Then Cody and I celebrated by taking a two-week trip to Paris with friends, and I prayed prayers of thankfulness and gratitude, and for Farema's guardian angel and Jesus to keep a closer-than-usual watch over her while we were out of the country.

When we returned to our home after the wonderful, still-hard-to-believe-we-did-it trip to Europe, all was well in the world according to me. I was freer than ever, thanks to a group of teachers and special advocates who had made it all possible. On weekends Farema would often visit our house and spend the night. I was living the dream.

I praised and thanked God for all he'd given our family, appreciating so much more what freedoms we now enjoyed since having known the years of such unpredictable odds. And yet, we were living like travelers on a train track of two parallel realities—the freedoms of the life Cody and I were coming to enjoy running alongside the reality that autism can be as precarious as shifting sand.

It was after Farema's move into the small upstairs apartment of her own that I got the call that made the tiny, invisible hairs on the back of my neck stand up and my heart race unlike any other time in my life. I woke up instantly the moment I heard the words about a "man"—and what was that? In her room?

I could hear her fast breathing into the phone as I pulled the sheet and blankets away and snuck out of bed, careful not to wake Cody. I grabbed my jeans off the chair and walked down the hall toward the back door where my purse sat on the kitchen table with my cell phone inside. I didn't want to get Cody involved—it was probably nothing, and I would be able to take care of her myself. Mostly, I didn't want to chance his demanding that she move back home. He had never been as convinced as I that living on her own was the best thing for Farema.

Her whispers were muffled, as if she were under something—most likely the bedcovers. I tried hard to hear and understand her words as I coaxed her, keeping my voice calm and even as usual so she would tell me more.

"Are you under the blankets? Can you see someone? Are you dreaming?" I repeated myself, knowing that my daughter's brain often needed more than one repeat to process verbal information.

The answer came back more distorted than it had begun. "I don't know— I think so—I don't know."

"Honey," I said calmly, "if you are having a nightmare, you know you will be just fine. You need to get up and turn on the light and you'll see there's no one in the room. Okay?"

I heard no response for longer than was comfortable. Then I repeated most of my previous sentence. I heard her sigh loudly, and then the sound of blankets being pushed away.

"I'm scared!"

Her voice was shaken and tearful. I was so sorry for her. Even in her dreams, the reality was always so intense; it had that way been each and every time since she was just a little girl. I had never forgotten the pure terror she suffered the year she awoke every night with the "veins" that disturbed all of our sleep when she was only ten years old.

As I fumbled with the phone while speaking words of reassurance and calm, I pulled on my jeans with one hand and picked up a jacket lying conveniently nearby. Barefoot and snatching up my car keys, I crept quietly out the back door into the garage. I turned on my cell phone and gave my frightened daughter careful instructions: "Okay, honey, I'm coming to get you, so you have to let me call you back on the cell phone so I can talk to you while I'm driving over—okay?"

I heard another muffled "Okay."

I assured her I would call back in two seconds. I hung up the phone, laid it on the stair ledge, and dialed her cell number while I groped in the dark to get the car door open, then climbed in.

The garage door was barely up high enough for my car to back through without hitting the roof when I shot backward out of the garage. Cody would have had a fit if he'd seen it. I could almost hear his voice in my head: *"Slow down!"*

Farema answered the phone with a whisper. "Hi honey," I said, "now you just talk to me and I will be there in a few minutes. It's late, and there are almost no cars, so I will be there faster than usual—you just stay in bed, and when I am near the apartment, I will tell you when to get up and you can go out into the parking lot and meet me. Okay?" She said okay so quietly this time, I could barely hear her.

As I drove down the hill I continued to assure her that a nightmare always *feels* so real. I reminded her that whenever she'd had them in the past, she was always all right after she woke up. But as I drove way over the speed limit, my heart raced and my hands felt sweaty and hot as I clenched the steering wheel. I was glad there were no police cars in view as I flew down the hill and through the center of town to reach my poor, scared daughter. Almost twenty years old, she still seemed like a child in many ways.

Farema calmed down as she listened to me talking to her softly all of the almost seven miles to her apartment. Finally she told me she could get up and turn on the light when I said I was turning into the driveway. I told her I would pull up and she could just jump in the car and come home with me for the night so she could get her sleep.

When I soared into the parking lot and put on the brakes, I saw that Farema had come out of her apartment on cue, pajama-clad, barefoot, and shivering. She hoped into my car, and in seconds we were headed back up the hill to our home, now traveling much more slowly. I looked over at her ashen face as she sat stiffly in the seat beside me.

"Honey, you've had dreams before; you know what a nightmare is, right?"

"Yes—but it was so real!" she said. Her eyes and her voice told the truth of her words. I knew she had believed there was a man in her room. It was a horrible, scary dream, to be sure.

For a normal young girl, living alone in an apartment in the middle of a busy part of town can be unsettling. But for a girl who is more like a child in her thinking, being alone and scared is a terrible thing. We'd tried, but we knew it was impossible to monitor each and every TV show and movie she might watch with her friends who lived in adjoining apartments. She announced recently she'd watched a movie called *Sixth Sense*.

"Is she really able to live alone?" one of us would say, usually Cody. He never would have initiated the idea that Farema live in her own apartment. Only because of my optimism and constant assurance of the possibilities did he dare to dream—to wish—it could be possible.

"I don't know. But someday, she will have no choice, will she?" the other would answer. Usually the conversation would end at that point, with both of us following our thoughts to "what ifs" and "what abouts" which took us nowhere but deeper into contemplation over what the future held for a child like her. Lisa, Lainee, and Farah had lives of their own, with families to care for and all the things life surprises us with; neither Cody or I wanted any of them to have the added burden of a developmentally disabled sister. And the fear of the future with its many unknowns continually haunted my thoughts.

Morning came, and after a good breakfast of her favorite, bacon and eggs, I took Farema back to her apartment to show her there was nothing to be afraid of. On our way over to her apartment, I glanced at her. I thought I saw a tinge of reluctance to return to where she'd suffered so much fright the night before.

When we ascended the steps to her apartment, the door was wide open, just as I knew she'd left it. We walked around and looked in every closet and under the bed. I tried to lighten the matter up with teasing about her thinking dreams were real. Finally she was grinning.

Nothing was missing; nothing was out of place. Her bedroom showed no signs of entry by anyone but her, and by the end of the day she was ready to stay there alone, knowing her friends lived across the hall and below her downstairs. But I was wondering now if Cody and I lived too far to help should anything real happen. We worried about the movies her friends brought to her apartment, that they might be coming alive in her dreams. Farema was different, and things that shocked her seemed to stay with her, as if they were constantly in the forefront of her mind. No one knew as well as I that this girl's ability to remember everything could be a most debilitating gift.

After Farema's nightmare, Cody and I decided to move closer to her, at least to her side of town. It was unsettling to think that if anything really did happen to Farema while she was alone, we might never forgive ourselves. And there was another reason for our decision to uproot again and move across town. Having Farema living on her own was too liberating a gift for us to let anything change it.

While Farema lived in the protective confines of a group apartment with classmates and then, still carefully monitored by the CLP staff, in her own apartment, Cody and I tasted the sweet morsel of peace—something we had forgotten we missed until we were given a sample. The years after our last daughter was born had been filled with continuous nights of crying and tantrums. As she grew older, the tantrums became nearly life-altering, whether in our home with only family or in public with the added discomfort of embarrassment. Then there were the months of lost sleep when she was obsessed with her veins. The never-ending anxiety over what to do about her lack of communication, her outbursts, her school issues with odd behaviors and inability to sit still and attend to classroom instruction, then the trips to Newburg, the endless search for entertainment and companionship—the list of what having Farema at home meant to me was endless. To Cody, the simple peace to watch television and hear what was going on was huge. The worry that Farema might never find her own place in the world as we aged also worried him deeply. Together, we agreed we would go to great lengths to help her manage in her own space, with her apartment and her friends nearby.

While we tried to sell our house so we could move across town, Cody entered into a business deal with an Iranian friend of his who wanted to buy a feed store. He'd enjoyed almost three years of semiretirement since selling El Kiosco in 1996 and thought it would be fun to do something so different. It was funny to me that a man who never heard of a "Feed and Seed" would suddenly be hauling hay and talking about livestock. For Farema, the feed store meant a new enterprise—baby bunnies. She learned all she could about the bunny-raising business, and soon she was selling her baby lop- eared bunnies for $25 each. While the bunnies were there to cuddle on weekends at the store, Farema continued to practice skating, work as a volunteer apprentice to the coaches, take additional off-ice classes at the rink, and in the fall of 2001, work the job she'd been offered at the City of Eugene on a janitorial crew.

Except for the fears that cropped up from time to time, hearing noises at night, or someone knocking at her door when she didn't expect it, Farema's independent life in her own apartment and her skating life were complete. I knew life couldn't be perfect, besides—look how far we'd come! I smiled at the successes and ignored the little inconveniences.

After all, didn't everyone's life have those?

Chapter 25

"I DON'T HAVE ANY FRIENDS NOW, DO I, MOM"

The CLP Life Skills training Farema received fulfilled every promise in preparing her for self-sufficiency. She was under their watchful eye and would be eligible for their direct support until the end of the school year after her twenty-first birthday in 2002. That would give her nearly three years to acclimatize to independent apartment living before she was truly on her own. Claire, her personal advocate, was worth her weight in gold during those years and beyond in teaching Farema how to shop, manage her money, and travel almost anywhere she wanted to go.

Farema was growing up and moving along almost like any other normal young adult, with all the independence possible for someone whom no one had guessed would ever live on her own. Her life was filled to the brim with activity.

Ever since she had started skating, February meant that Farema would be practicing for the annual ISI Love to Skate program that was a yearly event at the rink. It was also her birthday month. Along with all her usual ice classes at the rink, she was an apprentice to the coaches, and she helped me implement a Special Young Adults Bible Study, complete with pizza parties and ice cream socials. Then, as if she didn't have plenty to keep her busy, Farema began her part-time job at the City of Eugene as a member of their after-hours janitorial cleaning crew.

The city job was a fun thing for Farema at first. She loved the police officers, and they loved her back. It was very cool to know all the blue uniformed officers and say "Hi" to them when she was out with her friends, or tease with them while she was cleaning the offices. But the bus trip home late in the evening began to take its toll on her comfort.

After little more than a year, she began to fear the trip. I hated to see her keep doing it, but Cody reminded me that one day we would not be around to coddle and help her with life on her own. It was good for her to learn to manage alone. At the same time, her coworkers reported that she was having trouble seeing the dirt on mirrors, and they suspected something was wrong with her eyesight. A trip to the ophthalmologist confirmed she had a degenerative eye disorder of unknown origin called keratoconus, and in the following months she underwent two cornea replacement surgeries.

Farema's life was certainly full, more so than many of her counterparts with disabilities. I'd seen so many of the other girls happily living a "couch potato" lifestyle, happy to sit around each others' apartments watching TV or going to movies; I was grateful for Farema's active life. Occasionally she'd join them in the evenings if she didn't have skating or someone to go with her who liked to ride bikes or do something physical. She hadn't changed much since she was the child who wouldn't sit still for a minute if she didn't have to. For Farema, the real joy in life had been flying over the ice with the girls who befriended the strange and speech-impaired twelve-year-old, pulled her happily into their lives, and made her their own. But like autism, life was full of changes.

"Mom, I don't want to get old." I first heard her say those words in her own disjointed way as a girl of ten; then later she'd say it again, but in a sad, forlorn sort of way.

"You aren't getting old!" I'd say, "you're still a kid!"

I'd see the start of a smile, then a sparkle in her eyes as I went on to assure her that she was not getting old—only growing up. I tried to relieve her fears.

"Everybody has to grow up! You'll be young for a long, long time! Don't worry; you'll be young for many years to come, okay?"

"Okay," she'd reply, her smile an assurance that she believed me and all was well.

Telling Farema she was still young and not getting old became a weekly or monthly task. She was afraid of getting old and dying. The idea that a person just stops breathing and no longer exists in the tangible world was hard for her to comprehend.

I'd tell her that wouldn't be for so many years, and she'd accept my answers with complete faith that I knew what I was talking about. But each time Farema had to say good-bye to one more skating companion or wave to her sisters after a visit home with their children and husbands as they returned to their own cities and lives, she knew time was passing, and that with that, changes were coming.

Farema didn't do well with changes. Progressive changes, with years passing and people moving on and away from her, came with great distress. Then one day she turned to me on a ride home from the rink in my car and said, "I don't have any friends, do I?"

I was taken by surprise. I had feared she would take notice of how many people had gone and ask one day, but I'd not prepared myself for a good answer. I said all that I could muster on the spur of the moment.

"Honey, you still have lots of friends!"

Her wide, open-eyed stare back at me said that wasn't enough. I went on.

"Farema, you have all the girls at the apartments. And you have Anna, Julie, Cindy, and some others I don't know the names of, oh yes . . .and Allison!"

All of them worked at the rink, and all except Allison were older than her by many years. They had treated her like a sister or a daughter, and all had been in her life from the beginning. Allison had been a little girl just learning to skate when Farema was already a longtime rink accessory.

I drove on to her apartment with the rain drizzling down on my car, adding to my inner darkness and gloom. I hated to see her realize she'd outgrown her childhood and watch as old friends were replaced by new ones who themselves would move on to lives of their own. They were moving on, but Farema remained the same—a young woman whose social and emotional maturity was standing still.

I'd heard parents at the autism center talk about their grown children reacting to the loss of sameness. None said it had been easy, and many told of terrible upsets and sadness as their children, like mine, grew to adulthood, yet without the capacity to really grow up. There were stories of serious behaviors following puberty, and once I had feared those years, but Farema had come through them with flying colors—and ice.

Chapter 26

MY ANGEL

I had worried that growing older would make Farema see how different she was from those she felt were her peers. I also hated to see time pass and squelch her chances to show off her skating accomplishments, but at the age of twenty-one she was still a regular participant in the annual February Love to Skate competition. She entered whenever there was a home rink competition on weekends, and nearly every year she was a performer at the annual Lane County Ice Christmas Show. She was excited about skating in the wider world, too: Farema had always adored watching Olympic champion Scott Hamilton skate on television and cherished her copy of his book, Landing It, as well as a video of his past performances. She even collected articles about him, and after watching him perform live in the Stars on Ice production in Portland, Oregon, he became her one and only figure skating idol.

One day Farema told me she was going to do a spotlight in an upcoming ice show. I asked her what she'd like to do, and she knew immediately. She wanted to be an angel and skate to the song by Sarah McLachlan—the one that had so moved her at Angie's funeral.

The performance would be a poignant reminder for me of what challenges Farema had overcome and how wonderfully she'd grown. I sat in the bleachers at the rink that day, hoping the skating dress I'd made would look as good as I hoped it would when she was out on the ice.

The music began with the tranquil voice of Sarah McLachlan singing the words, "In the arms of the angel, far away from here . . ."

My eyes misted over as I watched Farema raise her head and unfold her arms gracefully from where they'd been crossed over her chest. Alone out there on the ice, in the spotlight that made her appear even more ethereal, she spread her arms open, first one and then the other, waving upward to show the billowy, pale blue "wings" of sheer fabric attached at the wrists and the side seams of her velvety pale blue dress. Then she took off on the ice to lean forward, one leg straight out and up into a flying camel. As Farema flowed over the ice with unusual grace and confidence, I glanced over at Cindy, whose presence in Farema's life had been no less than an earthly guardian angel as she watched her student from the shadows—compassionate tears streaming down her face. *Certainly,* I thought to myself, *this child has been existing as if "in the arms of the angels."*

The program was excellent. Farema did her waltz jump and a few others I couldn't remember the names of, and she looked more accomplished than I'd ever imagined she could be. Some of the teachers and aides from her CLP classes showed up to sit with Farah and me, and of course, she had the support of the staff from the rink who all now worked with her. When she ended her performance, they cheered and applauded as she'd become so used to hearing from past friends, now almost all gone to college or married like her sisters.

She so desperately missed the familiar girls, especially Gillian, who had gone out of state to college. Farema treasured the cards and letters she received from her friend and one-time coach, and my dream was that one day, Gillian would return to skate with her just like in the old days.

Farema continued to be busy as a volunteer skate guard and sometimes assistant to the coaches with the benefits of free ice time. It worked out perfectly for her: she would have been at the rink anyway, and she was learning skills that I hoped would one day materialize into a real job. My dream of her working at the rink was still alive in my daydream bank. Farema was constantly active, and her days were full of interaction and achievements. She'd been interviewed by a television news team about the accomplishments of a girl with autism. Eventually there would be enough interest in ice-skating from families with children with autism and other challenges that the rink would begin a new class for autistic children and those with other developmental problems. Farema would soon be asked to help assist the coach with the new ice-skating class to add to her full life. Keeping up with her lifestyle would have been a challenge for a normal young girl, but Farema loved it, and she still had the advantages of the connection to the Life Skills and Community Living Program.

Luckily, the apartment complex was strategically placed across the street from the bus stop, and Farema normally took the bus to the rink on her own. When her lesson and practice session ended, she would stay longer, helping the employees, who'd all become her friends, by retrieving and wiping off the skates, sweeping the big lobby floor, and helping any way she could to gain the favor of those she adored. It was obvious she was a happy participant in working alongside her skating pals. And then, when I least expected another dream to come true, I got the chance to look my husband in the eyes and kiddingly tell him, "Told ya so!"

Part of the Community Living Program's support was its dedication to finding volunteer work sites for students with the hope of finding their niche for paid employment. Farema had tried making jewelry at a local jewelry manufacturer, working for a candy company, and volunteering at the city animal shelter, which she loved. Her choice would have been to work with animals, but funding for the shelter fell through, and then she was offered the job at the city.

The position had been designed specifically for someone with a disability by supervisors at the City of Eugene. She worked from five in the evening until ten thirty; then she'd walk to the bus stop, a long block away. The bus would let her off at the Safeway store, about a five-minute walk from her apartment complex. It would be dark, and Cody and I were reluctant to let her do it, but I was told it was good for her to learn to be independent even in this, because the day would come when her father and I would no longer be there to pick her up and take her home. Still, I dreaded the nights she worked and took the bus home. Then, when I was teetering on the brink of calling her job to tell them I couldn't let Farema keep up the nightly trek home by bus, even against everyone else's advice, God intervened.

One typical day as I was dashing inside the rink to drop off some forgotten and necessary skating attire for Farema, Cindy caught me before I made it to the door on my way out.

"You know, Lauri, I've been thinking," she said. "Farema has been helping the staff here at the rink with things like sweeping and handing out skates—and now, since she is doing it anyway, I think she should be an employee, too!"

My heart took flight again, thanks to the gracious compassion of this woman. I knew God was again blessing us. It was another answer to prayer that she would no longer be riding the bus so late at night or walking the busy road back to her apartment. Once more, I thanked God for sending us to the rink, for the angel named Cindy, and for the acceptance Farema received with her new job in the one place she would rather be than anywhere else in the world.

Cody and I were amazed at how she'd grown, though to us she was still our little girl. No amount of achievements or years gone by would change that, and not only because we were the doting, ever-present parents we'd always been. Farema hadn't really changed that much from when she was only a child of eleven, running out across the street to swing in "her park."

I needed the reprieve of these years when Farema was fully occupied and busy. Though it had been harder than anything I'd ever done, I now felt like being Farema's mother wasn't always going to be the trial and tribulation it had been before the rink and its blessings consumed my daughter's once-lonely life. If anything, in those years with the Community Living staff at the apartments to look after her and the ice-skating that fulfilled her, I felt that Farema came so close to being cured of her autism that I could almost taste it. It was the flavor of sweet victory in my soul. My dreams took on a whole new dimension: Farema, the girl with the bizarre behaviors, the acute and extraordinary hearing ability, and all the other unearthly noises and things I'd never figured out, now appearing to all who came to know her—and even to me—as nearly normal.

While still pinching myself to see if it was real, I took advantage of no longer having a child to care for or attend to at home. I accepted a part-time job as a job developer for people with developmental and physical disabilities with Vocational Rehabilitation. Then I was asked to work a few hours in the kitchen at the Juvenile Detention Center in Eugene, and I took the position. I loved being busy and free to do so much and make extra money to pay for Farema's ever-increasing figure skating supplies.

For all the good and wonderfully happy things that were coming our way in 2003, heartbreak came as well. My sister Dianna, who'd been stricken with MS and appeared to be doing well, became ill and died. My heart broke, and I went to God for strength. Dianna had been a near and dear part of our lives, and most especially a precious aunt to my daughters.

Chapter 27

SKATING FOR SCOTT

2004

I ran up the concrete steps of the ice rink and pushed hard on the heavy double doors, feeling a rush of cold air as I entered the lobby. As usual, Farema had spent her entire day at the rink. Private skating lessons with Cindy in the morning, work in the afternoons as a skate guard, and evenings hanging out with friends and joining in the public skating sessions were a well-established routine. Everyone at the rink knew that this was Farema's home away from home. If she could have stayed there around the clock, she would have been thrilled with the prospect.

From the time Farema had started skating at the rink as a young teen, the other skaters had welcomed her like a little sister into their cliques, affectionately calling her their "Rink Mascot." She'd always thrived on the attention, joining in the girls' conversations whenever she could and imitating their teenage giggles and body language. She absolutely loved hanging out with her friends, and the hugs she shared with each of them whenever they parted company were the frosting on the cake. In those eleven years at the rink, friends came and went, but Farema always had a place to belong. I couldn't have been more grateful.

That evening, I walked through the lobby and headed for the place I knew I'd find Farema socializing if she wasn't out on the ice. Even though she preferred taking the bus home with a friend or coworker from the rink, I'd decided to stop by and offer her a ride.

As I rounded a corner into an open area near the rink, Cindy whisked by, her cheeks pink from her time on the ice, and called back to me over her shoulder, "Oh, Lauri, can you wait a few minutes? I'd like to talk to you."

Cindy's voice was as sweet as ever, but I had a sense this was something important. I smiled and called out that I'd stay put until she returned. As I waited, I wondered whether Farema might be in some kind of trouble, making a nuisance of herself by hanging around after she finished her work shift. Several of her friends were rink employees as well, working as cashiers, skate guards, and coaching assistants, and I was concerned that Farema might be keeping them from doing their jobs. I prepared myself for the possibility that Cindy was going to tell me that Farema needed to leave the rink if she wasn't working or skating. I knew Farema would be heartbroken, and I prayed that God would prepare me for the fallout when I broke the news.

A short time later, Cindy returned from the icy lower level of the building.

"Okay, Lauri, now I have a few minutes!" she said, shaking the ice particles off her gloves as she pulled them off. "Let's go in here so we can have a little privacy." She waved for me to follow her into her office.

As she closed the door, I took a seat in the chair opposite her desk, curious yet apprehensive about what she wanted to discuss. Cindy removed her warm jacket and hung it behind her chair before sitting down.

Smiling at me from across her desk, she began, "Well, Lauri, as you know, each year I attend the PSA Conference, and this year it's scheduled to take place during the last week of May in San Diego. Scott Hamilton will be there as well and is involved in a special training workshop for skaters with disabilities. I'd really like to have Farema come along this year and show him how well she can skate. Especially her footwork, since that's Scott's forte. What do you think?"

I could have fallen off the chair. Scott Hamilton, Olympic figure skating gold-medal champion, was going to watch my daughter ice-skate at the Professional Skaters Association Conference? And he wouldn't be the only famous skater attending, Cindy said. There would be professional skaters from all over the world whose names were synonymous with ice-skating. I was elated. No, I was in shock!

For years, Scott had been an avid supporter of adults and kids with developmental disabilities and was actively involved with the Special Skaters, a recreational figure skating program sponsored by the ISI for special-needs athletes of all ages. As I sat there listening intently to every word Cindy spoke, I remembered that the Special Skaters program had first opened the doors for Farema to enter the competitive realm of figure skating. As a Special Skater, Farema had not only found a place to belong as she integrated with her peers, but she'd also amassed a collection of medals and awards that had boosted her confidence and filled her with joy. "God bless the Special Skaters" was a prayer I'd uttered many times over the years.

I had known for some time that Cindy and Farema had been practicing a program especially for this event, hoping that Farema would eventually be able to perform for Scott at the PSA Conference. Things hadn't worked out the previous two years, but now, in 2004 it looked like the dream might actually become a reality! Cindy ended our impromptu meeting by encouraging Cody and me to seriously consider letting Farema attend. As far as I was concerned, there was nothing to consider. I was ready to leave for San Diego right that minute. Trying to maintain my composure, I thanked her for this amazing opportunity and told her we'd start saving up for the trip. No matter what, I'd find a way for Farema to go. Still in a daze, I floated out of Cindy's office with a new dream to cling to on my daughter's behalf.

I found Farema in the skaters' area gathering up her things and watched silently as she toweled off and covered her blades, packed up her skates in her skate bag, and hugged each of her friends good-bye. On our way out to the parking lot, I told her what Cindy and I were discussing, and when we reached the car, I turned to look at her.

"I can't believe we're going to meet Scott Hamilton! Aren't you excited?" I asked, nearly ready to explode with excitement myself.

Farema gave me a big toothy smile and calmly answered, "Yeah."

On the drive home from the rink, I wondered if the pressure to perform well for Scott, mixed with the joy and anticipation of seeing someone she admired so deeply, was going to be too much for Farema. But I was more than ready to set aside my own reservations so that my twenty-three-year-old could participate in this once-in-a-lifetime event. I was amazed as I thought back to how this new phase of Farema's life had transpired.

Soon after Cindy had offered to give Farema private skating lessons in 1993, she'd told me that Farema's learning style was unlike any she'd ever encountered. She'd discovered that Farema learned by watching and imitating Cindy's moves rather than by listening to verbal instruction. Then Cindy realized she mimicked everything she saw as if she were looking in a mirror. Farema would imitate every move, only in the opposite direction—a perfect mirror image. To accommodate this unique learning style, Cindy had developed a new method of skating instruction tailored especially for Farema.

Cindy's patience and expertise on the ice gently built Farema's confidence, and before long, with determination and practice, Farema was ready to take the next step. Cindy then told me about the Special Skater program, which would enable Farema to compete with others who, like her, had some sort of developmental delay or challenges. It had sounded like a perfect fit for my little skater. A chance to win medals and ribbons was reason enough for Farema to enter the competitions. I knew she'd be elated to add to her collection of spinning tops, watches, My Little Ponies, hair clips, and numerous other childhood fascinations.

The Special Skater program quickly became the driving force that made Farema want to do more—to perfect her skills and do her very best as a skater. When her skill on the ice improved beyond the abilities of those in her Special Skater class, Cindy decided to enter her in the regular ISI program so she could compete with other skaters at her skill level. I had been concerned about Farema's inability to keep up in the regular competitions, dreading anything that might discourage her and interfere with her new life at the skating rink. But Cindy knew her student well. When the class was announced and each contestant had performed, Farema held her own and won a medal. It was amazing to me how far she'd come since those early years at the rink.

Now, Farema was preparing for the most exciting experience of her life. March was just around the corner, and Farema was practicing a few hours each week with Cindy and another coach. She also continued working part-time as a rink skate guard, and on Wednesday afternoons, she helped a coach teach a skating class for small children with autism and other developmental disabilities.

While Farema was occupied with work and practice, I made lists of the things we needed to pack for the trip to San Diego in May. I knew I'd have to bring an inhaler because Farema had been diagnosed with exercise-induced asthma at the beginning of the year. I learned that this was a common ailment for those who spend a lot of time in cold, dry air. Many figure skaters were on steroid medications and inhalers for the same reason. As strange as it might

seem to most mothers, I felt almost grateful that Farema shared this condition with her peers. It was something else she had in common with kids who
weren't burdened with a disability, and I still desperately needed her to experience as normal a life as possible.

With all the wonderful and exciting plans to be made for the upcoming
trip, I barely noticed the dark hairs that were showing up more prominently
on Farema's fingers and toes. Then I saw the dark hairs on her upper lip and
at the sides of her face, like her hairline had extended. I'd seen patches of dark
pigment around her neck and underarms and figured her Persian ancestry was
the culprit. She and Farah had inherited their father's golden-brown skin and
were dark-skinned year-round. Still, this was strange. For just a moment I
questioned the steroid inhalants she'd been taking for her asthma. She administered it herself as needed, and on a couple of occasions I knew she'd run out
way too soon. The doctor hadn't been alarmed when I called and asked him to
refill it, although I told him I thought she didn't know how to use it correctly
and was wasting the medicine inside the disc.

Electrolysis was an easy answer to solve the facial hair problem. Then, just
when I thought her health issues were under control, Farema was hit by a car.

In early March, on a sunny afternoon while riding her bike the mile between
her apartment and our house, she was struck by a car pulling out onto the busy
highway she rode beside along the safety of the sidewalk. He hadn't seen her as
he looked at the oncoming traffic for a break in the cars.

I thanked God that Farema always wore her helmet. Though her new bike
was crushed, she escaped with only a few bruises and scrapes and even laughed
when the traumatized man who'd pulled out in front of her on the busy highway helped her to her feet. The man let Farema use his cell phone to call home,
and since I was visiting a sick friend at the time, Farah rushed over to pick
Farema up. Later that day, I took her to our family doctor for a thorough exam,
and he announced that all in all, she seemed just fine. I breathed a sigh of relief,
thankful that Farema had ten weeks to recuperate from her scrapes and bruises
before her once-in-a-lifetime performance. Her practice sessions on the ice continued as if nothing had happened, and the only complaint she had was that
she'd dented her bike helmet.

Yet I didn't rest easy. I was accustomed to my daughter's ability to ignore
pain, so for the next few weeks I monitored her activities more closely. It was

during that time that I began to wonder if Farema was getting enough sleep at night. When I picked her up at her apartment to take her to the rink in the mornings she looked exhausted. I begged her to stop staying up so late.

After endless preparations and weeks of anticipation, the morning of our trip to California finally arrived. In just a few days, Farema would be skating for Scott Hamilton! I still couldn't believe it.

"We're gonna have a lot of fun, honey," I said to Farema as I finished packing so we could leave for the airport.

She just stood there with a silly grin on her face, and I knew she was as excited as I was. This was going to be an extraordinary adventure for both of us, and the greatest thrill of Farema's life.

I had gone over the lists and reminders a dozen times at least to make sure we didn't forget the important things, like Farema's ice skates, her new red skating dress, her tights, and all the hair accessories she insisted we take along. I'd already had more than one nightmare about arriving in San Diego, getting lost on the way to the rink, and then finding out we'd forgotten to pack her skates. Needless to say, those skates were the focal point of my packing, and I intended to keep them in the bag and in my view all the way to California. Finally, we were on our way to Portland, two hours away, where we would leave the car in the lot called the Park and Fly.

A few short hours later, we boarded our plane. Cody was traveling with us as far as Santa Barbara, where his sister and her family lived, and Farema and I planned to continue on to San Diego by train a couple of days later on May 27. After our two-day visit, I was eager to begin the final leg of our journey to San Diego, where Cindy planned to meet us at the beautiful Manchester Grand Hyatt Hotel.

On the train ride from Santa Barbara to San Diego and the shuttle ride to the hotel, Farema was quiet and calm. I had a feeling that in spite of her silence, she was bursting inside, nervously anticipating the moment she would see her skating idol in person. With Farema, appearances were usually deceiving. Her reactions were never typical of kids her own age, and I'd learned that her silences often cloaked her true feelings. Once again, I wondered if the excitement of performing for Scott would be too overwhelming for her. I watched her carefully for a few long moments and then convinced myself that she would be okay once we settled into our hotel room.

We walked the few blocks from the transit train to the hotel, arriving around two o'clock in the afternoon. While checking into our room, I glanced around to see if I might find Cindy somewhere in the area. But I knew if I didn't find her, she'd find us, so we went up to our room to put our things away and freshen up. I suggested that Farema take a shower to help her unwind, and she hopped right in. She was still my water-baby: there was nothing better than water in any form to settle her nerves and make everything right in her world.

The room had a great view, and the afternoon sunshine filtered through the windows and welcomed us to sunny California. I was sure this was going to be a fabulous two days.

Later that afternoon, Farema finally loosened up and became her usual giggly self. With little else to do, I decided we might as well walk around and get acquainted with the huge hotel, so we took the elevator down to the main lobby, which looked about as big as my entire house.

As Farema followed me through the luxurious foyer, I heard her say in a quiet voice, "Mom, I think that's him."

"What?" I asked, glancing around, not sure what she was looking at.

When I spotted a man standing at the check-in counter with a couple of other people, I suddenly realized what had captured my daughter's attention.

"It's Scott!" I whispered back, trying to keep from raising my voice too loudly. "Farema, you're right. It's *him!*" I was thrilled that Scott was staying at our hotel. Maybe Farema would have other chances to see him, and even talk to him, during our stay.

Other kids Farema's age would have screeched in awe and pure delight at seeing Scott Hamilton standing just a few feet away, but my enigma of a daughter was totally composed. As I stood staring at her staring at him, it seemed odd to me that she didn't walk over and begin chattering at Scott, telling him who she was and reminding him why she was there. When she'd seen him performing at the Stars on Ice production years before, I'd had to restrain her from leaving her seat to run off and find him. My worries about Farema suddenly flooded to the surface again. Could she handle the stress of performing for Scott the following day? She showed no outward signs of anxiety, but I knew I needed to keep her on as even a keel as possible in the hours ahead. I silently prayed for her nerves—and mine.

The hotel was enormous, and there was a lot more to see. We walked through the wide hallways and past various sitting areas to an even larger foyer with massive white, wooden-railed stairs that spiraled dramatically upward. Overhead, huge crystal chandeliers hung from high ceilings, and giant paintings graced the walls.

When we climbed the stairs to the large convention center, we found Cindy with some other skaters and people she knew. After waving hello, I turned and peeked into one of the meeting rooms, where a large group was listening to a speaker at the far end of the room. I heard an explosion of cheerful voices and applause; then the clapping ceased, the doors opened wide, and Scott Hamilton came out, followed by a throng of fans asking him questions. Farema and I watched from the side while Scott greeted each person warmly and patiently answered every question. After the crowd thinned, Cindy, with her typical poise, escorted us over to the man adored by millions around the world. Farema's dreams were finally coming true. I watched in awe as Cindy walked right up to Scott and told him that there was someone who was anxious to meet him. "I'd like you to meet Farema," she said. "She's here to skate for you at the workshop tomorrow. She'd also like to get a quick picture of you two together."

He smiled and stepped right over to let me snap the picture of Farema and him together, arms around each other like old friends. I was impressed by the kindness of this man, who was a figure skating icon and yet acted just like any other person. This photo not only proved that miracles do happen, but that Scott Hamilton was truly one of the nicest people in the world. I knew that Farema would cherish that moment forever and would add the photo to her treasured collection of Scott Hamilton memorabilia.

The next morning, Farema and I arrived at the skating rink early so she could practice the routine she and Cindy had been working on. While I stood watching with other spectators outside the rink, Sandy Lamb, Scott Hamilton, and Michael Paikin led a workshop on the ice. Joining them were about a dozen coaches, along with Farema and five other skaters with developmental disabilities whose ages ranged from preteen to adult. Workshop leaders shared the challenges and joys of teaching special-needs students and presented the techniques used in the ISI Special Skater program. (I later learned that some of the skaters at the workshop that day went on to compete in the 2004 Special Olympics that summer.)

As the workshop progressed, skaters were asked to demonstrate the skills they'd learned, and when the tasks exceeded their ability, the skaters began to drop out one by one—except for Farema. She confidently kept on going, to the professionals' combined amazement, performing a waltz jump, a loop jump, a sit spin, a camel spin, a flip jump, and then a perfect lutz jump that totally blew them away. Someone asked if Farema had anything else to share, and Cindy told the group that she and Farema had prepared a program with music. There was just one little problem: only half of the ice was available for workshop participants. On the other half was a gathering of about one hundred coaches and several high-level competitive skaters demonstrating triple jumps.

No matter how hard Cindy tried to make Farema understand that she would have to skate her program on half the ice, she just couldn't seem to grasp the concept. I held my breath as I watched Farema take off across the ice to begin her routine. She plowed right through the professional skating group with speed and confidence. I was stunned when the coaches and skaters backed away from the center of the rink and gave Farema the ice. It was a magical moment.

I tried to capture her performance on my small video recorder so Cody and her sisters would see her doing her best, but it wasn't easy. The awesome way she glided across the ice with such grace was something I had never really noticed in all the years I'd stood and watched her practice her routines. She looked so normal, so *more* than normal, not like a person with autism but like a lovely young lady whose life had blossomed magnificently—it was hard to focus the camera as my eyes filled with tears of joy.

When Farema finished her routine, the crowd of onlookers gave her a thunderous round of applause. She flashed a huge smile at everyone and then skated quickly across the ice and into her coach's open arms. Cindy was full of praise and congratulations for Farema, and Scott told her she had done a great job. I was elated that he had taken the time to show an interest in her and her accomplishments. Farema glowed as she stood next to him on the ice for another picture.

Many others in attendance came up to Farema afterward to compliment her skating. One of the luminaries was Richard Dwyer, "Mr. Debonair," who had been Cindy's first pairs coach. With his usual grace and a beaming smile, he congratulated Farema on her great skating. Cindy told me later that Farema had "glazed over" by that time but had skated a flawless routine, the best Cindy had ever seen her perform.

I'd planned to stay and watch the rest of the day's performances, but Farema was ready to go home. I was exhausted too. Still, life couldn't have been better at that moment. The last thing I had expected was that Farema would want the day to end. But she did. It seemed she had accomplished all she wanted to do: she had skated for Scott Hamilton.

I watched her as she gathered up her skates and jacket and zipped up her skating bag, and then I followed her out of the rink. She never looked back, never said a word about the fairy-tale moment she had just experienced. In response to Cindy's profound approval and praise, typical Farema behavior would have been to let out a high-pitched squeal while stimming faster than ever, fingers fluttering like wings on a hummingbird while she twitched and quivered with uncontrollable and utter delight. Instead, she was quiet, pulling her small black skate bag behind her as we followed the sidewalk the few blocks from the hotel to the small train that would take us to the main Amtrak Train Station. We boarded at 4:00 p.m.

The long ride home to Eugene took us all night and till noon the next day. We had a sleeper room with a tiny bathroom, and when we were settled in, Farema continued to be quiet and reserved. I would later sadly recall how, on that day, it seemed like Farema realized this part of her life was over. In a very real sense, it was. But at the time, I was puzzled by the sudden change in her behavior. Situations like this reminded me that I would never fully understand what went on in her head. Since childhood, she had been prone to change in ways we couldn't possibly expect.

Sometimes I'd looked forward to a new phase, like when she was hearing her blood in her veins. This time, I wanted to keep her the way she was. I loved her happiness and her joy since she'd found her home on the ice. I hated the thought that she might be turning inward—retreating inside herself as she had when she was a child, deep inside her cocoon of autism. Ice-skating had pulled her out and kept her in our world; my greatest fear was that it might not last.

That night, instead of taking her back to her apartment, I told Farema to stay with us at our house. I thought a good night's sleep would ensure a return to her old self. In the morning, I took her to the rink for her off-ice class and told her to call when she was ready for me to pick her up.

Her first day back at the rink was reassuring: Farema was back in full force. The day took care of all the thoughts I'd had about her strange behavior in California. She was grinning from ear to ear with all the congratulations she received from her friends and the coaches. Thanks to our godsend—the ice rink and its staff—Farema was back to normal. Or so it seemed to me.

Lessons continued with Cindy, and there was talk in the air that something very "big" was coming Farema's direction. It was a secret, so I didn't ask more about what I heard, but one of the coaches said I'd know more when things were more definite. I let it go at that, since I'd seen the most fabulous dreams come true already and didn't think anything this side of heaven could be more wonderful.

Farema picked up where she had left off in her job, her lessons with Cindy, and helping with the class of developmentally disabled children. She continued to live in her apartment and spend time with her friends. No matter how many compliments and congratulations she received for meeting and performing for Scott Hamilton, she happily accepted them all with a big smile and a giggle. As I think back on how far she'd come in the past eleven years—from a lonely little autistic girl to a gifted young adult skater—I thank God for her life at the rink, for the many friends and coworkers who adored and accepted her, and for the generous and precious people who came into her life—Cindy and Scott.

Chapter 28

THE PERFECT STORM

SUMMER 2004

Life was back to normal—almost. There was one difference, cropping up a couple of weeks after we returned home: a change in how often Farema called me late at night with reports of noises that scared her. Long after she should have been asleep, the phone would ring.

"Hello, Mom, I could come home for tonight?" I knew what she meant, though her sentences were often disordered.

"Hi honey, are you awake? It's late; you should be asleep."

"I hear noise."

I always wanted to jump in the car and go get her. I hated to think of her lying in the dark in her bed—alone. But I was too protective. I knew that.

"It's only the wind—remember? I showed you the tree and the branches that rub on the window."

I spoke calmly and firmly, careful to never let my voice waver in the assurance that she was perfectly safe in her apartment, only a mile away from our house. She always agreed and promised to go back to sleep.

My first sure clue that Farema wasn't sleeping was when I passed her apartment on my way to my part-time job at the local youth detention center.

At five in the morning, as I passed her complex, I was able to see Farema's bedroom light shining from behind the mini-blind. My guess was that she'd heard a noise, turned the light on for comfort, and then left the light on all night. The next day I reminded her that she wouldn't get a good night's rest with lights on, but it continued to happen more and more often until I saw it on every morning I went to work.

At the same time, I was noticing other oddities. There had been an upsurge in physical complaints, as Farema frequently mentioned pain in her ankles, knees, arms, and neck. More than once she'd seen an orthopedist for pain in her knee, and he'd given her a variety of braces to wear when she was skating. Another time, when I took her to an appointment with her regular doctor with more complaints of pain in her legs and feet, I mentioned her lack of sleeping. He gave her an antianxiety medication called Lorazapam.

It wasn't long before I made another appointment and described to the doctor what seemed to me like a panic attack, making Farema's heart race and waking her in the middle of the night. She'd had such attacks in the past, and after her bike accident, she appeared more anxious and unable to relax. Around the same time, when I helped brush her hair it came out in handfuls, and the dark pigment change on her neck was still there. I'd told her to wash better and then realized it was the color of her skin.

Farema had started to be more dependent on me and Cody right after the accident. I knew it was normal that she should feel fragile after something so frightening, even though she had reacted so well at the time. The X-ray showed no broken bones. There were only a few bruises—but her confidence was shaken. The car incident had frightened her more than she'd shown at the time, and after it she seemed very clingy and told me she thought she should stay with us so we could "keep eyes on her." I'd laughed it off. But more than four months later, she still acted apprehensive—even frightened.

While trying to help the best I knew how and keep her focused on her independence, I began picking Farema up at her apartment and taking her to the rink for her early morning lesson with Cindy. In the past, she'd be ready for me by 7:45, but now, I'd find her still sleeping in her clothes from the night before. After I knocked loudly a few times, she'd open the door looking tousled and sleepy. Then I'd rush her around to get her washed up and grab her skates and jacket and off we'd go.

One September morning, I arrived to take Farema to work to fill in for someone who couldn't make it in. She sleepily opened the door, and I saw she had just barely awakened—again. I went inside, a little upset that once more we would get to the rink late. Then as I was going into the bathroom to get her toothbrush ready for her, I saw a glimpse of something odd on the bedroom floor next to her bed.

"What is that?" I asked, stopping at the doorway.

"Nothin,'" she said, trying to pull the bedroom door shut.

"Honey, did Anna spend the night again? Remember, we said no over-nights except on weekends!"

I'd made a rule about Farema and her friend taking turns sleeping at each oth-er's apartments after I was told they'd been seen walking to the twenty-four-hour grocery store in the early hours of the morning and getting coffee drinks at the Star-bucks inside. No wonder she'd not been sleeping! I continued to push the matter.

"Honey, did you make this bed for one of your friends?" I walked inside her room and saw a well-made little bed. She'd carefully formed it from a sleeping bag folded and placed on top of a couple quilts for softness, and there was a clean white pillow at the top and another blanket for a cover. Farema looked up at me with big eyes.

"Jessica comes to stay with me."

"Who? Jessica who?" I asked.

"From school."

"Farema, you mean the Jessica who moved away when you graduated?"

"Yes."

I knew the Jessica she was expecting was never planning to come spend the night with my daughter. Jessica was one of the regular students, a kind girl who'd treated Farema very nicely at the high school but would not have come for a sleepover. I was stumped at what would make Farema think someone she barely knew would come to spend the night with her.

I stood staring, first at Farema, waiting to go take her lesson at the rink, and then at the makeshift bed. The next thing out of her mouth would leave me speechless.

"When I am alone and scared, Jessica comes to stay with me. And she's so smart, Mom! She can walk in, right through the wall!"

To my daughter, this was the only necessary explanation—she wasn't sup-posed to open her door after 8:00 p.m. no matter what. She hadn't broken the rules. I turned and walked to the car with Farema following me. I didn't know what to say or where to go with this information. Had she dreamed something again? Or was she delusional? I didn't know.

All the way to the rink I tried to picture the Jessica Farema was talking about. I'd heard Farema speak of all the girls at school who treated her like a peer. While I tried to recall whatever I could about the girl who was, according to Farema, able to walk through the wall, I worried about all the extra pressure I'd allowed to be placed on my daughter. When I should have known she had enough going on, I had allowed her to take part in one more commitment. September had begun with a request from a company called Iris Media, who asked about Farema taking part in an exercise video produced specifically for developmentally disabled persons. It would be sold nationally for the purpose of initiating exercise in foster care and group homes, special schools for those with developmental challenges, and many other outlets. They offered $200 if she would participate. Farema didn't want to do it, but I told her it would be fun and that some of her friends would be there too.

Once more, I felt that it would be a great opportunity to mingle with other young adults, some with developmental challenges and some without. I knew that she needed to find new friends, young people she could turn to for companionship when the last of her skating acquaintances were gone. I'd never really wanted to face the fact that most, if not all, of her friends would find lives outside the rink, going off to college or marriage or careers. Few would remain at the skating rink with Farema.

I took her to the meeting place and assured her it would be a lot of fun. When she recognized others in the group, she decided to stay, and when I said I'd pick her up after the filming, she said she'd walk home from the meeting place with one of the girls from the Community Living Program. The walk was less than a mile, and the day was sunny and warm. I was relieved. Farema was going to be all right.

I had no way of knowing then that all the pressures of Farema's commitments, her constant inclusion in physical activities, and the everyday demands necessary to continue living in her apartment were mounting up like a rumbling pressure cooker of anxiety that was swelling to a volcano of immense proportion—soon to explode.

Life continued, and I let the incident of the ghost-like friend retreat to the back of my thoughts. Farema's schedule at the rink kept her busy and occupied with things she loved to do. She'd recently won acceptance as a member of the ice center's figure skating team, and she took part in some dance classes as they came up.

My one constant concern was that Farema get the right amount of sleep. When she was a child at home I was able to monitor her sleeping. But since she'd moved out from under our supervision, I was able to tell her to go to bed, but not able to know for sure what was happening after I said good night.

I was worried about Farema's health, both physically and mentally, but even I didn't detect the storm brewing. The unleashing of a tidal wave of family destruction was only weeks away.

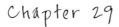

Chapter 29

BREAK

October 2004

The hospital smell of antiseptics, alcohol, and disinfectant cleansers permeated the air, overriding the calm generic music that echoed down the long halls as we followed the directions given us by the nurse in the ER. We walked close to each other, clutching each others' hands. A passer-by might imagine us an adoring couple, if not for the deer-in-the-headlights-look Cody and I wore on both our faces.

By the time we entered the main lobby of the hospital and turned down the hall toward the room referred to as the "Johnson Unit," we were walking fast, rushing but trying to look normal. We stopped to read a small sign pasted to the wall just to the right of a sliver of window. I bent down to look in as I read the sign aloud to Cody:

PLEASE PRESS THE BUZZER. THIS DOOR IS KEPT LOCKED.
SOMEONE WILL OPEN IT FOR YOU WHEN POSSIBLE.

I tried the door anyway. Nothing I could see through the small window looked all that private: people were sitting and some were milling around. It looked like a reception area—a visiting room for family and patients to gather. Some wore hospital gowns and others wore street clothes.

Someone came to open the door after we pushed the button, and we were told to see the person at the desk. We stepped up to the long counter and told a nurse, dressed in the typical white nurse's garb, that our daughter was supposed to be getting a room. We gave her Farema's name and ours, and immediately, responding to our overall look of distress, a white-jacketed woman with a clipboard in hand hurried out from behind the reception desk and motioned for us to follow her.

"Right over here, this way, and we will call someone," she said.

On the opposite side of the lobby, another buzzer was pushed beside another door with a small window. Through the wires embedded in the glass I could see more nurses in white and blue, walking around as if all was normal. The door was opened within a few seconds by a young woman in scrubs, and we were ushered in to see Farema rushing toward us. She was dressed in a two-piece blue outfit that looked almost the same as the scrubs worn by the nurses. For an instant I wondered how a visitor might know the difference between the patient and the staff. Farema grabbed onto me as if she were a little girl who'd been lost and was suddenly now found.

"Take me home, Mom; I want to go home!" It was almost too much for Cody and I to bear, but we had already agreed to let them keep our daughter one night to make sure she slept and that she was physically well enough to go home.

"Farema, this is just the hospital, you know, and they just want to help you get some sleep, okay?"

I expected her usual acceptance and trust in anything I suggested. She'd usually reacted that way in the past, and she had never minded going to doctors—other than those early hearing checks, of course. In fact, Farema was the one child of ours who rather enjoyed the doctor experience. I used to tease her about being a hypochondriac when she'd ask if she needed to see a doctor or go to the hospital over the smallest scratch on her skin. She was a child who never got sick and had little sense of pain, and wanting to visit the doctor was one of her eccentricities. While holding her close and trying to dispel her fears with a smile and calming words, I recalled years before telling others how I single-handedly supported the Johnson & Johnson Company when she was a little girl, purchasing a multitude of packages of colored and cartoon-branded Band-Aids which she enjoyed far more than new toys or dolls. As I tightened my arms around her, I would have given all my earthly treasures to be able to put a Band-Aid on her pain and watch it fade away. But instead, there was nothing I could do for her as she stood begging me to take her home with tears streaming down her face.

"I want to go home to my little dog! I promise I won't be bad; I'll be good, Mom! Take me home with you—don't leave me here! Pleeease!"

Farema clung to me and pulled on my sweater as if for her very life. I tried to console her while keeping my own composure intact.

"Honey, you just stay one night, and they will help you to sleep. Remember how you haven't slept? Well, they will give you some medication, and you'll get a good night's sleep. Okay?"

It wasn't okay. We walked away from Farema's pleading until she was out of earshot.

Although this day would be the beginning of a long and agonizing journey into the world of never-before-heard-of medications and great anguish, our road to the hospital and the decision to leave our frightened daughter overnight had begun two weeks earlier, on a night in mid-October. I'd answered a phone call from Farema that shattered our sleep for a night—and our lives for years to come.

The story about her friend Jessica who would come stay with her at night and sleep on the little floor-bed paled in comparison to what I heard after I picked up the ringing phone and knew it had to be Farema.

"Mom, can you come get me? Can I sleep at your house?"

I was tired and already in bed. I just wanted to go to sleep. "Honey, can't you just roll over and forget the noises and go to sleep? I'm really too tired for this tonight!"

I was determined to be firm this time, not to give in to her demands that I rescue her again. Then, instead of remembering the protecting and comforting qualities of guardian angels that we'd studied in the youth group for those with developmental difficulties I held at her apartment twice a month, she began to talk about "gang members." She talked fast and then began to cry and whimper uncontrollably. I knew she was afraid of something, and nothing I said would calm her down. I threw on my clothes and rushed out the door telling Cody to wait here, I'd bring her home.

She was waiting at the door and nearly ran over me to get to my car. All the way back she described an incident I knew hadn't happened. The apartment complex was surrounded with huge street lights, and she knew everyone living in the adjoining apartments—not to mention the teachers who came and went every night to check on the new students living in #50, the women's overnight apartment. I knew there'd been no "gang members" and that they hadn't attacked her. But whatever it was, dream or delusion, it was incredible.

With a wide-eyed stare and a look of pure terror, Farema gave me the horrifying details between sobs and tears.

"The gang members came . . . they put me in the bathroom, in the bathtub . . . and, and . . . they made me . . ." (uncontrolled sobs) ". . . drink blood . . . eat rats . . ."

Certainly, her nightmare had been terrifying.

I stared at her in shock. Then I forced myself to be calm—to speak more softly and firmly than at any time in my life.

"Farema—there are no gang members."

Instantly she responded with a loud, tearful shout back in my face.

"Yes, they *were* there!"

The tirade of tears and demands that I believe her, complete with facts of how the gang members were brought into her life by the girl next door, continued all the way to our house and after we'd gone inside. Once there, I helped her take off her clothes and put on a nightgown. I gave her a glass of milk and stayed beside her while she crawled into bed. After my sitting beside her for a long while and promising her that she was safe with us, and that she must sleep, Farema drifted off.

I'd first heard about the "gang people" from Farema after a neighbor girl with a mental disability told her about them. As she told me what she believed had happened to her, I knew she'd been deeply traumatized by something—a nightmare of horrific proportions or a movie she'd watched that had become real in her mind.

I would never know why her belief in the delusion was so strong, but I did know with absolute surety that she believed it had happened.

Cody was still awake when I went into our bedroom, and he waited for me to explain what was wrong with Farema while I turned off the lights and got back into bed. I whispered in the darkness as I lay on my back, staring up at the ceiling where the moonlight shone in from the big bedroom window.

"She thinks there were gang members in her apartment." I said in a whisper. "She's terrified. I don't know what's wrong with her. Let's talk about it in the morning."

Cody turned over in silence. I began to pray for God's protection, though I wasn't sure what from. Then I prayed for Farema to sleep and be back to normal in the morning.

Morning came, and Farema appeared to be better. I didn't mention the thing that had terrified her the night before. But I did make an appointment with Dr. Hall, her regular doctor, who was free that same afternoon. After hearing a synopsis of the story as it was told to me, the doctor's scheduler made sure we got in right away.

Farema had been taking an antianxiety medication for a couple of weeks as needed so she could relax and sleep. I trusted her to take them on her own, at her apartment, if she felt she needed them. She knew to take only one, but I never was sure if she actually slept after taking them. Claire, her advocate and dear friend, came along with us to the appointment to help me remember everything I wanted to say about Farema's delusional thinking, everything I wanted to talk about with the doctor.

The family physician was kind and sat listening as Claire and I took turns prompting an obviously noncompliant Farema to tell him all about her claims of gang members attacking her. She sat on the end of the examination table looking like a caged animal, with her eyes big and round as we told him pieces— looking first at the doctor's face, then back to hers—for affirmation the facts were as we stated.

"No! You can't tell!" Farema begged. "They don't want . . . no!" she pleaded.

The more I tried to describe her traumatic dream—or nightmare, as I tried to believe it was—the more distressed she became. Dr. Hall was not one to show any shock; instead, he wore a quiet calm in the face of anxiety and near panic. He asked us to go outside and wait while the nurse came and helped him give Farema a physical examination. I was thankful he'd thought of it, just so I could rest assured that nothing had really happened to her.

Farema had told me about her neighbor's connection to a group she called gang members, a bunch of street people who lived in Portland. By virtue of her autism, whether from unreasonable fears or not, Farema could imagine extraordinary complications to anything she repeated over and over in her own mind. Months earlier, I had told Farema to stop visiting the girl who'd scared her and assured her that no one was going to harm her. I told her never to worry, that the girl who spoke of these things wasn't really friends with those people and that she'd only made it up. It had seemed so silly to me back then. Now it was a serious matter.

The doctor said he had no idea what was going on with Farema, but he gave us a prescription for Risperidone, an antipsychotic often prescribed for children and adults with autism. He spoke with us about all the unusual behaviors connected with autism and how often, the hormonal changes that come with puberty and adolescence can set off all sorts of new and unexplainable behaviors, sometimes even causing delusional episodes. Farema was way past puberty, but it was the best he could come up with.

Farema continued her skating commitments, working as a skate guard, and attending her regular practice sessions. She spent her days as usual in her apartment, but slept nights at our house. I tried to keep everything as normal as possible, but in small ways she still appeared uneasy and anxious. She no longer wore her familiar, warm smile, only displaying it when someone she really liked, such as Cindy or one of her friends at the rink, asked her to.

One afternoon while Farema was at the skating rink, working her regular shift and assisting a coach with the Wednesday afternoon class for developmentally challenged children, Cindy noticed her out on the ice. Concerned, she quickly called me at home, saying I needed to come to the rink right away.

That same day I'd speculated about whether or not the pills she'd begun a couple days before would affect her balance on the ice. When I heard Cindy's voice on the phone, my earlier concerns flashed to the forefront of my mind.

I drove as quickly as possible to the rink and swung into the parking space, forcing the car into park as I threw the door open. I jumped out and ran up the concrete steps to the rink doors. What I saw, when I pushed open the big doors and rushed over to the window where Cindy stood watching her, was a dazed, expressionless Farema, all alone, skating round and round in small circles. She appeared catatonic.

After Cindy asked the coach to tell Farema to come off the ice, I thanked everyone, led her to the car, and took her home. Farema appeared to be exhausted, but no matter how hard I tried to get her to take a nap that afternoon, she refused to go to sleep. She didn't want to eat, and she didn't talk to us. I promised to stay with her on the bed and read while she fell asleep. It took hours, but finally, I heard her breathing steadily as evidence that she had finally succumbed to restful, healing sleep. I crept noiselessly out of her room and pulled the door shut. I felt relieved and hoped that morning would bring a change for the better. I stood in the hall for a moment and prayed that God and all the heavenly angels would come to her rescue.

"Stay by her side," I begged, "and please, Lord, make her the way she used to be."

I slept fitfully that night and awoke early in the morning, but not because I heard any noise. It was silent in the dark house; the sun hadn't come up yet. I lay in bed, mulling over what reason there might be for my daughter's first obsessing about Jessica, a girl she hardly knew and hadn't seen in years, and then this. The gang member story made me shudder. I rose to make a cup of coffee, and on my way to the kitchen I peeked into the room where Farema slept.

She wasn't there.

I went to look for her in the bathroom, but it was dark, and she wasn't there either. When I turned on the light in the kitchen and still didn't find her, I knew she wasn't in the house. Farema had risen before daybreak and left. I woke Cody and told him she was gone. He jumped out of bed immediately and dressed to go look for her. We both suspected she'd gone back to her apartment.

Cody drove straight over to the building, and when he arrived, he knocked lightly and then opened the door with our key to find Farema already asleep in her bed. She awoke at his entrance, and he told her to go back to sleep after assuring her he'd lock the door and that she was going to be all right. He returned home to tell me she was just fine, in her bed, safe and sound.

"I know she'll sleep for a while; she was really tired. She looked so bad, almost like she'd been up all night. Do you think she slept at all?" he asked.

Cody's question made me uneasy on more than one level. First, I couldn't understand why she wasn't sleeping, and I wasn't sure how long such behavior might have gone on. I was also concerned that it might be dangerous for her to take the antianxiety medication and then fight off its effects and stay awake. No one in our home had ever taken a drug to sleep, and we knew less than nothing about medications.

After her weird behavior at the rink, Farema's taking off in the dark hours of the morning was enough to send up a major red flag. Weeks earlier, after she had first started taking the antianxiety medication, she'd told me that she saw angels flying around her apartment living room and walking in the backyard, peeking in the windows at her. I had laughed and told her that God must have sent an extra few to watch over her. She had believed me and hadn't shown any fear. I thought she'd been dreaming. Then she acquired her nighttime fears, but they made sense—she'd never liked to go out in the dark or be alone at night, and I had expected it to be hard for her to learn to live alone. When she chose to walk alone, in the dark, all the way down a busy highway to her own apartment, I recognized a significant change in what was normal for her.

I should have sensed before now that Farema was coming apart, but it had never entered my mind until that day—the day before she was admitted to the psychiatric ward.

I was wary enough after Farema's abnormal night-time walk to call Claire again. Claire had been well trained in autism and worked with people with various mental and developmental disabilities. I trusted her to know what to do.

First, we called Dr. Hall, and when none of the doctors in his office could see her on Friday, we decided to take her to the hospital. Claire met us at the apartment and helped Farema get dressed and into the car with an explanation of going to check out her medication. She'd never before refused to do anything we asked, but I wasn't taking any chances.

After arriving at the hospital, we waited in the ER for hours until we were taken back to a room where a doctor finally looked into Farema's eyes, asked her a few questions, and told us that a woman who worked as a liaison to patients would come talk with us. Claire stayed with Farema while Cody and I followed the woman to a small family waiting room.

There, the woman told us that as a girl nearly twenty-four-years-old, Farema was an adult with all the rights of any other person. As parents, we could do nothing to protect her if the hospital wanted to admit her to the psychiatric ward and keep her there until they felt she was all right and able to return to her home. Worse, the State of Oregon could take over as her guardian if we did not legally hold that position. She told us it would be a good idea to apply for the guardianship of our daughter. Then she suggested we take Farema to a particular doctor who was experienced with autism before admitting her to the hospital. Amazingly, the liaison called the doctor and found there had been a cancellation in his schedule, and we had an appointment that day. We left the ER and rushed over with Claire and Farema in tow.

Dr. Finley's office was attached to the hospital by a long catwalk adjoining the Physicians and Surgeons Building next door to the main hospital. It was lucky for us, I said to Cody and Claire on our way over, that a doctor was able to see us so quickly. Then we all piled into the elevator and went to his floor, walked to the door, and stopped. I read the plate on the door. This doctor was a psychiatrist. I'd never known anyone who'd gone to a psychiatrist. Suddenly, my mind flashed back to the memory of Farema's earliest years, when a sign on a schoolroom door was the first, unwelcome clue to my child's future within the public school system. Gingerly, I opened the door, and we all piled into the small waiting room. After a short wait, we were ushered into the doctor's even smaller office, where we pulled extra chairs from the hall to make room for all four of us to be seated.

When I asked some questions as to what it was that he could do for our daughter, Dr. Finley told me he was primarily "a prescriber" and that he would manage her medications. I didn't understand what that meant. Unfortunately, and much too soon, I would find out.

He was a kind man, talking to all of us for a long while, and then prescribing medications he said should help. He was unable to diagnose anything specific, but he told us he'd seen many young people with autism and that the normal stresses of everyday life can be burdensome for the autistic person. Sometime during our appointment, the doctor mentioned another new and unexpected possibility.

"It is possible she is having a break." The term puzzled me. I wondered at first if he meant "breakdown"—or did he mean a "break" from reality? I'd never given much thought to what either word meant. I'd never had to. I heard his words, but my mind didn't process what he was implying. Or was it, I considered much later, that I didn't want to hear what he was trying to tell us?

We thanked him for seeing us so quickly, and Farema promised to take her meds and stay with us for a week or two without any more walks to her apartment in the dark so that we could monitor her sleep. We left feeling hopeful, if not relieved. None of us suspected that before another day passed, we would find ourselves back where we'd begun: in the ER, and under far more devastating circumstances.

The next morning, I had to work and left early as usual, and Cody was home with Farema. Both were sound asleep, or so I thought, as I crept quietly out the back door in the early morning hours. I'd assured Cody that soon the new pills would "kick in" and that Farema would be okay once they did. Isn't that what medications were supposed to do?

That afternoon, I was on break, sitting in the office at the detention center waiting for my coworker to return from a quick trip to the bread store so that I could go home. It was 1:15, and I planned to check out at 2:00.

The phone rang, and Cody's frantic voice summoned me to come home now! Something was wrong with our daughter. He didn't say what it was.

He hung up. I knew the situation was beyond anything he could handle, because my husband would never have made a call like that if he'd had any idea how to handle it himself. I made a fast and frantic call to my supervisor, and before she came in the door I was backing out of the parking lot to race home.

When I stepped in the front doorway at our house, I nearly ran into Cody. He was rushing to meet me outside to go pick up Farema. He and Claire had talked and they were meeting at Farema's apartment to get her, with a plan to take her to the ER immediately. I followed him back out the door, jumped in the passenger seat, and off we went. Breathlessly, he began telling me what had happened.

"She got up in the morning, and I thought she looked fine. I fixed her some pancakes, and when I went to tell her to come and eat she was in the bathroom."

Cody's accent and attention to detail made me want to scream at him, *Yes, she ate, or didn't eat, or whatever, but what happened?* Instead, I held my mouth shut tight and listened.

"Then, she said she wasn't hungry, so I didn't push her to eat. I went out back to mow the lawn, and I was in the garage and she kept coming out and saying she had to go home, back to her apartment. I told her to wait till you got off and then you'd give her a ride. Then around noon I went in to see if she wanted some lunch. She said she was going to take a shower."

Cody was driving toward Farema's apartment and was almost there when he finished the story.

"I heard the water running in the tub for a long time—maybe as long as twenty or thirty minutes. Then I went to yell for her to turn it off—that it was long enough for a shower." He looked over at me, and I could see the redness in his eyes as he fought the tears.

"There was no answer. I knocked on the door, but no answer. Then I knocked again, and still there was no sound from her. Then I got worried, and I tried to open the door but it was locked, and again, I yelled while pounding on the door for her to open up. She didn't answer me. I was really nervous then, and when I yelled at her to open up, I heard nothing but the water running in the shower. Finally, I went to get a nail to stick in the doorknob and it opened. When I went in, I found her lying on the bottom of the tub, with only the cold water on and the shower running full blast. She was just lying there, perfectly still and staring up at the ceiling. It was terrible . . . her eyes . . ." Cody stopped talking as his voice faltered.

Farema had been lying in the tub with a catatonic look on her face. With a towel in one hand for Farema to cover herself, Cody tried to pull her out of the tub and the freezing cold water. She'd looked at his face and screamed that she didn't know who he was. He knew something was terribly wrong with her. Then she ran naked with only a towel partially around her out the front door.

After Cody ran out and grabbed her and brought her inside, he promised her he'd take her to her apartment if she'd just put on some clothes. She put on a pair of jeans and a dirty t-shirt as he grabbed her shoes. She got into the car and waited while he found the keys, then he took her home to her apartment. When they arrived, she jumped out and ran inside, and he came home fast and called Claire, who promised to go straight over to check on her. Claire told Cody to call me at work and tell me to come home. Farema needed to go back to the ER.

Claire had a great knowledge of the side effects of various medications. She didn't tell us then, but she believed that either the medication we'd been giving Farema had affected her badly or that she was having a psychotic break from reality. Either one could have been life-threatening.

I expected to have Farema checked into a clean, white-walled hospital room where starched and pressed nurses would hurry about with lovely smiles on their faces to assure me all was well in the world. That was not where she ended up.

Instead of a bed all cozy and warm on the familiar hospital floor with rows of rooms, Farema was taken to the psychiatric ward in a wheelchair where she would be spending the night. Before we had a chance to absorb the seriousness of her admittance, Cody and I found ourselves staring at the buzzer outside the C.E. Johnson Unit. Until we arrived at that door and found Farema behind locked doors, we hadn't understood what it all meant. All I could do was rehearse the last few days in my mind and wonder how we'd come to this place in time.

The day before, the emergency doctor had questioned me about whether or not Farema had taken any kind of street drugs.

"Can you tell me if your daughter has taken some kind of medication today? Or if she may be using any kind of street drugs?" he'd asked.

I must have looked like any other parent sitting in there with a kid whose lifestyle had suddenly caught up with her, and I realized what he must be thinking.

"No!" I said adamantly. "She has never taken anything like that!"

I knew how I must look to him. He probably thought mine was a typical response to a doctor, called in for yet another young adult whose drug-induced high had inadvertently gone askew while the parents think their poor innocent little girl has some mysterious illness. I panicked just a little as I tried to calm myself and make him understand this was nothing like that. My child was innocent. My child was autistic!

"Doctor, my daughter is a high-functioning autistic, she has never had any kind of street drug, and the only kind of pill she has ever taken in the past is aspirin. She is extremely sensitive to all medications," I said.

I told him about the trial of Ritalin at the request of a teacher when she was very young, the short time she'd taken Busphar in her early CLP days, and the recent few doses of Risperidone, the antipsychotic that was the only drug the FDA had approved for children with autism. I said she had a prescription of Ativan for anxiety that she took at will, and that I hadn't monitored any of that. She was on her own, and she had said she'd only take it when she couldn't get to sleep. I assured him there was no possible way that Farema had been involved in some drug-infested party. She was sick, for sure, but it wasn't by any fault of her own. He appeared to believe me, but on our second admittance in the same number of days, I wondered if he'd believe me still.

Before Cody and I followed the route to the Johnson Unit, Claire assured us that Farema would be safe and went home with a promise to check with us the next day. We loved Claire and trusted her expertise with our daughter. But for me to leave my daughter, my childlike and trusting autistic daughter, in a psychiatric hospital ward with mentally ill adults was beyond anything I could have imagined doing in my lifetime. The crack in my heart began to break open even more at the sounds of her pleading for us to come back and not to leave her there, alone, as we walked out and away from the steel-wired door.

Cody and I were going home. Farema would soon be asleep, and we hoped morning would be a new beginning for all of us. I continued to turn and look back, and I felt like a traitor—a mother walking out on her child when she needed her most. Farema's cries for us to not go without her, to take her with us, and that she wanted to go home to her little dog followed us long after we'd closed the steel door behind us. I could hear her as I walked arm-in-arm with Cody, too shaken to turn and look back, too fearful to stop—but as I exited the door to the parking lot outside, I felt a cold shiver envelop my body, and for a moment, all I wanted to do was turn and run back, pull my child from the strange and scary place she'd been left in, and take her home.

Our drive home that evening was silent, but I could hear the doctor's words playing over and over in my mind. He said she just needed some help to sleep and then she'd probably be fine. In my mind that meant overnight—and that was all.

Chapter 30

PSYCHOTIC JUNGLE

The promise of one night rolled into five days. When we arrived at the hospital the following day, Cody and I were allowed to visit our daughter but told she needed a couple more nights of sleeping under medical supervision. When she was finally released, we agreed to keep her at home and continue to give her the medications they'd begun. There were names I'd never heard of. I would later learn that the pills were a mixture of antipsychotics and antidepressants. There was a mood stabilizer too. But with every dose, I could see the drugs were deadening her spirit.

We'd barely gotten home with Farema, and while she lay on her bed in a drugged stupor, Cody and I tried to make sense of what had happened so suddenly and so horribly to our daughter.

The days passed slowly and Farema stopped talking to us, staring blankly into space. It was different than when she had retreated into her own autistic world in the past. This was scary for us, and when her skin turned a pale yellow and she began to perspire what looked like shiny drops of oil, I called the doctor's office.

"Hello, is Dr. Finley in?" I asked hurriedly.

"No, he is out on Friday. Can I help you?" the receptionist said back.

"I need to see the doctor. Farema is looking terrible, and I think it's from the medications. Can someone else see her?" I was starting to feel a warm wave of panic washing over my composure. I was watching my daughter, who by now had not spoken for hours and was standing with her back against the wall in the kitchen, looking into space as if she had left her body. I feared she had.

The office was void of doctors on Friday, I found out, and the only other option I had was to call the hospital. I wasn't willing to chance taking her back in there. I knew it would devastate her if she came to her senses and could see where she was; and after the onslaught of pills we'd been given for her, I was terrified of what might be added to the mix. Yet my fear only increased as I watched my daughter fade away.

"Come with me, honey, we're going to the doctor's office. Let's get your coat on." My mind had taken over my body. I wasn't going to sit watching as my daughter retreated from our reality to an uncharted state of consciousness. I was taking her to the doctor whether he was there or not. I took her by the hand and led her to the car. On the way out, Cody helped me hold her arms out so I could slip on her jacket. It felt like I was leading a zombie—like I'd seen in the horror shows—out the door.

When we arrived at the office, I had to lead Farema into the elevator. Her feet shuffled along as if she was a robot that had been wound up to methodically travel wherever she was pointed. We rode up with a few other people, and I ignored their stares with a defiant resolve. I wasn't sure if their stares were the result of how Farema looked to them or of how I appeared, stressed and on the edge of panic. I didn't care what people thought, and when we walked into the small reception area of the psychiatry office I was trying to keep my anxiety under control.

"I brought Farema here to have you, or someone, look at her. I have tried to tell you all how she looks, but I want you to see for yourself." I tried to speak in calm, even tones. The woman seated behind the glass sliding window looked at Farema, and her face told me what she was thinking—she was shocked. She pointed to the small waiting area and asked us to take a seat. She said she'd send someone out to see us immediately.

Minutes later, Dr. Finley's nurse came out of the back and walked up to where Farema and I sat on a small leather couch. She spoke to me while staring intently at Farema, next to me, sitting motionless—arms dropped and hanging loosely at her sides, with a fixed stare coming from eyes that looked dead.

"Please wait right here—I'll be right back," she said. As if too stunned to say more, she backed away and disappeared through the door. After a few minutes, she returned.

"I called the doctor at home, and he wants you to stop all medication for now. He wants you to take Farema home and will call you in an hour or so and speak to you about what to do next."

Dr. Finley's advice was what I wanted to hear. I sensed that the pills she was taking had become a kind of poison in Farema's body. Never before that moment had I felt more helpless. I started to pray silently for Farema's health, that the Lord would keep her safe—alive—until the doctor could reverse whatever was happening to her. We left, with me leading her silent, robotic form out the door and down the long hall to the elevator. All the way home in the car I restrained my emotions. I was afraid of frightening Farema, though she showed no sign of being aware of where we were, where we'd been, or even who we were. I prayed without stopping.

All the way home I kept watch over Farema, sitting semiconsciously next to me in the front seat of the car. She didn't talk, and she didn't look out the window. She just sat there, staring straight ahead. When we arrived home, Farema lay on the bed, and Cody and I waited anxiously for Dr. Finley to call. The phone rang an hour later, and the doctor told us to stop the medications. We could bring her into his office on Monday.

"Monday?" Cody and I repeated the word in unison when I hung up the phone and told him verbatim what the doctor had said. We were to hope she survived, with us, for two more days until Monday.

We were the first to see the doctor that Monday morning, and Farema was a little better. She didn't talk, and she still looked pale yellow, but she was moving on her own and had eaten a little at each meal. The doctor replaced one medication with a new one. Others were changed, and after only a week or two, changed again.

As the drugs were absorbed into her brain, Farema began to exhibit more bizarre beliefs, and when I told the doctor what she was seeing and hearing, he said something I was unable to digest. Its implications were bad enough—but worse, he said it as though it made sense, and the truth was it didn't make any sense to me at all.

"You know, with science and medicine, nothing is really definite, and in some people a medication will work fine and do the job it was designed for. But there are some instances where the drug will create the thing it was created to control or cure."

Farema was afraid to be alone for a second. From the first night she stayed with us after leaving the psychiatric ward, I slept next to her in her bed, and sometimes the tears rolled down my face and over my arms as I tried to cover my head to muffle any sound for fear of waking her and escorting her back into the psychotic nightmare that had become her every waking moment. I wondered, in my stream of prayers, if Cody and I would be able to endure this until it was over. I wondered if it would ever be over.

While we cared for our daughter at home, I worried about Farema's sisters and their families—our grandchildren. I was concerned they would feel left out, as we were unable to spend much time with them with our attention so totally focused on our sick daughter. There just wasn't time for anyone or anything else. I didn't want the little ones to see their aunt Farema and how she'd changed. I didn't want anyone to see her until she was well, her old self again.

From the time we brought her home, Farema stayed on her bed in the guest room at our house and hid under the covers. I stayed next to her, listening to her breathe while trying to keep her comforted and assured that her illness would soon pass. When she woke up after a long drug-induced nap, she turned over to face me, and with tears in her eyes, asked me a question I could not answer.

"Mom, can the doctor make me well? Will the pills make them go away?"

I wanted to grab her, wrap her in a soft, warm blanket, and hold her close like I did when she was sick as a baby and allowed me to do such things. I wanted to run away with her too, and let my mother's love heal the pain that was so evident behind the pools that flooded her eyes when she was awake. I wanted to be her comforter, her healer—but nothing I could do would change the hellish prison my child was now existing in. As the drugs took her deeper into her psychosis or the stupor they created, she simply cried out, sobbing, "Help me! Please! Help me!"

Time passed slowly, but as it did, not much changed with our daughter's illness. She was given all kinds of medications, and with each new drug her delusions came back. I tried to impress upon the doctors that she had been much better before the medications were given, before they gave her pills to make her sleep that first day at the hospital. But when I was honest with myself, I had to accept that she was already having some sort of break from reality before we took her to the hospital. Still, it was difficult to know if her delusions were simply a new phase of her ever-changing autism combined with a desperate lack of sleep, which we'd seen for a few weeks.

I called the doctor daily, asking questions. I left messages with his assistant, and she'd talk to him, then call back with advice. When I told her about Farema seeing things that weren't there, she said she'd make an appointment with the doctor. We'd take Farema in to see him, and usually the medication was increased, decreased, or changed. I asked if she was psychotic, and he said he couldn't be sure because the autism made the problems she had so much more complex.

Most frightening was the parade of characters in Farema's world. Most worrisome was her fear of them, and how she looked around me as if there was a crowd of people—none of whom sounded like they were friends—standing or sitting all about us. She spoke to some, telling them to leave her alone. I tried to tell her they weren't real. She screamed back at me that they were, then stared wide-eyed over my shoulder while moving her head slightly to the right or left, as if she was watching someone who was peeking back at her from behind me. I'd turn to look at what she had fixed her gaze on, then back to her, each time wishing I could see what she saw so I could explain it away and calm her fears. If they weren't talking or pointing at her with vicious remarks, they threw things at her, and she would snatch fistfuls of something invisible and pitch it forcefully to the floor. Finally, she'd lower her head and cower into the cushions on the couch. Each time, my heart broke all over again, while I tried to hide the tears I could no longer control. Most times I joined her in tears.

During the night and evening hours, when Dr. Finley's office was closed, I'd call the Johnson Unit and speak to the doctor on call. I'd describe the latest weird thing Farema was seeing or talking about. Most of the doctors I spoke with suggested I ask her doctor for a new medication, telling me that maybe the one she was on wasn't working well enough to override the psychotic symptoms. I wanted to scream into the phone that the medication was the *reason* for the psychotic symptoms! Not the *cure*! I didn't say anything except "thank you" before hanging up. I knew they would never believe it. They were in the business of handing out drugs to people like Farema, and I couldn't truly say they were wrong. I was just as lost as if I'd been left on an island and told to find my way back. Cody was quietly coming apart in his own way. It grieved him to the depth of his soul to see Farema and I talking about, and her talking to, beings that no one else was able to see.

One evening after she'd fallen asleep, I crept out of the bedroom to find my husband sitting in his chair staring at the television with eyes red and filled with tears. When he turned to see me coming into the room, I saw that his chin quivered. My heart ached for him.

Christmas Eve came, and the tree I put up and decorated went unnoticed. I told everyone we would most likely stay home and have a quiet—and solitary—celebration. Cody and I led Farema into the living room and sat together on the couch near the tree. I gave her the presents I'd wrapped with hopeful visions of her miraculously coming out of her stupor, of her smiling and laughing over her new clothes and gifts. Reality, however, was nothing like that. She wouldn't open anything, and when I did it for her, exclaiming in my most animated voice how lovely the gifts were as I held them in front of her face, she turned away as if she didn't know what they were. After a few minutes she returned to her bed.

A few days after Christmas, Farema asked to go shopping. I was nearly ecstatic to see her interest return to a much-loved pastime, and Cody volunteered to take her to the mall with her Christmas money. He allowed her to buy whatever she chose, not realizing what was happening. While there, she asked to go to the bathroom. He waited for her in the hall outside, and she went in and changed into her new black jeans and black sweatshirt, the hood pulled up over her head. She had purchased a pair of black tennis shoes, bra, and underwear. When they walked in the house later that day, I was speechless. Farema looked every bit like the gang members she'd been so terrified of. None of my pleadings for her to take the new clothes off moved her, and when she did finally remove them to crawl back into her bed, she slept in a drugged stupor.

Some changes in the medications kept Farema sleeping up to sixteen hours a day. Cody and I took turns watching and sitting next to her while she slept, day after day and night after night. I worried that she might sleep her life away. Then I thanked God that, at least for now, she was sleeping instead of wrestling with the creatures and ghostly characters that came and went with her waking hours.

Many nights, I lay awake next to Farema in her bed, listening to her breathing. Often she seemed so deep in sleep that, though for those hours she was at peace, I feared she might not wake up. Every few hours I would lean close to her face and put my ear down next to her mouth to be sure she was breathing.

While I spent so much time imprisoned in Farema's bedroom, I told myself this would end soon, it wouldn't be much longer, and I prayed for healing. I thanked God for the patience he'd instilled in me. On my own I'd have never survived the lockdown in the bedroom. I asked for wisdom for myself and for the doctors who appeared confused by what they saw in her. Most doctors quickly admitted they knew little about autism, and all said they'd never seen anything like Farema.

As I sat next to her on the bed, I searched my heart and my Bible. When I thought I would no longer be able to contain my grief, I called out in utter despair to God.

"Father God," I prayed, "if there is a cure, show us where to find it. And God—I don't care about the autism! Let her be the girl she was before this sickness attacked her! Make her the way she was—not *normal,* Lord, I don't care about that anymore! But make her the way she was!"

I meant every word. I didn't care if she was autistic. I only wanted her to not be so *crazy*—like she was now! Never in my life had I prayed more earnestly to my Heavenly Father. When Farema was a baby and I walked the floors wondering if I'd ever again sleep a full eight hours, I thought then that I'd prayed my hardest. What was happening to her now proved to me that I hadn't begun to beg and plead for God's blessing and healing hand. Those days now seemed like a moment's inconvenience.

The black outfits Farema insisted she wear at Christmastime were slowly given up, and as more and more drugs were sent into her brain and system, she began to quiet down and sleep for longer hours every day. As much as I hated to see her sleeping her life away, I was thankful for the hours she was excused from her daytime nightmare.

We went for rides in the car and ate our meals in silence so not to bring on any of the fearsome creatures that were invisible to us. They appeared only to her, especially when she was hungry and tried to put food into her mouth. Cody had long been the cook in our kitchen, as his talent and enjoyment of cooking far exceeded mine. While Farema was in our home, he fixed only those meals that were her favorites. His berry rice, a mixture of cranberries and tiny sour berries from Iran mixed in a succulent and flavorful semisweet sauce with raisins and other ingredients and served with baked chicken was a dish she especially loved. But when she sat down to take her first bite, her torture began.

"They won't let me eat," she'd say, with tears streaming down her cheeks.

"Honey, you can eat all you want! They have nothing to say to you; they are not your boss!" we'd respond simultaneously, if not in unison.

But no matter what sort of authority I tried to exhibit, they won the battle. Her fear of "them" was too powerful, and she would put her fork down and push her chair back from the table, leaving her father and me to sit and stare at each other. Cody looked to me like a man hopelessly lost in despair as he watched his youngest, most helpless child hungry and sitting before the special meal he'd prepared for her—and unable to take one bite. She'd push her chair away from the table and shuffle back to her room and to her bed where the host of invisible intruders would converge around, over, and under where she lay.

Months passed, and the creatures varied according to the change in medications. Some were less frightening than others, and some were almost funny. When Farema said there were small people in the room, I asked, "You mean like Smurfs?"

"Yes, they are the Smurfs. And they're blue," she told me.

I would have laughed if it hadn't been so horribly real. I tried to imagine what she was seeing. But no matter how hard we tried, Cody and I were baffled by the strange things our daughter described as if we should be seeing them too.

"Mom, put a blanket over the window," she whispered one evening as she lay awake next to me in the self-made prison of her bedroom. "The birds are looking for me. And they keep yelling at me."

Argument didn't change the fact that she saw black birds, bigger than most, and heard their screams. I found a blanket and rigged it up over the entire window, hammering a small nail into each side of the window frame at the top and then hooking the corners of the blanket over the nails to block any place where the light—or the birds, could peek in.

In the middle of the night I would slip out of bed, sit in the darkness of the living room, and cry out to God for her healing. Some nights I just sat quietly, hoping that God would speak to my heart and offer something—anything— to give me a hope to cling to.

During those long months, our daughter suffered so much and so long that neither of us could complain about any personal discomfort. The weather turned from cold to springtime rain. Farema stayed the same, and Cody and I tried to support each other with words of encouragement that neither of us completely believed. We hoped the very uttering of them might bring about a break in the nightmare that had become our home and Farema's total existence.

Chapter 31

WAITING FOR HEALING

Every day for the first few weeks after that first day of her admittance to the psychiatric ward, each and every morning I expected to find my daughter back to her old self.

With the limited knowledge I had of medications, I assumed the right pills would help her, along with a few good nights' sleep—just like the doctor had said—and things would start to get better.

I'd heard of adults with autism suffering huge meltdowns, and when Farema lived at the apartment, I'd witnessed some of the boys—actually, young men—who'd displayed bizarre and emotional outbursts. I'd heard stories from other parents like me about traumatic behavioral issues with their grown kids. I'd read that things might get worse when autistic children reached puberty, and later, when they enter the adolescent years. What I'd heard and read scared me.

Yet I didn't know that delusional thinking was part of the meltdowns, especially in someone as highly functional as Farema. I would learn more about autism and its mysterious changes and effects on those afflicted with the illness than I ever wanted to know. Though I'd ignored everything I'd read early on about the differences—and similarities—between children diagnosed with childhood schizophrenia and autism, I pushed all of it from my conscious thoughts.

I would live to regret many things, not the least of which would be the stubborn and persistent way I'd pushed away the inner voice that told me to pay attention and heed what might look like a falling down in Farema's persona. Now I tortured myself with thoughts of how, if only I'd had a warning,

I would have taken my daughter out of her apartment and kept her close by—right under my nose for protection. But I was not to have life-altering foresight. And by the time I found out how common the drastic and devastating mental crashes could be, I knew much more about the disorder that was fast becoming nationally known as the "most devastating developmental disorder."

Day after day, from that first week in November 2004, I waited with anxious anticipation for the moment my daughter would return to the girl who, one beautiful day, at the moment of waking, would greet the morning with her typical bounce out of bed to start the day at a run.

Instead, she didn't wake up until noon or later. While I sat and watched her sleep, visions of her doing just as she'd always done invaded my thoughts like a home movie—scenes of the past, when she was still our little girl, tucked nightly into her own bed under our watchful eyes, and later, as a young woman, when her busy schedule left her with little time on her hands.

"Mom, where're we going today?"

Farema's questions always had action applied to them.

"Do I have a class? Where are my skates?"

My greatest desire was to see her once more jump up in the morning and throw on her warm-up pants and sweatshirt, grab her skates where she'd left them against the wall by the closet, and head for the car. Even after she'd moved out, my phone would ring before she'd rubbed the sleep from her eyes, jump-starting my day at a run just to keep up with her.

I look over at her now, lying on the bed. I notice the pair of tan, professional skates—size five—on the floor, leaning up against the wall inside her closet. All I can do is get up off the bed and shut the closet door. It is too much for me to bear.

A multitude of factors may have played a part in Farema's meltdown just before Christmas. There were the steroid inhalers she used at the beginning of the year, in January, the pressure to do well, the new medications she'd been given to sleep; there were the physical changes that must have had some part in it, her hair falling out and the pigment changes in strange places that had led a Portland physician to suspect Cushing's Disease. And there was the bike accident, the loss of her beautiful life with so many friends, lifestyle changes that were inevitable, and the change of the complex manager when the young woman the CLP kids all called "Mom," moved away with her new husband. That unexpected loss caused some of the autistic young adults to freak out, cry uncontrollably, and exhibit unexpected behaviors when they realized she'd gone. Farema had always had a hard time with change, and when the longtime manager was gone, her reaction was noticeable. I'd told her that most likely her friend would one day be back, and at the time, it seemed to appease her.

Ultimately, in barely more than six months Farema's world had begun to come apart—to break away like pieces of shattered glass. It was crumbling around her and she was following suit.

One thing my daughter had that many others like her did not was a large group of supporters: in the friends she had at the apartment, the girls and coaches at the rink, and her big family of sisters with their children and husbands. Everyone loved her, and she knew it. Still, I knew she tried hard to live up to our expectations. And she had always done it well.

I wondered if Cody had been right.

"Don't let her do so much, *she isn't normal!*" he'd warned over and over. Cody had worried that an apartment of her own might be too much.

"Didn't you say that with autism stress is not good?" He was right, but to me, Farema was so close—so *almost* normal.

Spring arrived, and still I was waiting and expecting Farema to wake up one morning and be back to her old self. Then I had a new thought. Maybe if I took her out of town, away from the things that reminded her of her downfall, she might recover. Maybe she only needed a fresh new look at the world. My random thought soon became a tangible plan.

In April, with the changes of medications more precarious than before, I reserved airline tickets to go to San Jose and visit my friend Georgia. She and her husband were probably the only people I knew who would agree to open their arms and home to two visitors such as we—one overly anxious mother and her behaviorally unpredictable daughter.

Only days before we were to fly to San Jose, California, Farema cried to me about how mean her invisible visitors had been. Scooby-Doo was not nice, and the witches and bats and Popeye were mean to her as well. My concerns about the side effects of the medications had finally alerted her doctor to think it might be good to take her off everything, since they only brought more hallucinations instead of eliminating them. By her last appointment before we set off on our flight, Dr. Finley had taken them all away with the suggestion that we begin a new one if things didn't go well. In barely two weeks, she'd gone from taking the antipsychotic, antidepressant, mood stabilizer, and benzodiazepine medications to only using a small dose of Ativan, a benzodiazepine commonly used for anxiety, as needed. I was learning much about the capricious treatment of someone with mental instability.

The airplane ride was uneventful. We arrived and walked up the long ramp from the plane to the airport terminal, where we found Georgia and Naish waiting to take us to their home. It would have been a perfect vacation—if the trip I'd hoped would be the turning point in my daughter's nightmare-ridden life had continued on as it began. It didn't. In fact, it became a new and terrifying delusion for her and a new test for me, not to mention my poor friends, who'd never encountered anything like what they were forced to endure upon our arrival.

Naish pulled the car up into the long driveway that passed through a tall black wrought-iron gate, and stopped parallel to the back door leading into their house. The garage was straight ahead, and for what reason we will never know, Farema climbed out of the car, took one look at the closed garage door, and stopped in her tracks.

"Mom! The garage door is in my stomach! And the alligator is there!"

The three of us stood dumbfounded and staring at her, not yet aware that we had only just begun to see the direction our vacation week was about to take.

Georgia and Naish were quick to disregard the odd statement and lead us inside, putting us up in the guest room. Just like the entire home, our room was beautifully decorated with ceiling-to-floor floral draperies, a matching coverlet on the bed complete with canopy over the top, and big puffy pillows to lean back on for watching TV. Before long, the lovely room would be the place of unbelievable terror and frightening commotion. Farema and I would hold our ground atop the overstuffed comforters and pillows.

Farema's first strange exclamation led to more of the same, with a replay of scenes from the scariest movies she'd watched when I still thought she was doing fine at her apartment. Dr. Finley had intended to try a new antipsychotic in a couple weeks, called Seroquel. Again, I was sure this new medication would be the long-awaited *answer*. After a frantic call from me that afternoon, he told me to start the new antipsychotic immediately—not to wait as we'd planned. He faxed the prescription to California while Farema yelled in the background.

For the entire week we were there, Farema would cry and scream, fending off the ghosts of characters locked in her brain. I tried to keep her calm and hold her tight against me for fear she might hurt herself as she lurched back and forth, trying to avoid the slashes of the knife she said "Chuckie" was jabbing at her.

I remembered having found a DVD on her bed the same week she'd told me about her nighttime friend Jessica. It was the movie *Child's Play*. I had asked her whose it was, and she said it was her friend's movie and that they'd watched it together. I was appalled that she'd seen so horrific a movie, a story about a doll that comes to life and tries to kill everyone in the family. That same summer she told me she had also watched *Sixth Sense*, about a boy who could see "dead people." I made her promise not to allow any more scary movies in her apartment and told her she should never watch them. But Farema was on her own, and I wasn't there to screen out the things I knew would harm her.

While we were sequestered in their guest room, Georgia and Naish brought food in to us and patiently waited in case we needed anything else. Farema ate very little. I tried to read to her, to talk to her, and we all tried to help her forget her visitors and enjoy our time in sunny California. Nothing changed. The onslaught of Chuckie went on, and between his knife and the alligator in her stomach, we were destined to just survive the week, only able to leave the confines of our safe place to visit the bathroom a few feet away. After five long and terrifying days, we were to board the plane and head for home.

My friends drove us to the airport and said good-bye with sad looks and an invitation to "try it again when she feels better." I had never felt such unconditional love and acceptance as I did in that week at their home. And though I knew the invitation was true and from their most generous hearts, I promised I wouldn't do this to them again.

My hope that a trip out of her usual environment, a new medication, and a week in sunny California with friends would be the recipe needed for Farema to return to her old self was dashed. The return home on the plane was not as bad as I expected; the only strange thing she did was turn to me with tears streaming down her cheeks and say, "Mom! I stole Disneyland! They're here with me, on the airplane!"

I told her it was okay. We'd return them when we got home and had time to box them up properly. Then I turned my face toward the little window and let the tears fall as I gazed out at the billowy white clouds and imagined how very wonderful heaven would be.

When we returned home, I withdrew from life as I'd known it to remain home with Farema and help her dodge the visions and ignore the sounds of creatures, imaginary people, and flying things. My poor girl, who'd once known so much happiness, was now suffering a mutiny within her own mind.

At the same time, I could see that the long months of caring for our daughter was taking a toll on our marriage, if not on our very existence. Cody's inner grief for what had taken hold of his youngest daughter was shattering him. Since she was a baby, he'd held her and called her "my heart," a Persian term of endearment, meaning "precious" or "dearly loved." Both of us knew we were helpless to give her relief, and while I searched the Internet and read pharmaceutical information for hope of something that might help her, Cody internalized his pain. Cody's heart—and Farema, *his heart*—were broken.

When we did talk about it, Cody said he couldn't face more disappointment and that I should give up. For us, there would be no common ground in the agonizing ordeal that had become Farema's life. And for us, life would march on, as if there was nothing happening to deter it. Then, amid our tortured existence, tragedy struck again, in another way.

Farah and Brett suffered a terrible loss of a baby who, for no reason known to the doctors, died before it was born. Her sister's heartache was noticeable in Farema's countenance when she overheard us talking, and I worried again that she was absorbing the sorrow with no means to understand. At the same time we all were devastated for the baby Farah and Brett had longed to hold and to raise.

Farah and Brett and their little Ariana faced the sorrow with much prayer and faith, and a year later they were blessed with a joyful bundle and sister for Ariana, named Alexa Grace. Cody and I took turns visiting them as we did with all friends and family, since having them at our house was too much for Farema. Sometimes we tested the waters and family members would come by for dinner, but most often Farema stayed in her room, separated and alone. Before the end of Farema's independent life, we'd had a busy and fulfilling social life—that too was a thing of the past.

While we kept Farema with us at home and tried to face the world with stoic smiles and heads raised, I never for a second forgot there were other doctors we hadn't consulted, though it seemed we'd seen them all.

Cody and I took Farema to see an endocrinologist and came away with high hopes that there'd been a discovery and that healing was just around the corner.

The doctor ordered blood tests and prescribed a strong steroid medication for the Congenital Adrenal Hyperplasia that he diagnosed at the same time. He explained this was something she would have inherited, something not terribly rare, and that the steroid would have no effect on her behavior. What we didn't know then was that the steroids would play a major part in the upcoming disaster that would take us from our place of deep concern for her physical and mental health and drop us once more smack in the middle of a tempest of gale proportions.

Chapter 32

STEROID-INDUCED PSYCHOSIS

Nov. 2005. Farema still throwing stuff back at 'them'—not much talk." I wrote the words in a diary I'd begun keeping of Farema's torment. Hopefully, one day I might look back at my entries and laugh at the bizarre happenings in our home. Suds drifted past me, accompanied by the clank and splash of dishes. I sighed and looked up at Farema, standing at the kitchen sink up to her elbows in soapy water. Cupboards stood open all around her head, their dishes dragged out to join the din.

Day after day Farema would start out washing a few breakfast dishes, then return to the kitchen sink to go over the same dishes. I'd tried at first to take over and offer to let her do something less bothersome, less hazardous. But Farema ignored me as if I were a fly in her field of vision, standing her ground and planting her feet dead center at the kitchen sink. When each dish was scrubbed hard more than five or ten times, she'd turn to the cupboards to pull the cups and glasses out and give them a once-over, the sink brimming with hot water and suds. I'd stand back a few feet and watch the water fly around her and over the drain boards, all the while wondering what kind of inner comfort she could possibly be getting from the motion of scrubbing dishes. Water was the only part of the new obsession that I could understand. It wasn't surprising that comfort for her would have some element of water, hot or cold.

As the days passed, Farema's obsessive washing became more frantic. Faster and wilder, she'd snatch the plates and the bowls from the surrounding cupboards, then go into the dining room and remove all the little crystal treasures I'd collected over the years from happier days rummaging through antique stores with my friends. No longer important to me, those once-adored little delicacies barely survived the bubble baths she'd inflict on them. Remarkably, none were ever broken.

"Doctor," I said during one of our appointments, "Farema says her tongue and her lips aren't going the way she wants. And her hands are always in the same position; she says they're stiff. They look stiff, the way she holds her fingers straight out. She's sleeping sixteen hours a day."

I talked quietly so as not to sound as hysterical as I felt. I'd read the terrifying side effects of neuroleptic drugs, and Risperdal, a medication often used for people with autism, was one of the most powerful. We added it to the list of medications that had been tried and excluded, a common practice, I'd been told, in finding the "right one."

In less than two years Farema had tried drugs with names like Zyprexa, Depakote, Seroquel, Navane, Zoloft, and many more. I'd tried the best I could to talk Cody and the doctor into letting me try to decrease her intake of antipsychotics and antidepressants. Their response was always the same. The "right one" would make all the difference in the world.

Adding to the already mind-boggling list of medications, the endocrinologist had prescribed a steroid I'd never heard of. Dexamethasone was as new to me as any of the others, but the OHSU doctor frowned when he read her chart and saw it listed. "I don't know why she's taking this," he said. "Prednisone is strong enough." Even so, he didn't change anything. I wondered if doctors were careful not to interfere with each others' diagnoses—right or wrong.

With the trade of one antipsychotic for another or a change in dosage, Farema's phantom visitors would diminish or increase. When they sporadically vanished, I whispered "Thank you, Jesus!" He knew what I meant. Each and every time my daughter's happy self returned, I assumed, with a grateful heart, that another miracle was being worked in her life. Then her sweet, chatterbox happiness would fade, and the darting looks and glances return. I'd ask myself, "Have I used up all my miracles?"

As the end of the year closed, Farema's hyper giggle and insistence on washing every dish in our house over and over became more and more frantic. It was as if her OCD and energy level was increasing with each day.

It was impossible to take her out in public. She went to Starbucks with Farah one day, and before her caramel macchiato was ready, she acted out and yelled at her invisible abusers. Farah, a quiet, reserved, and somewhat shy young woman, tried to settle her down with soft words of assurance that all was well. It didn't work. Before they exited the crowded coffee store, Farema struck out at her sister and frightened a few patrons. Farah was forced to take the outrage of a sister who'd once been her closest confidant and dearest friend.

Farema became more agitated and defiant with everyone around her. The hallucinations and things she heard increased, making her respond in anger and rebellion. My frequent calls to the doctor brought no solution other than to give her more medications. Once more, I worried that the drugs were part of the problem, but no doctor would discuss such things with me.

One quieter than usual evening, while we sat around the dinner table with Farah and Brett and their girls, Farema asked if she could take her little dog, Taco, for a walk to the park less than a block from our home. Normally I would have been glad to see her take part in a once-typical Farema endeavor, but this time I insisted she wait for me to go along with her. "It's dark, honey. I don't want you to go on your own."

When we'd finished eating and started to clear the table, someone asked, "Where's Farema?"

I frowned. "She wanted to take the dog for a walk to the park, but I asked her to wait. Maybe she's left without me," I said.

Before there was another reply, a knock sounded at the door. It was a neighbor girl. "Hi, Lauri," she said when I opened the door. Her expression was earnest and worried. "Taco is loose—I tried to catch him, but he ran off." She cleared her throat. "And Farema's down at the park. Over by the school with the police."

My heart froze. Something was horribly wrong. I dropped the dish towel and ran out the door toward the park and the adjoining elementary school grounds.

When I arrived alongside the school, only a few feet from the park where the neighborhood children played on swings and slides, I saw my daughter sitting on the grass with her legs straight out in front of her. Her eyes were devoid of sparkle. She seemed to have vanished, even more so than when she'd periodically retreated to her autistic world. She looked lost—unreachable. Two men—I'd learn later that they were teachers—stood alongside her, and a young blonde policewoman with a sweet smile stood in front of her, talking. I was breathless, but able to ask what happened.

"Well, I was just asking that same question myself, and as I understand it, your daughter—what is her name?" the officer said.

I told her Farema's name.

"Farema! I know you!" she said as she bent down near Farema's face, smiling. Farema smiled up at her.

"You used to clean my office at city hall. Remember me?"

Farema didn't respond except to smile vacantly. I took a deep breath as I listened to the young police officer tell me how she'd come to be there, with my daughter sitting silently at her feet on the grassy lawn of the elementary school with neighbors and school employees and various students surrounding us as if watching a performance of great excitement. None of them could know that the performance playing out before them was a tragedy.

"What these gentlemen have told me is that this couple . . ." She turned to look for a man and a woman who'd apparently left the scene. "Well, they may have gone on home by now, but they were walking their dog and passed by here at the same time Farema was pounding on a glass door over there while screaming and crying." The young officer pointed to a door at the back side of the school where a small light still cut the darkness around that part of the building.

"They assumed she was just a teenager with some anger issues and approached her from behind. The woman reached out to pull her back from the glass—they both said she'd been kicking it as well—to keep her from getting hurt if it broke and to ask what they could do to help. Then Farema swung around and grabbed the woman's shirt by the front and ripped it apart, and really scared them. The after-hours activity class that was going on in the gym heard someone scream, and the teachers rushed out here to see what was going on."

I looked over at the two big men standing aside my daughter, still seated and dazed on the grassy school grounds. They had grabbed my daughter by the arms and thrown her to the ground, and one of them actually sat on top of her to keep her from getting up. When she stopped crying so loud and thrashing to get out from under him, he released her and let her sit up where they stood watch until the moment I arrived.

My heart had already started to sink into a pool of despair. I didn't utter a word as I listened to how the neighbors came to see what was happening, how the police had been summoned only an hour earlier to an incident with an autistic boy across the street, and how they were just leaving that boy's home when they saw the crowd that had gathered at the school. They'd stopped by to see what was going on. I stood listening, absorbing the words along with a mental picture of the tragic falling down—not only physically, but emotionally—of my daughter, who no longer resembled who she had once been.

So many years of maneuvering an autistic child through the world of public venues and bewildered and strained school systems had taught me how to tuck away my true feelings and paste a smile on my face as I uttered "thank you" and "yes, we will be calling a doctor," and "no, I can take her home, we live nearby." I glanced only momentarily at the large men who hadn't moved from their stance beside Farema. But for the cover of darkness, they would have seen the utter disgust in my eyes.

With no help from the men, Farema got up when I reached down to her and took my hand as I led her off down the little concrete path to our street. I could feel the eyes of the crowd watching us disappear into the darkness.

Then they took her to the ground. The words the officer had used to describe how Farema came to be sitting on the grass came back to haunt me. I couldn't bear to remember how she'd looked.

The park incident happened on the sixth day in February, 2006. The downward spiral of our lives was gaining velocity. I knew the future might hold more than I was able to endure. It was obvious that Farema's mania and agitation were more elevated than I'd known, worse even than when the drugs transported her to places of strange beings and visions.

When we got back to the house, I urged her to climb into a warm bath. As I helped her undress, I saw large square shapes with dark purple and blue crisscross marks on her buttocks. I'd never seen anything like it. The marks were all around her stomach, and there were almost inch-wide red streaks that looked like stretch marks but worse—as if the skin had actually torn apart and was bleeding just below the surface. The marks were in patches all over her body, on her arms and down her legs.

I called the OHSU emergency number and requested a call back as soon as possible. Within an hour the doctor called me back. He listened to my story of what had happened in the park and told me to stop giving her the steroid medication she'd been taking for more than eight months.

"Those marks are a sign that she has way too much cortisol in her system. It sounds like steroid-induced psychosis. She must not have any more steroids!"

Three days later we traveled to the OHSU, where a misdiagnosis by a previous physician was revealed. Farema's steroid treatment had been a mistake. They brought in a photographer, and he took photos of the huge purple marks and the strange wide stretch marks. The doctor said her chart would reflect the allergic reaction to the steroids, creating a thinning of her skin, the purple marks, and the frantic, out-of-control behavior she'd been exhibiting. He said the steroids would slowly leave Farema's system, but it would take time, up to a year, depending on her body's ability to expel them.

It was good to know I'd been right about the drugs, but the revelation was frustrating at the same time. It wouldn't be easy to tell Cody, especially because the expelling of cortisone from Farema's system meant more hard times ahead for us. I wondered how long Cody and I would be able to endure the pressure of caring for our daughter and still remain caring for each other. Statistics claim that 89% of parents divorce because of the pressures of raising a child with autism, and I couldn't help contemplating what our situation might add to the odds. Could we find a place of harmony before our marriage became one of the statistics?

The new diagnosis meant waiting for Farema's body to release the high amount of cortisone. Her life would be a roller coaster of highs and lows. Our home life would ride the waves of ever-changing plans, therapies, and more medicines while the steroid slowly dissipated from her body and the extreme manic behavior began to settle down. But long before that happened, I became weary of the path I'd been traveling. My once- persistent resolve to find a cure for my daughter imploded inside of me. We admitted Farema to the now familiar Johnson Unit. Finding a "place" for her to live would be the next step. Peace was coming, but not in the way I'd hoped or imagined—not as a result of the miraculous recovery I'd so longed for.

During my most desperate moments of doubt for her future, I had never imagined I'd give in to the suggestion that we find some sort of "placement"— another kind of home for my most vulnerable child, even though it would mean freedom to leave my home after months of hypervigilance, keeping Farema with me twenty-four hours each day. The fear of what might become of her and how drastically her life would change far outweighed my longing for a little freedom—even though going to the bathroom by myself had become an oddity since the beginning, when her first imaginary characters showed themselves—before the steroids attacked her system. My reluctance to send her to a new and more restrictive environment under the care of strangers brought me to tears—and to my knees.

During that third and last time Farema was in the care of the psychiatrists and physicians at the local hospital psychiatric ward, I took to my place of refuge once more—to the chair by the living room window, where I'd found solace in prayer so many times during her illness.

Again, I prayed for my daughter—now a young woman—and for her healing. I'd prayed so many times before, just like this. I'd prayed for her and for me, for her sisters and for Cody, for her healing and for our endurance.

This time, while I sat with tears streaming down my face, I lifted my arms up to the ceiling, and as if handing over my child, I offered her back to the God who'd been there from before her conception.

God had been there to watch as she was formed in my womb. He'd known the girl she would become before I even knew I was pregnant. And he'd known she was going to be born with autism. I held her life up and offered my autistic and desperately ill daughter back to the Father in obedience, and I *cast all my burden on him* (Matthew 11:28).

It wasn't the first time I'd made a conscious effort to give my daughter and all her frailties over to God. But it was the first time I began to make a purposeful and lasting step in truly letting go.

Chapter 33

THE HAPPY ENDING

[18]I consider that our present sufferings are not worth comparing
with the glory that will be revealed in us. [28]And we know that in all
things God works for the good of those who love him,
who have been called according to his purpose.
ROMANS 8:18, 8:38 NIV

There would be a lovely Cinderella ending to this story if life was a fairy tale and this a perfect world. Farema would go on to wow fans of figure skating, maybe even to perform on a national television program and display the possibilities for someone with the profound developmental condition known as autism.

She would continue to enjoy the attention of figure skating compatriots at the rink, and in her late twenties and thirties, and maybe even her forties, would stay on as a regular patron of the place that would never forget the miraculous "awakening" she'd come to be famous for. Her life would be full, and her accomplishments would outshine her autism. No one would ever hurt or tease her, and she would live happily on her own, with help, in her little apartment across from the Safeway shopping center.

I'd often check in with her, and when necessary, replace those who aided her in her independent living as their lives moved them along and out of her life. By the time Cody and I approached the last years of our lives, Farema would be well-versed in living without us.

But this is not a perfect world.

It is doubtful now that Farema will ever again be the happy and carefree, accomplished—though autistic—young person she once was.

Only by God's grace am I able to admit to that truth in these days as I have come to accept that there is no happily-ever-after—at least not here in this world. Life will never be the way I planned it. Unless God sees fit to bless us with another miracle, the happy ending I expected, prayed for, and finally allowed to pass away from my longings will have to wait until we are all made perfect in mind and body (Philippians 3:21).

On that day, the ending will be just the beginning. Farema and her sisters, along with a precious host of family and loved ones, will join to see miracles happen on a daily—eternal—never-ending basis. We'll finally have our happy ending!

For the rest of life here, there are lessons learned.

If I'd never come face to face with the world of autism, I might not have heard God's voice calling me to pay attention. I've often thought that my worship of him would be so much less had it not been for the years since Farema's birth. I do know that God uses our pain and sorrow to pull us closer; C. S. Lewis said in *The Problem of Pain* that God whispers to us in our pleasure, speaks to us in our conscience, and *shouts in our pain,* and one of the first things God taught me is that he uses our circumstances to get our attention.

I learned humility early on. It's nearly impossible to feel anything but humble with a screeching, writhing, and flailing child at one's feet on the filthy mall or grocery-store floor—even more humbling when that child is screaming and babbling incoherently as an adult and one is trying every possible way to speak calmly and entice her to come along, to go outside and away from the staring, accusing eyes of sometimes frightened and confused strangers. Keeping my composure and a calm demeanor with a smile on my face was the only way to appease Farema when something would trigger such an event, for if I were to show my true dismay she'd only become worse. It was not an easy lesson, but one that has affected many areas of my life—not least in showing me that I am not the one who controls life and its twists and turns.

Cody and I have survived the statistics. Instead of running out on my marriage when it seemed there was no hope, with new God-given patience and forgiveness, I have let God's love fill the empty places in my heart and remind me that this time, there is always hope. With the odds against us, and the future we envision for our daughter as diverse and opposed as the distance between the worlds we grew up in, Cody and I have endured the nearly impossible strain on our marriage. Sometimes my Moslem-born husband reminds me to "Ask Jesus to take care of Farema" when he sees she is having a difficult time. I am each time refreshed to know that my prayers are going to be answered—for both of them.

Ever since that frightening night when I came home and found my ten-year-old had miraculously survived a plunge into the icy Willamette River, I've read and reread, and written upon the tablet of my heart, the 139th Psalm that tells me of God's overwhelming love for me.

Through David, God expresses how completely he *knows me!* Whether I am sitting or standing, he knows my "every thought"—and when I lay myself down to sleep, he knows. Before I speak, he knows what I will say; he blesses me "with his hand upon my head" and is in front of and behind me as well.

Could I escape his Spirit if I tried? No. If I go to heaven, or to the depths of hell, he is with me—if I were able "to rise up on the wings of the dawn, or on the far side of the sea," even there his hand would be leading me along the path he has planned for me. In the darkness of the darkest night, he sees me as if in daylight. He created me, seeing my unformed body as he wove me together in my mother's womb—amazingly—for his works are so very wonderful.

All the days he has given to me, he gave "before even one had come to be." Above all—his thoughts of me are "precious" and countless! My heavenly Father protects and shelters me with his overwhelming love!

In the old days of testing and denial, Farema met every one of the criteria for classic autism. It took me years to accept it because I allowed my own feelings of guilt and shame to overwhelm me. But the truths of the Bible have slowly healed those hurts and allowed me to embrace the girl who is. When asked by his disciples if the reason for the blind man's loss of sight at birth was the sin of his parents or his own, Jesus said it was not due to anyone's sin. It was so that the work of God could be seen. Farema's birth was just as it should have been. God was there, in control, even then. Farema was born to be the girl she is now, to fulfill her place in God's perfect plan in ways that only she can do.

Passing by the little park across from the house where we lived, or traveling through town and driving by the ice rink, I am suddenly aware of the miracles—both big and small—that were bestowed on us in those places. I will never forget the experience of knowing God's presence next to me as I watched Farema take to the ice as if she'd always known how to skate. That day was not just the beginning of a new life for her, but the stark and awesome answer to so many years of prayer. In that instant I knew that God is still a God of miracles.

Recently I was looking for something I'd put away. Unable to remember where I'd put it, I found myself searching through the closet in what is now called "Farema's room." While pushing aside the clothes hanging there, I saw a red velvet skating dress. Immediately my eyes welled up, and I was transported to past days when I stood along the rink wall and watched Farema fly over the ice with a smile of indescribable joy. Usually when this happens, I stop only momentarily to dry my eyes and then go on. This time I was reduced to sobs. But now I remember that God has a plan and a purpose for every tear shed and every hopeful prayer I've uttered. I've learned to see *that God causes everything to work together for the good of those who love God and are called according to his purpose for them* (Romans 8:28). And I know that *God, who began the good work within her (and me!), will continue his work until it is finally finished on that day when Christ Jesus comes back again* (Philippians 1:6).

I'll continue to wonder about the rest of God's plan. Maybe, I've secretly pondered, I'll open my eyes one morning and there will be a new discovery—a pill, a therapy, anything that means Farema can find herself once more—the *old* Farema, with autism but minus the ghosts and irrational fears. It will never be easy for me to forget what might have been, and I will never stop praying for one more miracle, according to God's will. I'll never give up on my quest to be informed should a good and safe remedy for autism or the ever-changing symptoms of Farema's medications arise, but I know for sure, I cannot fix her. Only God can do that.

I no longer fear the future, for God alone knows the end of this story. I will trust him and wait. Whether God's plan includes healing Farema in this world or in the next, I will thank him for the lessons learned and for reaching down and lifting the weighty burden I was so reluctant to let go of. I know God will be there every step of the way, and when I am weary, I will find rest in the shadow of his wings (Psalm 17:8). Our Lord Jesus Christ is ever present and willing to heal our broken hearts (Psalm 147:3), to count our tears (Psalm 56:8), and to mend our shattered lives. He is there to pull us up when we fall under the weighty burden of caring for and loving our autistic child or adult, and unlike ours, his strength never fails (Matthew 11:28).

A MOTHER'S EPILOGUE

Today Farema and I go for a drive up Highway 126 West, toward the Oregon coast, where we can escape reminders of everyday struggles and relax and share quality time. As we travel between tall fir trees and rocky slopes on either side of the road, I marvel at the beauty of fall.

There are trees of all sorts mixed in among the firs, big-leaf maples and others. Orange, yellow, and green leaves cascade down and enhance the lush undergrowth with thick green moss and endless valleys of fern. A song from the past is playing on the radio, and the vocalist sings:

It must've been love, but it's over now, it must've been good, but I lost it somehow; it must have been love, but it's over now . . .

I am surprised and warmed to hear Farema singing along, and I am reminded of the days when we would be alone in the car together on a weekend evening headed to the ice rink. Winter or summer, rain or calm, I'd roll down all the windows in the car and turn the volume up as loud as I could bear when we heard our favorite song by Johnny Ocean: "Get Out of My Dreams, Get Into My Car." Together we'd sing at the top of our lungs while laughing and dancing wildly in the seat. I'd make Farema giggle and laugh by exclaiming, "I hope no cops are watching!"

Today I am joyfully reliving the scene—she and I doing what once came so naturally, and had been lost so completely—until she stops singing, looks worriedly over at me, and says, "It's over now!" She sounds distraught.

"Honey, that's a song. Just a song," I calmly respond.

"It is?" she replies, with a little girl voice.

In many ways, Farema is still very much like a girl—certainly not at all like a twenty-eight-year-old woman. But no matter how she sounds, I am grateful just to hear her voice. Not so long ago, I'd feared she had lost her will or ability to converse. Cody and I had believed she might never speak again.

"Do you think she will never talk to us again?" I asked Cody during those most tragic months in the beginning. He'd been unable to respond optimistically, unable to say that she would.

I'd surrendered my dreamer's optimism, and, so reminiscent of when Farema was diagnosed with autism long before, mentally bidden farewell to the girl I knew and resolved to find a place in my heart for the person, so unfamiliar, who was left.

Now she sits beside me in my car, looking like she did before the mysterious so-called break with reality—a pretty girl with striking big blue eyes accented by the longest lashes some say they've ever seen. Farema is down now to one new, mild medication, and with God's help, one day soon even that will go. One day we hope she will be free of the chemicals with their dangerous side effects. Her long, golden-brown hair is pulled back in a ponytail, and she is looking as beautiful—and normal—as always, while talking constantly. I smile at her as if I've been given a long-awaited gift. And yes, I know, I certainly have.

I can hear her voice, and I can have a real conversation with her. That is enough, for through it all I have found the greatest of all God's gifts to me: the absolutely free expression of his lovingkindness—his boundless and amazing grace—unearned and undeserved.

ॐ

[Grace] is the unbroken circle of God's astounding lovingkindess. Think of grace this way: Grace is whatever you may need, whenever you need it. Do you need strength? Grace begets strength. Do you need wisdom? Grace bestows insight. Do you need peace? Grace stills the waters. Do you need comfort? Grace soothes the soul and spirit.

But grace does more than this. Because the fountainhead is God himself, grace gives and gives and gives. The grace of God is not just barely enough to scrape by with. It exceeds and surpasses our most pressing demands. Grace carries you from strength to strength. It gives wisdom liberally. It grants peace that never wanes. It brings comfort that heals and sustains.

CHARLES STANLEY, *A Touch of His Peace*

For more information on autism resources and to see a video of Farema skating, visit www.lonelygirlgraciousgod.com

Contact Lauri through her website or write to her at:
laurikhoda@comcast.net or
Lauri Khodabandehloo
2262 Dale Ave.
Eugene, OR 97408

Autism Resources
Autism Today: www.autismtoday.com
Autism Speaks: www.autismspeaks.com
Autism Research Institute: www.autismresearchinstitute.com
Autism Society of America: www.autismsource.org

Medicines Prescribed and Taken

Neuroleptics:	Antidepressants:	Anxiety/Sedation:	Mood Stabilizers:
Abilify	Lexapro	Ambien	Depakote
Geodon	Zoloft	Ativan	Topomax
Navane	Trazedone	BuSpar	
Risperdal		Klonopin	
Seroquel		Benadryl	
Zyprexa			
Fluoxatine (Prozak)			

Agitation/Blood Pressure:
Clonodine
Propanolol

Additionally, Farema took various vitamins to counteract the numerous side effects of the neuroleptic drugs, including a prediabetic condition. For the misdiagnosed metabolic disorder, she was given steroids.

NOTES

In the early 1990's, Dr. Rimland and his colleague, Stephen M. Edelson, Ph.D., conducted the first empirical study on the efficacy of AIT in autism. The results were quite promising (Journal of Autism and Developmental Disorders, 1995). They have also conducted two additional studies which also showed positive effects from AIT (American Journal of Speech-Language Pathology, 1994; and one submitted for publication). 1967-2010 Autism Research Institute, 4182 Adams Avenue San Diego, CA 92116

95539